Seeking Awareness in American Nature Writing

Henry Thoreau
Annie Dillard
Edward Abbey
Wendell Berry
Barry Lopez

Scott Slovic

D1559018

University of Utah Press
Salt Lake City

∞ The paper in this book meets the standards for permanence
and durability established by the Committee on Production
Guidelines for Book Longevity of the Council on Library
Resources

Library of Congress Cataloging-in-Publication Data

Slovic, Scott, 1960–
    Seeking awareness in American nature writing: Henry
Thoreau, Annie Dilliard, Edward Abbey, Wendell Berry,
Barry Lopez / Scott Slovic.
        p. cm.
    Includes bibliographical references and index.
    ISBN 0-87480-362-4 (pbk. : alk. paper)
    1. American literature – History and criticism. 2. Nature in
literature. 3. Thoreau, Henry David, 1817–1862 – Influence.
I. Title.
PS163.S56   1992
810.9'36 – dc20   91–24313
                                                                    CIP

To Analinda and Jacinto

Contents

Acknowledgements

Though completed among the live oaks and prickly pears of Central Texas, this project began in the bookish surroundings of the Horace Mann Building at Brown University. A University Fellowship at Brown in the fall of 1989 allowed me to write the early chapters without much interruption. Many individuals at Brown also supported this project, either through direct response to my ideas or through less tangible forms of encouragement. In particular, I would like to thank Barton L. St. Armand for his "cordial" and stimulating mentorship. Mutlu K. Blasing and Geroge P. Landow provided important advice at the early stages of my writing. The Americanists' Reading Group, which listened to a trial version of the Annie Dillard chapter, offered lively human contact as a break from self-absorbed writing during my final year at Brown.

There are many other friends and scholars around the country who deserve thanks for listening to my speeches about nature writing, which were sometimes solicited and many times not. Thanks, especially, to Alicia Nitecki of Bentley College for the invitation to talk about Annie Dillard at the 1989 Society for Literature and Science Conference, and to Terrell Dixon of the University of Houston for giving me similar forums to pitch my ideas about Wendell Berry (the 1990 North American Interdisciplinary Wilderness Conference) and Edward Abbey (the 1990 College English Association Convention). I presented an early draft of the chapter on Barry Lopez at the 1990 Twentieth-Century Literature Conference in Louisville. While writing this book, I also benefited from talks and correspondence with Ken-ichi Noda, John Daniel, John Elder, Robert Finch, Edward Hoagland, Lawrence Buell, Glen Love, William Rossi, Paul Bryant, Betsy Hilbert, Don Scheese, Cheryll Burgess, Sean O'Grady, and other members of the growing community of "nature readers." John Tallmadge provided insightful and generously detailed criticism of the manuscript. More recently I have enjoyed the encouragement of my colleagues in the English Department at Southwest Texas State University and the members of The Live Oak Society, an interdisciplinary environmental reading group on campus. Miles Wilson chipped in with excellent editorial advice at the last minute.

Olga Camacho of the *New York Times* provided valuable research materials and saved me hours of squinting at microfilm.

Finally, I want to thank Analinda and Jacinto for their special contributions to this book. Jacinto, during our many walks on the country roads of San Marcos, has taught me to slow down and look at the world when my own impulse is to hurry home and start reading again. Analinda, with her combination of patience, good humor, and skepticism, sustained me before this book began and still does.

I do not propose to write an ode to dejection, but to brag as lustily as chanticleer in the morning, standing on his roost, if only to wake my neighbors up.

—Henry David Thoreau, *Walden* (1854)

When we are with Nature we are awake . . .

—John Muir, Journal entry (June, 1890)

When one pays close attention to the present, there is great pleasure in awareness of small things.

—Peter Matthiessen, *The Snow Leopard* (1978)

We teach our children one thing only, as we were taught: to wake up. We teach our children to look alive there, to join by words and activities the life of human culture on the planet's crust. As adults we are almost all adept at waking up. We have so mastered the transition we have forgotten we ever learned it. Yet is is a transition we make a hundred times a day, as, like so many will-less dolphins, we plunge and surface, lapse and emerge. We live half our waking lives and all of our sleeping lives in some private, useless, and insensible waters we never mention or recall. Useless, I say. Valueless, I might add—until someone hauls their wealth up to the surface and into the wide-awake city, in a form that people can use.

—Annie Dillard, "Total Eclipse" (1982)

One of the oldest dreams of mankind is to find a dignity that might include all living beings. And one of the greatest of human longings must be to bring such dignity to one's own dreams, for each to find his or her own life exemplary in some way. The struggle to do this is a struggle because an adult sensibility must find some way to include all the dark threads of life. A way to do this is to pay attention to what occurs in a land not touched by human schemes, where an original order prevails.

—Barry Lopez, *Arctic Dreams* (1986)

CHAPTER 1

Introduction: Approaches to the Psychology of Nature Writing

Sharon Cameron has suggested in her book *Writing Nature: Henry Thoreau's Journal* (1985), that "to write about nature is to write about how the mind sees nature, and sometimes about how the mind sees itself" (44). I believe this statement holds true not only for Henry David Thoreau, to whom Cameron is referring specifically, but also for many of Thoreau's followers in the tradition of American nature writing. Such writers as Annie Dillard, Edward Abbey, Wendell Berry, and Barry Lopez are not merely, or even primarily, analysts of nature or appreciators of nature—rather, they are students of the human mind, literary psychologists. And their chief preoccupation, I would argue, is with the psychological phenomenon of "awareness." Thoreau writes in the second chapter of *Walden* ([1854] 1971, 90) that "we must learn to reawaken and keep ourselves awake." But in order to achieve heightened attentiveness to our place in the natural world—attentiveness to our very existence—we must understand something about the workings of the mind.

Nature writers are constantly probing, traumatizing, thrilling, and soothing their own minds—and by extension those of their readers—in quest not only of consciousness itself, but of an understanding of consciousness. Their descriptions of this exalted mental condition tend to be variable and elusive, their terminologies more suggestive than definitive. Thoreau himself (drawing upon classical sources and daily cycles for his imagery) favors the notion of "awakening"; Dillard and Abbey use the word "awareness" to describe this state, though for Dillard such activities as "seeing" and "stalking" are also metaphors for stimulated consciousness; Berry, at least in his major essay "The Long-Legged House" (1969), emphasizes "watchfulness" as a condition of profound alertness; and for Lopez, two complementary modes of "understanding" natural places, the "mathematical" and especially the "particularized" (or experiential)—serve as keys to mental elevation.

Both nature and writing (the former being an external presence, the latter a process of verbalizing personal experience) demand and contribute to an author's awareness of self and nonself. By confronting face-to-face the separate realm of nature, by becoming aware of its otherness, the writer implicitly becomes more deeply aware of his or her own dimensions, limitations of form and understanding, and processes of grappling with the unknown. Many literary naturalists imitate the notebooks of scientific naturalists, or the logbooks of explorers, or even the journals of non-scientific travelers in order to entrench themselves in the specific moment of experience. The verbalization of observations and reactions makes one much more acutely aware than would a more passive assimilation of experience. As Annie Dillard bluntly puts it in describing one of her two principal modes of awareness, "Seeing is of course very much a matter of verbalization. Unless I call my attention to what passes before my eyes, I simply won't see it" (*Pilgrim*, 30).

Giles Gunn writes that "modern man tends to view the encounter with 'otherness' . . . as a mode of access to possibilities of change and development within the self and the self's relation to whatever is experienced as 'other.'" We associate reality, he continues, "with the process by which we respond to [other worlds'] imagined incursions from 'beyond' and then attempt to readjust and redefine ourselves as a consequence" (*Interpretation of Otherness*, 188). The facile sense of harmony, even identity, with one's surroundings (a condition often ascribed to rhapsodic nature writing) would fail to produce self-awareness of any depth or vividness. It is only by testing the boundaries of self against an outside medium (such as nature) that many nature writers manage to realize who they are and what's what in the world.

Most nature writers, from Thoreau to the present, walk a fine line (or, more accurately, vacillate) between rhapsody and detachment, between aesthetic celebration and scientific explanation. And the effort to achieve an equilibrium, a suitable balance of proximity to and distance from nature, results in the prized tension of awareness. According to Alain Robbe-Grillet, "This oscillating movement between man and his natural doubles is that of an active consciousness concerned to understand itself, to reform itself" ("Nature, Humanism, Tragedy," 69). Geoffrey Hartman, in commenting on Wordsworth, uses different terms to say something similar: "The element of obscurity, related to nature's self-concealment, is necessary to the soul's capacity for growth, for it vexes the latter toward self-dependence" ("The Romance of Nature," 291). In other words, the very mysteriousness of nature contributes to the independence and, presumably, the self-awareness of the observer. This dialectical tension between correspondence and otherness is especially noticeable in Thoreau, Dillard, and Abbey, writers who vacillate constantly between the two extreme perspectives. Berry and Lopez, however, do not vacillate so dramatically. Their sense of correspondence with the natural world in general, or with particular landscapes, does fluctuate, sometimes seeming secure and other times tenuous. But for the most part these two writers assume an initial disjunction (that of a native son newly returned from "exile" in Berry's case, and that of a traveler in exotic territory in Lopez's) which is gradually, through persistent care and attentiveness, resolved. The result, for Berry, is a process of ever-increasing "watchfulness"; for Lopez, one of deepening respect and understanding.

For all of these contemporary American nature writers, the prototypical literary investigation of the relationship between nature and the mind is Thoreau's Journal (*The Journal of Henry D. Thoreau*, hereinafter referred to and cited as Thoreau's Journal). The Journal, far from being a less artful and therefore less interesting subject for scholars than the works published during Thoreau's lifetime, is actually an example of nature writing at its purest, with no conscious attempt having been made to obscure and mystify the writer's intense connection or disconnection with his natural surroundings. In the works published during Thoreau's lifetime, the temporal element tends to be muted (by extensive philosophical digressions in his 1849 *A Week on the Concord and Merrimack Rivers* and by the somewhat concealed seasonal movement in *Walden*, for instance) and the authorial self often dissolves into multiple personae. The Journal, on the other hand, generally presents consistent temporal and spatial locations. We receive almost daily entries from a consistent narrator and it's usually clear exactly where Thoreau was and what he did or thought. The Journal gives us the sense throughout of Thoreau's actual presence in the natural world, something we encounter only intermittently in the other works, even in the many essays organized according to the excursion format. And not only is the author's proximity to nature more consistent and concrete in the Journal, but there is also a more explicit testing of the boundaries of self against the "other world" of nature.

One of the major issues of the text, which covers more than twenty years of Thoreau's life, is whether there is, in Emersonian terms, a "correspondence" between the inner self and the outer world, between the mind and nature. This is a question that Thoreau never answers finally—and thus results the rich tension of identity forging. The Journal, an almost daily record of observations, shows the author's efforts to line up his internal rhythms with those of external nature. There are times when Thoreau takes pleasure in the apparent identity of his own fluctuating moods and the "moods" of the passing seasons. At other times, though, it is nature's very "otherness" which fascinates and delights him: "I love Nature partly because she is not man, but a retreat from him" (4:445). The idea of nature as distinct from man gives the cranky author more than mere refuge from the annoyances and trivialities of the human world. This understanding, which comes from constant and thorough observation of natural phenomena, helps Thoreau both to enlarge his minute self by anchoring it in nature and, conversely, to become more deeply conscious of his human boundaries. Virtually all nature writers in Thoreau's wake perpetuate his combined fascination with inner consciousness and external nature, but I have chosen to focus my study on Dillard, Abbey, Berry, and Lopez because they represent with particular clarity modern variations of Thoreau's two opposing modes of response to nature: disjunction and conjunction.

For the purposes of the writer at the time of the actual observation (or of the journal-writing, which may, in Thoreau's case, often have occurred back at his desk), a journal is simply the most expedient way to keep a record, to protect observations from the foibles of memory. But even more importantly, as Dillard suggests in the quotation above, putting things into language helps people see better; and this can happen either at the moment of confrontation or in retrospect while sitting at a desk hours later. Of course, it is possible to record observations without strictly keeping track of chronology, but for the nature writer the omission of time of day and time of year would betoken a vital lapse of awareness. Nature changes so dramatically between noon and midnight, summer and winter, and sometimes even minute by minute, that the observer fails to grasp the larger meaning of phenomena if he or she overlooks the temporal aspect. Also, by making regular entries, the writer establishes a consistent routine of inspection; the condition of awareness thus becomes more lasting, and is not consigned to occasional moments of epiphany alone. For the reader, the journal form of nature writing (either the private journal or the various kinds of modified journals and anecdotal essays) effects a vicarious experience of the author's constant process of inspecting and interpreting nature, and heightens the reader's awareness of the author's presence in nature.

My interest in the way nature writers both study the phenomenon of environmental consciousness and attempt to stimulate this heightened awareness among their readers has led me to consult some of the scientific literature on environmental perception. Stephen and Rachel Kaplan edited a collection of essays entitled *Humanscape: Environments for People* (1982), which I have found particularly useful. In his introductory essay, Stephen Kaplan cites William James's seminal definition of the perceptual process: "Perception is of probable and definite things" (31). "By 'probable,'" Kaplan writes, "[James] meant that we tend to perceive what is likely, what is familiar, even when the stimulus is in fact not familiar. By 'definite' he meant that we tend to perceive clearly, even when the stimulus is vague, blurred, or otherwise ambiguous" (32). In other words, rather than attending fully and freshly to each new experience when we look at the world, we tend to rely upon previously stored information—what Kaplan and others refer to as "internal representations" (33). Although we may generally feel certainty when we perceive external reality, we are actually making what Kaplan calls "best guesses" (32) and *not* perceiving everything thoroughly, in detail. The reasons for this perceptual process are, of course, understandable. Often we don't have the time for thorough inspection—when we round a bend in the mountains and glimpse a large gray object, it is useful to decide quickly whether we have seen a dozing grizzly or a mere boulder. What especially interests me, though, is the implication that even when we feel certain we *know* our natural environment, we probably do not—we may not even have really looked at it.

It seems to me that Annie Dillard and Edward Abbey, in their efforts to stimulate our attentiveness to nature and to the foibles of our own minds, our delusions of certainty, take pains to invoke and then upend precisely the system of perception which, echoing James, Kaplan describes. Also in the *Humanscape* volume, William R. Catton suggests in an article entitled "The Quest for Uncertainty," that "one important type of motivation underlying the recreational use of wilderness by the average devotee may be the mystery it holds for him" (114). The attraction of mountain climbing, he explains, "is not in reaching the summit but in carrying on the task in the face of doubt as to whether the summit will be reached or will prove unattainable" (113). With a similar sense of the excitement of uncertainty, Dillard and Abbey tend to place special emphasis on the startling, sometimes even desperate, unpredictability of the natural world. They capitalize on the harsh and chilling features of the landscapes they love, recounting with particular avidness experiences in which perception has not been probable and definite. The emotional results are disgust, horror, annoyance, surprise, and almost always (at least in retrospect) satisfaction with the intensity of the experience.

Critics have traditionally been thrown off track by the flashy catchwords of Dillard's *Pilgrim at Tinker Creek*—specifically, the language drawn from either religion or natural science—and by their own desires and expectations. Think of the book's title, for instance. This in itself indicates the usual poles of critical response. Many readers approach the book expecting (and frequently finding) a "pilgrim," a person on a quest for spiritual knowledge, or one fulfilling a spiritual commitment through meditation on wonders of divinely mysterious origin. Others dwell upon the words "Tinker Creek," which are suggestive of a natural place. They expect to read meditations on nature or on man/nature interaction, and these readers are often put off by what they perceive as the work's anthropocentrism. Hayden Carruth, in an early review, deplores Dillard's abstractness and her failure to attend "to life on this planet at this moment, its hazards and misdirections," and refers to Wendell Berry's writing as being more responsible and "historically . . . relevant" than Dillard's ("Attractions and Dangers of Nostalgia," 640). Still other readers combine the two "poles" of the title and label Dillard a "visionary naturalist," though not always a successful one (Lavery, "Noticer," 270).

But Dillard is not now and never has been precisely a religious mystic or an environmentalist. She calls herself an "anchorite" on the second page of *Pilgrim* and a "nun" in her next book of prose, *Holy the Firm*, which appeared in 1977 and in which one of the few characters other than Dillard herself is an accident-scarred girl named "Julie Norwich." But despite her beguiling hints and suggestions, Dillard is not a latter-day Julian of Norwich, nor is she Rachel Carson's literary daughter, alerting the nation to the urgent problems of the environment. She is, rather, a kind of hybrid—if we were to push this hypothetical lineage to absurdity—of Thoreau and William James. The "wake-up call" of Thoreau's chapter "Where I Lived, and What I Lived For" in *Walden* reverberates throughout her works, as does the process of psychological experimentation demonstrated in the Journal, the alternating closeness to and estrangement from nature. Dillard is—and here I believe I deviate, at least in emphasis, from previous readers of her early work—a devoted student of the human mind, of its processes of awakening, its daily, hourly, and even momentary fluctuations of awareness. In this way she is much like William James, an investigator of the varieties of human consciousness. However, whereas James dwelled upon the varieties of religious experience, Dillard's emphasis (especially in *Pilgrim*) is on the varieties of natural experience—or, more precisely, on the experience of both heightened and dulled awareness of nature.

I do not wish to discount entirely the important religious and natural historical currents in her work, but I do think the central focus of her writing has always been the psychology of awareness. Even *Living by Fiction* (1982), with its concern for how writers working in various fictional and nonfictional genres experience "the raw universe" (145) and transform this experience into literature, is, to a great degree, psychological. In *Pilgrim* and *An Amer-*

ican Childhood (1987), Dillard displays with particular vividness her habit of provoking insight and wonderment by estranging herself from ordinary scenes and events. Fecundity and death, the opposing processes of nature so prominent in *Pilgrim*, are probably the most fundamental and therefore most common processes in the natural world. Yet Dillard, in her dreamlike observations of a giant water bug sucking the life out of a frog, or in her representation of a mantis reproducing ("I have seen the mantis's abdomen dribbling out eggs in wet bubbles like tapioca pudding glued to a thorn" [*Pilgrim*, 167]), uses unexpected language to transform the quotidian into the cataclysmic, thus snapping herself alert to the world and to her own thought processes. By verbalizing experiences, as she herself notes in the chapter of *Pilgrim* called "Seeing," she makes herself a more conscious, meticulous observer of the commonplace, an observer able to appreciate the strangeness, or otherness, of the world. Through her encounters with nature and her use of language, she awakens to her own participation in and distance from the organic world and to the dimensions of her own mind.

Edward Abbey, too, has often found his work co-opted by readers who needed his voice for their own purposes. In his tongue-in-cheek introduction to *Abbey's Road* (1979), Abbey claims to recall an incident which occurred after he gave a reading "at some country campus in Virginia." When a student accused him of not looking "right," not fitting the image of "a wilderness writer," an "environmental writer," Abbey supposedly responded with the following indignant self-definition: "I am an artist, sir, . . . a creator of fictions" (xxi–xxii). But the student is certainly not alone in his failure to sort out Abbey's intriguingly overlapping literary personalities. The critics also have often been baffled, either ignoring his work altogether or applying rather predictable labels to it. Virtually all of Abbey's writing, both his fiction and his nonfiction, defies easy categorization—much like George Washington Hayduke, the Green-Beret-turned-ecoterrorist in *The Monkey Wrench Gang*, Abbey's 1975 novel. Abbey's language feints one way, dodges capture, hides out until the coast is clear, then parades itself once again before carrying out yet another daring escape.

Desert Solitaire, his most famous work of nonfiction, exists for many readers as pure rhapsody – indeed, as an elegy for the lost (or, at least, fast-disappearing) pristineness of the Canyon Country in Utah. *The Monkey Wrench Gang*, on the other hand, is usually read as a straightforward call to arms for environmentalists, and such radical preservationist groups as Earth First! have even claimed it as their Bible. But neither reading is adequate. Ann Ronald encompasses part of the truth when she explains, in *The New West of Edward Abbey* (1982), how he uses "his sense of humor to pronounce a sobering message" (200). I have tried to push this explanation one step further in my chapter on Abbey by suggesting that his abundant humor – which typically takes the form of wordplay, like the pun in my chapter title on Abbey – is merely one aspect of his broader devotion to the aesthetics of language. I believe that Abbey's true project, his essential consciousness-raising effort, hinges upon the conflation of pure aesthetics with volatile moral issues (such as the sacredness of the wilderness, the inviolability of private property, and the appropriate use of public lands). This tension between aesthetics and morality is evident throughout Abbey's work, but I will focus on *Desert Solitaire* and, particularly, *The Monkey Wrench Gang*, reading the latter work as the *Lolita* of the environmental movement. Just as Vladimir Nabokov's *Lolita* throws its reader into richly conflicting states of disdain, pity, admiring sympathy, and aesthetic pleasure, Abbey's novel heightens our attentiveness to issues of the environment (while providing little explicit dogma) by presenting disturbing extremes toward both preservation and development of the land, within a literary context aimed to *please*. Obviously, *The Monkey Wrench Gang* is a novel and hardly a journal-like one at that. But it demonstrates a bold extension of the exploration of human awareness which Abbey began in *Desert Solitaire*, a more direct echo of Thoreau's own psychological journal.

I selected Wendell Berry and Barry Lopez for this study because they contrast so vividly with the more flamboyant and whimsical modern nature writers. Whereas Dillard and Abbey tend to emphasize disjunction and unpredictability in their efforts to prompt awareness, Wendell Berry and Barry Lopez take the opposite approach, mirroring the correspondential swing of

Thoreau's mental pendulum. For Dillard and Abbey, the most effective stimuli of intense alertness are change, surprise, disruption of facile certainty implied by the Jamesian concept of perception. But Berry and Lopez assume ignorance or limited awareness to begin with, then proceed to enact a gradual and almost linear progression toward a deepening of awareness. What most people merely perceive as "probable and definite" in the external world, these two writers attempt to make evermore solid, evermore certain. Neither of these writers ever claims to have achieved a fully developed consciousness, an unsurpassable plateau of awareness. Like Thoreau, they emphasize the ongoing process of mental growth, but they deviate from the dazzling erraticness of Thoreau's other heirs, Dillard and Abbey, in their steady and (perhaps to some readers) tediously persistent movement toward the world.

In "The Long-Legged House," the lengthy essay which is the primary focus of my chapter on watchfulness, Berry presents the history of his attachment to his native place along the Kentucky River, showing "how a person can come to belong to a place" (145). It was only after contemplating Andrew Marvell's poetry about humanity's place in nature that Berry began "that summer of [his] marriage the surprisingly long and difficult labor of *seeing* the country [he] had been born in and had lived [his] life in until then" (141). Thus Berry's work implies the need to move beyond complacent acceptance of our "internal representations" of the places where we live or visit, the need to see things consciously, to become aware — and it indicates also the role of literature in inspiring and guiding "awakening" (to use Thoreau's word) in its readers. The essay sweeps through many years of Berry's life, recounting the history of the place where he eventually, after years as a wandering academic, came back to live and revitalize his roots. Berry also digresses from direct discussion of this place, known as "the Camp," in order to reflect abstractly on connections between the self and the natural world, and on ways of coming to know intimately a specific natural place. The place, he says, will reveal its secrets to the human observer, but it takes prolonged contact: "The only condition is your being there and being *watchful*" (169 — my emphasis).

This necessary watchfulness is enhanced by the process of writing. At the point in the history when Berry and his wife have returned to the Camp and he has vowed to become (as he later puts it) "intimate and familiar" with the place (161), he recalls that he began writing "a sort of journal, keeping account of what [he] saw" (146). Immediately after he mentions this, the style of the essay changes—it becomes much more detailed and concrete, the pace of the narrative slowing to allow the presentation of specific natural observations, examples of how "the details rise up out of the whole and become visible" to the patient observer (161). What is interesting to me about this process of observation is that Berry associates it explicitly with the act of writing, a connection manifested even in the way the prose of the essay changes, becoming more journal-like and immediate, at the point in the history when the author is finally making contact with the place. The result of this increasing intimacy with the Camp and the nearby river landscape, despite the deepening sense of attachment, is an awareness that the man belongs to the place without the place belonging to the man. So there remains a disjunction between Berry and his most familiar natural place—the separation lessens, but is never erased entirely. This awareness does not mitigate the author's feeling of attachment, but it does result in the distinctive humility of Berry's work, in the frequent reminders that people are part of a vast world.

Although Berry narrates this process of return and reconnection most thoroughly and explicitly in "The Long-Legged House," he also meditates compellingly on exile, homecoming, and belonging to a place in such works as "Notes from an Absence and a Return" (a 1970 essay/journal which tersely parallels "The Long-Legged House"), the Odysseus section in *The Unsettling of America* (1977), and "The Making of a Marginal Farm" (1980). In the most recent of these essays, Berry makes an important distinction between writing about a place from afar, treating it merely as subject matter, and actually living on the land. He writes,

> In coming home and settling on this place, I began to *live* in my subject, and to learn that living in one's subject is not at all the same as "having" a subject. To live in the place that is one's subject is to pass

> through the surface. The simplifications of distance and mere obser-
> vation are thus destroyed. . . . One's relation to one's subject ceases
> to be merely emotional or esthetical, or even merely critical, and
> becomes problematical, practical, and responsible as well. Because it
> must. It is like marrying your sweetheart. (*Recollected Essays*, 337)

For Berry, awareness or watchfulness is indeed an exalted state of
mind, but it is not an innocently blissful one. "The Long-Legged
House" tends to emphasize the difficulty of achieving watchfulness
and the pleasure of paying attention to the subtleties of place once
one's mind begins to get in shape. However, "The Making of a
Marginal Farm," written a decade later, admits that paying attention can reveal horrors as well as delights. In this essay Berry is
particularly attuned to the problem of erosion, a problem so severe
along the steep slopes of the lower Kentucky River Valley that "It
cannot be remedied in human time; to build five or six feet of soil
takes perhaps fifty or sixty thousand years. This loss, once imagined, is potent with despair. If a people in adding a hundred and
fifty years to itself subtracts fifty thousand years from its land, what
is there to hope?" (335). Despite this expression of despair and futil-
ity, Berry's life and literary work are both processes of reclamation,
rehabilitation. To write about a problem is not necessarily to produce a solution, but the kindling of consciousness—one's own and
one's reader's—is a first step—an essential first step.

   One of the important issues in contemporary nature writing
is determining how this literature translates into concrete changes
in a reader's attitude and behavior toward the environment.
Cheryll Burgess, the author of a paper entitled "Toward an Ecological Literary Criticism"—delivered at the 1989 meeting of the Western Literature Association—argues that it is the responsibility of
critics and teachers to point out the environmental implications of
literary texts, or, in other words, to engage in "ecocriticism." At
the panel discussion "Building a Constituency for Wilderness,"
which took place during the Second North American Interdisciplinary Wilderness Conference in February 1990, such writers and
editors as Michael Cohen, Stephen Trimble, and Gibbs Smith
contemplated more specifically the likely audience for nature writing and the possible effects—or lack thereof—that this writing

might have. Are nature writers "preaching to the choir," or do their voices reach out even to the unaware and uncommitted? With the 1990 Earth Day celebration now more than two years behind us, it is clear that the Thoreauvian process of awakening is not merely a timeless private quest, but a timely—even urgent—requirement if we are to prevent or at least retard the further destruction of our planet. But how can nature writers lead the way in this awakening, this "conversion process"?

This is, of course, the problem Barry Lopez presents movingly in the prologue to *Arctic Dreams*: "If we are to devise an enlightened plan for human activity in the Arctic, we need a more particularized understanding of the land itself—not a more refined mathematical knowledge, but a deeper understanding of its nature, as if it were, itself, another sort of civilization we had to reach some agreement with" (11). The book itself consists of nine chapters, which could be said to represent such academic categories as anthropology, geology, biology, history, and aesthetics. Much of this material, however elegantly worded, is discursive—that is, non-narrative. And this alone is not enough to achieve the special understanding Lopez seeks for himself and his readers. But what he does do is crystallize all of his scholarly passages around vivid kernels of personal experience, demonstrating his own profound engagement with the place and thus soliciting his readers' imaginative engagement as well, the first step toward active concern.

In his interview with Kay Bonetti, Lopez explains that "the sorts of stories that I'm attracted to in a nonfiction way are those that try to bring some of the remote areas closer for the reader by establishing some kind of intimacy with the place, but also by drawing on the work of archeologists and historians and biologists" (Bonetti, "An Interview with Barry Lopez," 59). This passage demonstrates the approach in much of his work, including *Arctic Dreams*. It is a process of venturing to exotic, seldom-experienced landscapes, of describing terrain, flora, fauna, and human inhabitants, and of reporting back to his North American readers in a detailed, respectful mode of storytelling calculated to generate in his audience a concern, not only for the specific subject of the narrative, but for the readers' own immediate surroundings. As Lopez asserts at the Fourth Sino-American Writers Conference held in 1988, "The goal of the writer, finally, is to nourish the reader's awareness of the world" ("Chinese Garland," 41).

The chapters in *Arctic Dreams* are frequently aloof, factual, and coolly prophetic, but then Lopez suddenly presents a pulsing human heart amidst the frozen landscape, pushing understanding beyond the merely mathematical, the intellectual. The personal anecdotes do not show the author melting easily into the landscape, despite his intimations of reverence for its beauty and the inspiring abundance of Arctic life—rather, the emphasis tends to be, for instance, on the author's insecurity, his vulnerability, as he stands on the edge of an ice floe which could without warning break adrift or be shattered by the predatory battering of a submerged polar bear. The work depicts insecurity, alienation, even gawking wonderment (at the appearance of icebergs, for instance), yet there is also a sense of deep respect for the place, an awareness of the simultaneous fragility and power of the landscape and its inhabitants. Lopez achieves his thorough understanding of the Arctic by coupling academic research with personal experience of its otherness, of its separate, inhuman reality. He makes use of the personal anecdote to recreate the experiential moment and thus guides his audience through a vicarious conversion.

One of the purposes of Lopez's writing, a goal he hopes to extend to his readers, is to develop an "intimacy" with the landscape that does not interfere with attentiveness (by causing excessive comfort and ease), but rather fuels it and deepens it. When asked by Kenneth Margolis how he served the community, Lopez responded that "There has always been this function in society of people who go 'outside'. . . . If you come face to face with the other you can come home and see the dimensions of the familiar that make you love it" (Margolis, "Paying Attention," 53). The writer who goes "outside" in order to help himself and his audience understand both the exotic and the familiar requires his readers to draw upon their capacity for metaphor, to associate their own landscapes with the writer's, their language and conceptual patterns with those of the story. Lopez's own multidisciplinary approach, as he suggests in his public dialogue with E. O. Wilson (in Edward Lueders's *Writing Natural History: Dialogues with*

Authors, 1989), has profoundly impressed him with the idea that people "all see the world in a different way." He continues,

> And I lament sometimes, that there are those who lack a capacity for metaphor. They don't talk to each other, and so they don't have the benefit of each other's insights. Or they get stuck in their own metaphor, if you will, as a reality and don't see that they can help each other in this inquiry that binds people like ourselves together. So this issue arises for me: what do we know? how do we know? how do we organize our knowledge? (14-15)

In my discussion of *Arctic Dreams*, I will discuss not so much what Lopez has come to know about the Arctic, but how he has organized this knowledge so as to prompt his readers' engagement with a multiplicity of eye-opening metaphors or alternative modes of perception/conception. Much like Thoreau, who demonstrates a constant shuffling of perspectives in both *Walden* and the Journal, Lopez interweaves the perspectives of various disciplines, cultures, and physical vantage points in an attempt to make us conscious of the constraints of static perspectives. I believe that both Berry and Lopez attempt in their work to demonstrate and explain the process of achieving "intimacy" with the landscape, but while Berry (to adapt his metaphor) establishes a monogamous relationship with one particular place and peels away layer after layer of surface appearances to come to know the place, Lopez travels to remote locations throughout the world and then returns to Oregon to write about them. However, just as Thoreau dreamed of world travel before deciding it was challenging enough to become "expert in home-cosmography" (*Walden*, 320), Lopez has told recent interviewers, "I'd be happy for the rest of my life to just try to elucidate what it is that is North America" (Aton, "An Interview with Barry Lopez," 4).

My goal in this study is to illuminate the purposes and processes of "paying attention" in American nature writing since Thoreau. By examining Thoreau's Journal, we can see demonstrated the two principal relationships between the human mind and the natural world—"correspondence" and "otherness"—which recent writers have continued to investigate. Thoreau's Journal marks the obvious starting point of this psychological tradition in

American nature writing because it records the author's empirical scrutiny of his own internal responses to the world. The more recent works considered in this book differ in important ways from Thoreau's Journal—I have not traveled to Tucson to read Edward Abbey's Journal, nor have I bothered Barry Lopez for a peek at his (though he told Bonetti that he has kept one since the age of nineteen as a way to "make sense—daily sense—out of [his] life"—68). Instead, I have tried to focus on what I consider to be the primary investigatory genres of each author: Dillard's coherent, episodic collections of nonfiction essays; Abbey's aestheticized prose in *Desert Solitaire* and, more exaggeratedly, in his fiction; Berry's individual essays of exile and return; and Lopez's psychological essays in *Arctic Dreams* and self-reflective interview performances (he has participated in so many interviews in recent years that perhaps it would be reasonable to view "the interview" as one of his chief modes of communication).

There remains more work to do along these lines. For instance, the political and historical contexts of these literary investigations of awakening could use further attention. Although I recognize that several of these writers have political agendas, I prefer to view them as epistemologists, as students of the human mind, rather than as activists in any concrete sense of the term. Ray Gonzalez titled his 1990 interview with Barry Lopez, "Landscapes of the Interior: The Literature of Hope," and this captures precisely the approach that I try to take in this book. Nature writing is a "literature of hope" in its assumption that the elevation of consciousness may lead to wholesome political change, but this literature is also concerned, and perhaps primarily so, with interior landscapes, with the mind itself.

Lopez once said: "The two ways I have learned to pay attention are to read and then to go to the place myself, to walk around in it, to see what the ground feels like under my feet, to listen to the sounds of the birds . . . " (Bonetti, 59–60). I, too, value the complementarity of literary experience and direct sensory experience, and my understanding of what Thoreau, Dillard, Abbey, Berry, and Lopez have achieved in their writings derives not only from hours spent cooped up with heaps of books and papers, but from what happens when I put down the literature and step outside. For this reason – and with the support of John Elder's insight in *Imagining the Earth* (1985) that "It seems important to acknowledge that natural scenes engender and inform meditations on literature as well as the other way around" (3) – I have concluded the book with several brief, summarizing "Excursions" (outdoor narratives) and "Incursions" (parting thoughts on the aims and contexts of psychological nature writing).

CHAPTER 2

The Inner Life and the Outer World: Thoreau's "Habit of Attention" in His Private Journal

Not the sun or the summer alone, but every hour and season yields its tributes of delight; for every hour and change corresponds to and authorizes a different state of the mind, from breathless noon to grimmest midnight.
                    —*Ralph Waldo Emerson, Nature (1836, 6)*

Watching the Seasons:
A Journal of Correspondence and Otherness

Two modes of apprehending the natural world predominate in Thoreau's Journal. The more commonly recognized approach is that of "correspondence," a belief in the subtle mirroring of man and nature, a sharing of vital rhythms; this notion pervades the work of Thoreau's fellow transcendentalists, particularly in Emerson's *Nature*. The other mode, which Thoreau inherited from Coleridge, suggests that a fertile tension, a rise in consciousness, results from the recognition of the "polarity" of man and nature rather than their connection; but even this idea rests upon the possibility of engaged interaction between the two poles. Sharon Cameron goes so far as to argue that "when the mind sees nature what it sees is its difference from nature, is the way in which correspondences fail to work out. . . . The harmony and confluence so central to Thoreau's other works and to Emerson's *Nature* (with which Thoreau's Journal can profitably be compared), in which nature and the mind evoke each other, is posited by the Journal so as to be frustrated" (*Writing Nature*, 44–45). This is frequently the case, but not always. What we encounter in reading the Journal is the writer's exploration of his own mental processes, processes which coincide intermittently with those of the natural world. "The poet must be continually watching the moods of his mind, as the astronomer watches the aspects of the heavens," he proposed on August 19, 1851. The poet and the astronomer are united in the keeper of "a meteorological journal of the mind" (2:403). Thoreau's Journal may have begun as a self-conscious workbook for the preparation of public lectures and essays, but it gradually evolved into a testing ground of consciousness. In particular, attentiveness to the passing of the natural and internal seasons became, as years went by and journal writing ceased to be an artificial activity, Thoreau's principal habit of mind.

In the early decades after Thoreau's death in 1862, his closest friends were granted access by Thoreau's sister Sophia to the "nearly seventy handwritten volumes" (Howarth, *The Book of Concord*, 5) of his private journal. Emerson, savoring the aphoristic brilliance of the Journal, made a series of scattered extracts available to the public in his memorial essay shortly after Thoreau's death. But when it came to the publication of more extensive selections of the Journal, Bronson Alcott advised Harrison Blake to refine and reorganize the chronological but erratic sequence of observations and meditations in the original notebooks; and thus Blake came up with the seasonal format for its initial publication, compressing over twenty years' worth of journal entries (1837–1861) into the four seasons of a single, undated year. Perhaps Blake found his precedent for this act of artful compression in Thoreau's own presentation of the two years he spent living at Walden Pond as a single year in his literary account: a year, however, in which the passage of the seasons is surprisingly obscure and unemphasized when compared to the highlighting of seasonal changes which one finds in the "raw" version of the Journal.

Then there is the idea, expressed by William Ellery Channing in *Thoreau, the Poet-Naturalist* (1873, 1902), that Thoreau himself hoped eventually "upon a small territory—such a space as that filled by the town of Concord—[to] construct a chart or calendar which should chronicle the phenomena of the seasons in their order, and give their general average for the year" (67). Emerson, too, sensed that Thoreau had been working on an enormous, synthesizing project when he died, and Emerson felt it "a kind of indignity" that "he should leave in the midst his broken task, which none else can finish" ("Biographical Sketch," 33). The mere fact that so much of the Journal remains intact, not yet mined for lectures and essays, suggests that the author died before he could put his notes to their ultimate use. The notion that the Journal was intended as a working draft of some literary product other than itself, together with the conspicuous attention to the seasons, seems to have inspired his posthumous publishers to adopt the seasonal format. The choice of format had little to do with an understanding that Thoreau's extreme attentiveness to the seasons resulted from his testing of the transcendental theory of correspondences, his ongoing scrutiny of the overlappings and oppositions between himself and nature.

It was logical for Thoreau's friends to assume that his Journal was not an end in itself but rather an inchoate testing ground of words and ideas; this was an assumption truly based on intended faithfulness to Thoreau's secret goals, but I think it diminishes the flights of imagination and the recurrent cycles of observation to remove them from their natural chronology. The Journal in its original year-by-year form displays what Thoreau intimated already in his early statement that "The highest condition of art is artlessness" (1:153). This appreciation for rough form and artless expression emerges again and again in the Journal, suggesting implicitly that Thoreau valued the crude form of his Journal above the more crafted form of his published works, in which he bowed to the demands of publishers and, to some extent, to the palates of his expected readers. His well-intentioned posthumous editors, in determining how to present the Journal to the public, actually relied more upon their own notions of a finished work of natural history than on the Journal's internal clues regarding Thoreau's literary values.

But this is not to say that Thoreau did not place great emphasis on seasonal progression in his daily Journal entries. In a sense, every natural observation he made was a kind of sighting, a note regarding a seasonal landmark, or timemark. "On *this* day at *this* hour at *this* location, I saw *this* plant or animal doing *this* or having *this* done to it," Thoreau seems to say in his most characteristic entries. Sometimes the sightings are less individualized, consisting of lists of sightings and dates that run for pages. But what was the real reason for this meticulous record of the emergences and disappearances that mark the progression of the seasons? Was this all merely raw material for an eventual "chart or calendar," a Linnaean work of factual natural history? I don't think so. The Journal is, in a sense, the opposite of the usual post-Baconian scientific approach to nature, the attempt to establish objective distance between the human observer and the natural phenomena under scrutiny.

The Journal is particularly useful as a means of tracing Thoreau's interest in the effect of nature upon the human mind, and especially the effects of specific seasons and times of day. The Swedenborgian doctrine of correspondence, received by way of Emerson, seems to have had a profound influence on Thoreau's understanding of nature and human psychology. Thoreau echoes Emerson's *Nature* (1836) repeatedly in his observations of the correspondences between the seasons and the mind, asking in August, 1853, "Is it not as language that all natural objects affect the poet? He sees a flower or other object, and it is beautiful or affecting to him because it is a symbol of his thought. . . . The objects I behold correspond to my mood" (5:359). Four years later he suggested a specific correspondence between the external seasons and his own internal rhythms:

> These regular phenomena of the seasons get at last to be – they were *at first*, of course – simply and plainly phenomena or phases of my life. The seasons and all their changes are in me. I see not a dead eel or floating snake, or a gull, but it rounds my life and is like a line or accent in its poem. Almost I believe the Concord would not rise and overflow its banks again, were I not here. After a while I learn what my moods and seasons are. I would have nothing subtracted. I can imagine nothing added. My moods are thus periodical, not two days in my year are alike. The perfect correspondence of Nature to man, so that he is at home in her! (10:127)

"After a while I learn what my moods and seasons are." It takes time for Thoreau to assimilate the natural seasons within his own mental seasons, but the convergence eventually, after years of close observation and note-taking, guides his understanding of how his own mind works. His own attunement to the seasons, even to the minute passage of time from day to day, suggests to him a broader identity between himself (and perhaps all people, though they may be ignorant of it) and nature. Thoreau writes elsewhere in the Journal that "The poet is a man who lives at last by watching his own words" (2:428); he is thus extremely *self-conscious* even as he proceeds to record intricate observations of the outside world. He can never look only at himself or only at nature, but must always employ a kind of double vision, a way of seeing which acknowledges the subtle, vital unity of the self and the world.

This preoccupation with himself is particularly conspicuous in the early years of the Journal, especially in the entries written while Thoreau was still in his twenties. As the writer ages, the external world takes on greater independence and solidity and becomes, it frequently seems, a realm worthy of contemplation for reasons other than its correspondence with man. William Howarth has suggested that in the mid-1850s "the Journal had become more external and comprehensive, taking in a larger image of the world lying around him. No longer [was it] just an autobiographical mirror" (*Book of Concord*, 108). Similarly, Judy Schaaf Anhorn observes in her study of *The Maine Woods*, that "From at least 1852, Thoreau's work illustrates his attraction to a more objective, even empirical, study of natural fact" (1). But even in the Journal's later entries, despite Howarth's sense that "aging turns men into realists" (110), Thoreau remains fascinated with the possibility of correspondence—or rather, with the stimulating alternation of otherness and correspondence. Along these lines, in his 1986 study William Rossi provides an illuminating discussion of Coleridge's theory of "polarity" in the context of Thoreau's frequent opposition of civilization and wildness. Rossi suggests that the very independence of the two realms (and, on a smaller scale, the individual human observer and the specific natural phenomenon) creates a vital tension that binds the poles together ("Laboratory of the Artist," 57–103).

One reason why it was not particularly appropriate to publish the Journal according to the progression from spring to autumn (with winter inserted after summer because of the "rhyming" relationship) is that this pattern implies a steady "bud, bloom, blight" movement not consistently evident in the Journal itself. There are, of course, numerous instances where Thoreau notes the special qualities of each season and the effects these have upon his mood—for instance, he writes the following with springish exuberance on March 15, 1852: "My life partakes of infinity. The air is as deep as our natures" (3:350). A year and a half later, he writes with Decemberish sobriety that "In winter even man is to a slight extent dormant, just as some animals are but partially awake, though not commonly classed with those that hibernate" (6:38). He regularly tries to pinpoint seasonal peculiarities with observations such as "The wind is Septemberish" (4:327), which may be less descriptive than suggestive in a more abstract way of the special seasonal quality of the wind. Similarly, he writes that during November, "whose name sounds so bleak and cheerless," even "men are more serious" (11:312). Still, rather than emphasizing in sweeping terms the general climatic characteristics of the distinct seasons, Thoreau seeks to attune himself to the precise conditions of each particular day, often noting changes during individual days. In 1860, near the end of his life and his career as a journalizer, he explained his approach to natural observation, one of the dominant modes in the Journal:

> In keeping a journal of one's walks and thoughts it seems to be worth the while to record those phenomena which are most interesting to us at the time. Such is the weather. It makes material difference whether it is foul or fair, affecting surely our mood and thoughts. Then there are various degrees and kinds of foulness and fairness. It may be cloudless, or there may be sailing clouds which threaten no storm, or it may be partially overcast. On the other hand it may rain, or snow, or hail, with various degrees of intensity. It may be a transient thunder-storm, or a shower, or a flurry of snow, or it may be a prolonged storm of rain or snow. Or the sky may be overcast or rain-threatening. So with regard to temperatures. It may be warm or cold. Above 40° is warm for winter. One day, at 38 even, I walk dry and it is good sleighing; the next day it may have risen to 48, and the snow is rapidly changed to slosh. It may be calm or windy. The finest winter day is a cold but clear and glittering one. There is a remarkable life in the air then, and birds and other creatures appear to feel it, to be excited and invigorated by it. Also warm and melting days in winter are inspiring, though less characteristic. (13:106–7)

The successive entries of the Journal betray Thoreau's perennial interest in both the characteristic and the anomalous. Even the minute fluctuations of temperature and precipitation often seem to constitute characteristic seasonal conditions, but Thoreau was ever ready to note a change which was out of the ordinary. And any external condition, he suggests in the passage just quoted, makes a "material difference" in "our mood and thoughts." This is a rather mundane expression of Emerson's often repeated, abstract intimations "that inner and outer correspond" (as quoted from the Journals by Hotson, "Emerson and the Doctrine of Correspondence," 48), but it also indicates that Thoreau's own understanding of the doctrine, his own tentative and intermittent acceptance of it, is based upon empirical, experiential tests: his almost-daily "walks and thoughts" among the elements, recorded in his Journal. One of the interesting and suggestive features of the previous passage is the possibility that animals display, in their physical behavior, a similar correspondence with the weather; this is perhaps a more stable and incontrovertible type of correspondence than the transcendental one to which Emanuel Swedenborg and his American followers adhered.

But what Thoreau seems especially intent on doing in his Journal, with only occasional explicit references to the idea of correspondence, is to record the transitions from season to season, not merely isolate the traits of each. It is as if these temporal "borders" between the different phases of the natural year, much like his own spatial and psychological "border life" ("Walking," 130) between the wilderness and civilization, provide a particularly rich realm in which to prompt awareness of harmonies and discords, of shared and individual identity. This is a profoundly exciting process for Thoreau—perhaps the essential project of the Journal. It is the source of much of the boyish energy within even the more factual passages of observation. Even toward the end of his life (specifically in 1860, when he was forty-three years old), he wrote with childlike eagerness, with true Romantic innocence, about his love for the raucous upheaval as winter gave way to spring: "It excites me to see early in the spring that black artery [the river] leaping once more through the snow-clad town. All is tumult and life there, not to mention the rails and cranberries that are drifting in it. . . . These are the wrists, temples, of the earth, where I feel its pulse with my eye" (13:138). This transitional phase between winter and spring is the time of year when "a certain dormant life awakes in [the writer]" (7:104), too. Yet this mood of exhilaration is not linked strictly to the theme of regeneration typically associated with spring itself. Thoreau, over the years, displays a special love of variation, of change in general, and thus he exclaims one March day in 1859: "What a variety of weather!" (12:58).

The idea that particular seasons correspond precisely to particular moods seems forgotten when the writer rhapsodizes in autumn about the beauty of decaying things:

> How much beauty in decay! I pick up a white oak leaf, dry and stiff, but yet mingled red and green, October-like, whose pulpy part some insect has eaten beneath, exposing the delicate network of its veins. It is very beautiful held up to the light,—such work as only an insect eye could perform. Yet, perchance, to the vegetable kingdom such a revelation of ribs is as repulsive as the skeleton in the animal kingdom. In each case it is some little gourmand, working for another end, that reveals the wonders of nature. There are countless oak leaves in this condition now, and also with a submarginal line of network exposed. (7:495–96)

The writer's own emotional response to this natural observation evolves quickly into a meditation on the variability of perspective, on the possibility that a natural phenomenon which produces aesthetic pleasure for one observer will repulse another; for Thoreau, though, this relativization of perspective spans the organic world as a whole, not merely differentiating between human viewers. By becoming so alert to the idiosyncrasies of his own emotional responses to nature, Thoreau achieves a sense of personal boundaries. While on some occasions he intuits the effects of weather upon "birds and other creatures," his inclination is to emphasize commonality. Many other times he highlights difference, difference between the observer and the observed, and between various observers.

Another example of an aesthetic response which defies the conventional correspondences between moods and seasons occurs in midwinter, when, captivated by the perfect crystalline structures of snowflakes, he writes: "Nature is full of genius, full of the divinity; so that not a snow-flake escapes its fashioning hand"

(8:87). Beauty is available to the willing-and-able beholder at all times of the year, not only during the benign and lush seasons of warmth and fruition. In fact, Thoreau suggests explicitly at one point in the Journal that the source of feeling is not nature itself but the mind of the human onlooker: "The nature which to one is a stark and ghastly solitude is a sweet, tender, and genial society to another" (9:337). Anyone may experience a variety of attitudes toward the same season, depending on the mood.

So which comes first: the mood or the season, the mood or the natural phenomenon? Thoreau occasionally seems to make unequivocal statements of association, such as, "The objects I behold correspond to my mood." But it's unclear from this particular comment whether his eyes select things to observe according to his mood, whether his internal condition colors the external world, or whether his mood results from whatever he happens to be experiencing in the outside world. Of course, the poet-naturalist sauntering through the woods near Walden is bound to take in many random impressions from his surroundings—many connected with the season at hand. But when he actually sits down to record his experience, he writes: "I find some advantage in describing the experience of a day on the day following. At this distance it is more ideal, like the landscape seen with the head inverted, or reflections in water" (6:207). It may well be his mood at the time of writing which guides his choice of natural images.

Thoreau's frequent remarks about the living language of nature hark back not only to Emerson's section on language in *Nature*, but even to the earlier Puritan efforts to read the book of nature, to decipher the divine "hieroglyphs" (Thoreau's own word: 1:363). But I believe Thoreau is rather original in suggesting that it is his own fundamental kinship with the natural world that enables him, that requires him, to call upon natural symbols and analogies in order to express his moods and thoughts. He writes at one point, "My thought is part of the meaning of the world, and hence I use a part of the world as a symbol to express my thought" (4:410). The first part of this statement reiterates Thoreau's frequent assertion that the very significance of nature, or in particular of a naturalist's observations, is dependent upon the disclosure of the observer's relationship to the object observed. Elsewhere he writes: "Your observation, to be interesting, i.e. to be significant, must be *subjective*. The sum of what the writer of whatever class [poet or scientist] has to report is simply some human experience . . . " (6:237). But why the reliance upon natural symbols and tropes for the expression of human ideas? Thoreau offers an explanation when he states:

> [T]he roots of *letters* are *things*. Natural objects and phenomena are the original symbols or types which express our thoughts and feelings, and yet American scholars, having little or no root in the soil, commonly strive with all their might to confine themselves to the imported symbols alone. (12:389)

Thus Thoreau feels that he is working with a primal, potent form of language when he relies upon his own immediate natural surroundings for his imagery; for him, the language of nature is not merely something to receive and interpret (as it was for the Puritans), but rather a medium for his own communication. It is especially important to note his reliance upon personal observations of his own native place; in this way he strives to summon the raw vigor of "indigenous" words—"words which are genuine and indigenous and have their roots in our natures"—rather than resorting to the "spurious and artificial" words of the scholar "who does not stand on solid ground" (10:233).

It is true that much of the Journal, including many of its richest and most beautiful passages, was not written explicitly for eventual publication. In 1851, Thoreau suggested that the motto of the Journal should be "Says I to myself" (3:107). Yet he never releases himself from the demand that he write with as much "gusto" as possible: "It is always essential that we love to do what we are doing, do it with a heart" (2:441). He yearns "to have [his] immortality now, that it be the *quality* of [his] daily life" (3:351). And what he spent his daily life doing was observing and contemplating nature, then attempting to put his ideas into appropriate words. The best words available to him, the words he traced directly to the soil beneath his feet, were those of the peasant rather than the high-flown preacher (1:255–56) or the effusively eloquent English essayists (2:418). He criticizes DeQuincey and Dickens, for instance, because "They never stutter; they flow too readily" (2:482). Thoreau, on the other hand, hoped to plant good sentences in his Journal much as the farmer tried each year to plant good corn (1:313), making his work "concentrated and nutty" (2:418). Likewise, his criticisms of scientific language emphasize its distance from life and nature: "I look over the report of the doings of a scientific association and am surprised that there is so little life to be reported; I am put off with a parcel of dry technical terms. Anything living is easily and naturally expressed in popular language" (6:237–38).

Many times Thoreau succeeded in expressing his mood merely by describing external nature without extensive commentary, but at other times nature served as an explicit analogy for the workings of his own emotions. The following is a good example of this, as well as of Thoreau's sense of the transience of moods:

> The mind of man is subject to moods, as the shadows of clouds pass over the earth. Pay not too much heed to them. Let not the traveller stop for them. They consist with the fairest weather. By the mood of my mind, I suddenly felt dissuaded from continuing my walk, but I observed at the same instance that the shadow of a cloud was passing over [the] spot on which I stood, though it was of small extent, which, if it had no connection with my mood, at any rate suggested how transient and little to be regarded that mood was. I kept on, and in a moment the sun shone on my walk within and without. (2:340)

Here Thoreau hesitates to attribute his dark mood to the little cloud passing overhead (indeed, the brief anecdote is so generalized as to seem a kind of parable rather than a genuine report of experience), but he does show here that the external world can bear a profound resemblance to our own minds—and passages such as this one help to substantiate his claims of identity with the natural world.

It is not necessary to have four dramatically different seasons, to have humid summers, vivid autumnal tints, snowy winters, and startling springs, in order for an observant and articulate person to become deeply enmeshed in the rhythms of his or her surroundings. In fact, although Thoreau does occasionally praise his native

Concord with understandable patriotism, the process of his interior migration, of making himself as awake to familiar surroundings as travelers might be to new places, is not specific to New England but to Thoreau's kind of mind. And anyone who can say for himself "I am a mystic, a transcendentalist, and a natural philosopher to boot" (5:4) is potentially capable of producing a journal such as Thoreau's. It is not enough, though, simply to possess such a mind, to desire awareness. The act of keeping a private journal, requiring as it does the close and persistent attunement to experience, makes this desired state of alertness an actuality.

Testing Perspective:
The Journal as Means of Experimentation

Thoreau did not accept correspondence wholesale, nor did he take it for granted. To a great extent, the Journal is a forum for testing this very notion. Frequently, the connections Thoreau makes between nature and humanity seem based not so much on observed similarities as on dissimilarities, the sense that nature could provide a useful model for the reform of human behavior or society. One example of this comes early in the Journal, when he first observes that "Nature never makes haste; her systems revolve at an even pace. The bud swells imperceptibly, without hurry or confusion, as though the short spring days were an eternity"; and he asks, "Why, then, should man hasten as if anything less than eternity were allotted for the least deed?" (1:92). The implication that nature changes at an "even pace" may well be a faulty description of the world, a description deriving more from the observer's intended moral comment than from objective openness to natural truth. However, this possible mistake in scientific inspection does not result from a sense of external nature's intrinsic correspondence with human nature, but rather from Thoreau's sense of a distinction which ought to be erased by modifying man. The reform of his own species, or even of himself (this note did, after all, appear in a private piece of writing), is hardly a certain result of such an observation; what is more certain, and perhaps more meaningful, is the way Thoreau's discernment of regular changes in nature accents his awareness of and disenchantment with the haste and erraticness he experiences as a human being. Another time he remarks, "I think the existence of man in nature is the divinest and most startling of facts" (2:208), suggesting that man is not simply a natural being, that the strange incongruity between man and nature is itself pleasantly "startling." The Journal's record of Thoreau's successive encounters with the natural world thus serves as an ongoing prompter of awareness, nature affording him both an object for intense scrutiny and a kind of mirror (often a distorting one) reflecting his human reality.

This use of nature as an external mirror of humanity is not merely a youthful self-deception. Even as he ages and grows, becoming more factual and empirical in his journal notations, Thoreau discerns in himself the very essence that he most cherishes in external nature – its "wildness":

> It is in vain to dream of a wildness distant from ourselves. There is none such. It is the bog in our brain and bowels, the primitive vigor of Nature in us, that inspires that dream. I shall never find in the wilds of Labrador any greater wildness than in some recess of Concord; *i.e.* than I import into it. (9:43)

This is perhaps the most enriching of Thoreau's conceptions of nature. Here, for a fleeting moment, he thinks of it not simply as an extension of man or as a wholly alien realm, but as a wild other within his own "brain and bowels." This concept of the "inner other," so to speak, appears infrequently in Thoreau's work, though it may underlie such famous remarks as "in Wildness is the preservation of the World" ("Walking," 112). The significance of this statement in the present context is that it calls precisely for new awareness of the human self, a Darwinian awareness (although *Origin of Species* would not appear for three years) of the wild self participating in the natural order. With a mind open to such ideas, how can it be that Thoreau ever felt, when inspecting external nature, that he was doing anything but looking inward? But this alliance of self and nature, even for Thoreau, was not constant, not easy. "We must go out and re-ally ourselves to Nature every day" (9:200), he writes. Like keeping a journal, the quest for sanity and self-awareness is a daily activity.

Was Thoreau a good scientist, keeping his Journal as a sort of laboratory notebook? Barton St. Armand asks if the Journal itself could constitute "a 'secret' natural history of Concord, or an escape from the formal undertaking of that task?" ("Topics for Discussion," 2). Perhaps a good place to begin a response would be to consider Loren Eiseley's assessment of Thoreau-as-scientist, which suggests that Thoreau was not a genuine scientist in the modern sense, that he was not dispassionate and strictly objective, but rather that he glimpsed, in his examinations of the natural world, the human implications of the mysterious universe:

> [I]f it be true that Thoreau . . . was on occasion, weak in the identification of birds, he is cherished for quite other reasons, and these reasons, though now forced back into obscure corners of the modern mind, are still not without a certain power. They are the ineradicable shadows in the murky glass which can never be totally cleansed by Bacon's followers. For when the human mind exists in the light of reason, and no more than reason, we may say with absolute certainty that man and all that made him will be in that instant gone. ("Enchanted Glass," 482)

The gist of Eiseley's argument is that the Journal serves not only as a storehouse of Thoreau's spontaneous comments about the aims and methods of science, but as evidence of his approach to nature and his use of writing as a way to fathom his own place in the universe and his perspective on things. For Eiseley this concern for the human implications of nature makes Thoreau a quintessentially modern nature writer. Sherman Paul has even gone so far as to suggest that Thoreau's fundamental motivation as an empirical observer of nature derived from his desire to verify his belief in the correspondence of man and nature. "[B]ecause the mind did not make nature," Paul writes, "one had . . . to study her phenomena more closely. For when one could no longer project his mood *on* nature, he had instead to find his mood *in* her; he had to know her ways so intimately that he could anticipate them" (*Shores*, 258).

No less than do Annie Dillard and Barry Lopez, Thoreau viewed the study of nature as a human and humanistic enterprise, thus deviating from the inductive method favored by the followers of Francis Bacon. But unlike Dillard and Lopez who, while writing about their own encounters with nature, also rely upon the work of experts for precise explanations of natural phenomena, Thoreau actually developed himself into a patient, careful observer. In a recent essay, Don Mitchell points out that Dillard's famous description of the female praying mantis who eats her mate during copulation is based upon misinformation appropriated from the writings of the nineteenth-century entomologist Henri Fabre, and "amounts to sustaining a hundred-year-old libel on praying mantises, and investing it with startling new symbolic meanings" ("Dancing with Nature," 195). The antidote to such mistakes, Mitchell asserts, is to have "the writer get committed to a life of authentic involvement with nature. . . . And then to be extremely patient about deciding what 'Nature' means . . . " (196). Even if he occasionally made mistakes when attempting to identify birds and other aspects of nature, Thoreau nonetheless demonstrated Mitchell's exalted "third level of engagement, . . . Involvement or Investment" (192). Despite his occasional Emersonian impatience to see the ideal in the actual, Thoreau was an exceptionally patient, faithful, and industrious observer.

Still, Thoreau's criticisms of formal science, beginning early on in the Journal, are so passionate and so consistent in their argument, that it seems quite clear that he did not intend to produce typical science. This is not to say that he did not hope to achieve some sort of lasting understanding of nature, to grasp at Truth, but rather that he felt already at the age of twenty that the mere accumulation of facts would not lead to genuine understanding. Echoing Emerson's critique of Linnaeus's and Buffon's "dry catalogues of facts" (*Nature*, 16) a year after the publication of Emerson's first book, Thoreau wrote the following in the Journal under the heading "FACTS":

> How indispensable to a correct study of Nature is a perception of her true meaning. The fact will one day flower out into a truth. The season will mature and fructify what the understanding cultivated. Mere accumulators of facts—collectors of materials for the master-workmen—are like those plants growing in dark forests, which "put forth only leaves instead of blossoms." (1:18)

Thoreau saw himself as more than an "accumulator": rather, he sought to be an experiencer and interpreter of nature. One of the few aspects of science which he praised unequivocally was its practitioners' relentless, even heroic, quest for Truth. He writes, "Science is always brave. What the coward overlooks in his hurry, she calmly scrutinizes, breaking ground like a pioneer for the array of arts in her train" (1:98). But even in these words of praise it is evident that Thoreau values the subsequent "array of arts" above the preliminary collecting role of the scientist.

Thoreau came more and more to realize that typical science cut off the mind from the heart, from the rest of human experience, and his own poetic spirit balked at this narrowness of vision. He felt a great need to speak from "full experience," even when attempting to describe observations of nature. Close, careful inspection of nature – the supposed activity of the scientist – was never something Thoreau sought to avoid; in fact, he appreciates the notion that "Nature will bear the closest inspection. She invites us to lay our eye level with her smallest leaf, and take an insect view of its plain" (1:92). To take the "insect view" is to momentarily leave behind the human perspective in an effort to understand both the object under scrutiny and the limitations of the human mind. Because of its externality, its otherness from the human viewer, nature will bear such close, active inspection in a way that the human mind might not. And the compulsion to pry into the secrets of the natural world gives Thoreau an opportunity to test his own point of view without needing to pause and attempt direct self-scrutiny. Early in his career as a journal-writer, he realized the difficulty of learning about himself through any direct means of inspection. Thoreau's project was "forever [to] go in search of [himself]" (2:314), but he knew the value of circumspection. In 1841, he wrote:

> It is only by a sort of voluntary blindness, and omitting to see, that we know ourselves, as when we see stars with the side of the eye. The nearest approach to discovering what we are is in dreams. It is as hard to see oneself as to look backwards without turning round. And foolish are they that look in glasses with that intent. (1:253)

He learns, though, that the outward-looking perspective of the naturalist often works as the most efficient approach to "discovering what we are," that external inspection complements the introspection of "dreams." However, it is always necessary, even for the naturalist, to find new perspectives, new sides of the eye from which to view nature and thus to avoid the "head of medusa" which "turns the man of science to stone" (5:45). "What is a horizon without mountains," Thoreau exclaims at one point (2:57)—the goal of the naturalist, like that of the self-exploring poet, is always to discern a graspable, appreciable texture in the object of scrutiny. A "horizon without mountains" is like a flawlessly familiar self.

Thoreau values his experiments with different points of view, but seems to carry them out mainly in the hopes of deepening his sense of nature's meaning for man, always returning to what he considers the human perspective on the natural world. In June of 1852, he writes:

> Nature must be viewed humanly to be viewed at all; that is, her scenes must be associated with humane affections, such as are associated with one's native place, for instance. She is most significant to a lover. A lover of Nature is preëminently a lover of man. If I have no friend, what is Nature to me? She ceases to be morally significant. (4:163)

Years later he even asserted that "What we call wildness is a civilization other than our own" (11:450), an idea closely echoed in Barry Lopez's prologue to *Arctic Dreams*. For Thoreau, this "wildness" is an ideal quality of nature, a source of refreshment and awareness. And this particular sentence suggests that what leads us to discern wildness is the mere hint that something is alien to ourselves—thus the key to wildness is otherness. Still, this does not revoke the distinction between man and nature. Despite the implications here that nature influences human feelings and even possesses a moral significance for the observer, there is no merging of subject and object, no moment of "Emersonian or American Sublime" when, as Harold Bloom puts it, "the spirit, transparent to itself, knows its own splendor, and by knowing that knows again all things" ("Emerson," 158).

We need to observe Thoreau's sense of priority. It is tempting, at times, to read Thoreau's celebrations of "wildness" as evidence of his yearning to escape his human nature, to find salvation in the nonhuman. Even in his Journal, he notes, for instance, that "By my intimacy with nature I find myself withdrawn from man. My interest in the sun and the moon, in the morning and the evening, compels me to solitude" (4:258). But in actuality, Thoreau's hope is that intense contact between the human and the nonhuman, between himself and nature, will have a beneficial effect upon his human self, both emotionally and morally. And in order for nature to have such an effect, it cannot be wholly akin to the human observer: a certain distance or difference is necessary. It is in this spirit that Thoreau notes,

> I love Nature partly *because* she is not man, but a retreat from him. None of his institutions control or pervade her. There a different kind of right prevails. In her midst I can be glad with an entire gladness. If this world were all man, I could not stretch myself, I should lose all hope. He is constraint, she is freedom to me. He makes me wish for another world. She makes me content with this. (4:445)

This sentiment betrays Thoreau's pre-ecological sensibility, his unawareness of how man's "institutions" would come to "control or pervade" nature, throwing off kilter many of nature's fragile systems. However, one of the first expressions of this idea appeared in 1864, shortly after Thoreau's death, when George Perkins Marsh published *Man and Nature: Or, Physical Geography as Modified by Human Action*. But Thoreau's view has endured vibrantly, and it underlies many works of contemporary nature writing. As did Thoreau, the writers working today "love Nature partly *because* she is not man*," because in nature's very otherness it is possible to find a refreshing refuge from the self and from civilization. Thoreau's remark that "a man needs only to be turned round once with his eyes shut in this world to be lost" is not a complaint about the alienness and mysteriousness of the world, for he believes that "not until we are lost do we begin to realize where we are, and the infinite extent of our relations" (5:64). We need this sense of disorientation, of being in an unfamiliar place, in order to realize eventually what our true relationship with the world is. H. Daniel Peck has noted a similar tension in *A Week on the Concord and Merrimack Rivers*, an "interplay" between the "reflection" inspired by "the condition of river travel" and "its continual opening of new and unexpected scenes [which] periodically commands renewed attention and observation" (*Morning Work*, 24). Whether the result of travel or other shifts in perspective, the disruption of ease and familiarity calls us to attention, as Annie Dillard and Edward Abbey show so strikingly in their recent works.

William Rossi implies a similar elevation of awareness (or insight) in his comments on the Journal and the essay "Walking": "The dynamic sense of that relation [between the landscape and the self]—in which the invigoration of human power and consciousness is felt as the renewed experience of its source—is represented as a feeling of simultaneous independence from and identity with the spectacle" ("Laboratory," 78). Excessively facile acceptance of some sort of fundamental correspondence between man and nature would preclude such "invigoration of human power and consciousness." The semiregular (but not lifelessly predictable) structure of the Journal provides an appropriate form for the expression of this living, changing relationship. Even in "Walking," one of Thoreau's more polished works, Rossi finds that "An active sense of creatively seeing the landscape—and, correlatively, the self—anew is not bestowed at the end of the quest [for the Wild] but is a quality of the questing activity itself" (84). The Journal is, likewise, a "questing activity"—not the record of a quest, but the quest itself. Because of its direct roots in lived experience, the Journal cannot follow a static, predetermined path of inquiry and observation; instead, it shadows the author's mental forays into the nature of life.

In an attempt to distinguish between Emerson's notion of the viewer's fusion with external nature ("I become a transparent eyeball; . . . the currents of the Universal Being circulate through me . . ." *Nature*, 6) and Thoreau's more removed apprehension of nature, Perry Miller quotes the following 1839 journal entry which describes "The Poet":

> He must be something more than natural—even supernatural. Nature will not speak through but along with him. His voice will not proceed from her midst, but, breathing on her, will make her the expression of his thought. He then poeticizes when he takes a fact

out of nature into spirit. He speaks without reference to time or
place. His thought is one world, hers another. He is another
Nature,—Nature's brother. Kindly offices do they perform for one
another. Each publishes the other's truth. (1:74–75)

To Miller, this suggests a "duality of vision" ("Context," 150), a
merging of the "natural supernaturalism" typical of Romantic literature and the more scientific naturalism which we frequently
consider an especially modern development. Miller argues that
Thoreau's "life was an unrelenting exertion to hold this precarious
stance," to inspect nature microscopically and, "at one and the
same time," to make experience "intelligible" through spiritual
interpretation. But this magical "duality" occurs only once in
Thoreau's work, according to Miller, and that's in *Walden*. In this
book, "he had for a breathless moment, held the two [perspectives]
in solution, fused and yet still kept separate, he and Nature pub-
lishing each other's truth" (151). If *Walden* is the apex of Thoreau's
achievement as a writer (indeed, "one of the supreme achievements
of the Romantic Movement—or to speak accurately, of Romantic
Naturalism," ["Context," 156]), then the Journal is merely a workbook and, later, an ignoble project to which the obscure writer
resigns himself. This, at least, is how Miller interprets Thoreau's
undated comment from the mid-1840s that his journal entries,
which roughly record the writer's "inspirations," would eventually
be "winnowed into lectures, and again, in due time, from lectures
into essays" (1:413). By 1857, however, Thoreau's literary aspirations had been largely disappointed, leading Miller to read the
line, "Is there any other work for [the poet] but a good journal?"
(10:115), as a statement of resignation (*Consciousness*, 21).

More recent readings of Thoreau's Journal are less disparaging, however. Critics such as William Howarth have begun to
reverse Miller's evaluations. Howarth writes:

[F]or all its merits as a public statement, *Walden* was also a compro-
mise with Thoreau's private notions of his art. In the Journal since
1852 he had evolved new goals for his writing: to appreciate the myriad phenomena of nature, to replicate its processes, to distill from its
order an exact but suggestive fable. After years of tedious revising

and editing, little of this natural spontaneity survived in his text. (*Book of Concord*, 98)

The conscious reworking of the text of *Walden* not only diminished its replication of nature's rhythms, but also drained it, at least in part, of its experimental inconsistency, its vacillation of perspective. What prevents *Walden* from becoming an arid, unconvincing piece of rhetoric is its retention of at least a little of its journal roots, which themselves derive from vivid primary experience. Still, as Howarth observes, Thoreau's central goals of "appreciat[ing] the myriad phenomena of nature" and (I would add) studying the nuances of his own identity are better served by the private journal than by his more public forms of expression. Howarth finds this increased respect for the Journal occurring primarily in the early 1850s, but a statement such as "the highest condition of art is artlessness" suggests that Thoreau was inclined to feel this way as early as 1840.

Even in the experimental forum of the Journal, it is never enough for Thoreau simply to try out one perspective or another, either the insect's microscopic view or the more distant human view. The failure to combine, or at least to alternate points of view, results in a kind of stultification, a lapse in acuity. On July 14, 1852, he asserts that this narrowness of vision results even in the crippling of expression: "A writer who does not speak out of a full experience uses torpid words, wooden or lifeless words, such words as 'humanitary,' which have a paralysis in their tails" (4:225). Words suffering "paralysis in their tails" must be the linguistic analogue of men suffering mental dullness or lack of awareness. Thus it may not be too much to say that Thoreau's own effort to vary — and sometimes even overlap — points of view in his writing demonstrates his seeking of awareness. But most fundamental to this prompting of awareness and to the basic expressive act is the reliance upon personal experience, not merely secondhand reports of experience. "The forcible writer," says Thoreau, "stands bodily behind his words with his experience. He does not make books out of books, but he has been *there* in person" (3:276).

When Thoreau seems to be presenting rather plainly his observations of nature, closer inspection of his descriptive lan-

guage reveals that he is not merely providing unaesthetic, un-
digested facts. On May 7, 1855, he writes:

> I observed a middling-sized red oak standing a little aslant on the
> side-hill over the swamp, with a pretty large hole in one side about
> fifteen feet from the ground, where apparently a limb on which a
> felled tree lodged had been cut some years before and so broke out a
> cavity. I thought that such a hole was too good a one not to be
> improved by some inhabitant of the wood. Perhaps the gray squirrels
> I had just seen had their nest there. Or was not the entrance big
> enough to admit a screech owl? So I thought I would tap on it and
> put my ear to the trunk and see if I could hear anything stirring
> within it, but I heard nothing. Then I concluded to look into it. So I
> shinned [sic] up, and when I reached up with one hand to the hole to
> pull myself up by it, the thought passed through my mind perhaps
> something may take hold my fingers, but nothing did. The first limb
> was nearly opposite to the hole, and, resting on this, I looked in, and,
> to my great surprise, there squatted, filling the hole, which was about
> six inches deep and five to six wide, a salmon-brown bird not so big
> as a partridge, seemingly asleep within three inches of the top and
> close to my face. It was a minute or two before I made it out to be an
> owl. It was a salmon-brown or fawn (?) above, the feathers shafted
> with small blackish-brown somewhat hastate (?) marks, *grayish* to-
> ward the ends of the wings and tail, as far as I could see. A large
> white circular space about or behind eye, banded in rear by a pretty
> broad (one third of an inch) and quite conspicuous perpendicular
> *dark*-brown stripe. Egret, say one and a quarter inches long, sharp,
> triangular, reddish-brown without mainly. It lay crowded in that
> small space, with its tail somewhat bent up and one side of its head
> turned up with one egret, and its large dark eye open only by a long
> slip about a sixteenth of an inch wide; visible breathing. After a little
> while I put in one hand and stroked it repeatedly, whereupon it
> reclined its head a little lower and closed its eye entirely. Though
> curious to know what was under it, I disturbed it no farther at that
> time. (7:364–65)

This long paragraph shows both Thoreau's effort to observe nature
faithfully—to discern its facts through careful, empirical inspection—and at the same time his use of vibrant language in order to
avoid "paralysis." Measurements and descriptions of colors neither
dominate this narrative of discovery, of engagement, nor freeze it

into a static record of observation. The process of perception itself is at the heart of this passage, which displays a subtle shifting and sometimes blending of perspective. The narrator recounts his own movement through space, an approach closer and closer to the small owl inside the "middling-sized red oak standing aslant on the side-hill"; at first, he can only speculate about the possible inhabitants of the "cavity" in the tree (and he does present a few guesses, even though he must know at the time he writes this entry what he ended up finding), but eventually he both sees and touches the actual owl inside.

Although we have no reason to doubt the accuracy of Thoreau's description of the owl, we quickly realize that this is not ordinary modern scientific writing: what's missing is the air of detachment, of depersonalized analysis. Instead we receive an account of interaction, the mental processes of the human observer becoming as significant a feature of the text as the external information. Repeatedly, Thoreau writes "I thought x," "I concluded y," or "I made out z," thus taking his retrospective self and his posthumous readers through phases of engagement with an elusive natural entity; and the effort to figure out the nature of this phenomenon (even to discern its mere physical characteristics) provides Thoreau with an opportunity to exercise his ability to inspect, to become aware. This is not a neutral, taken-for-granted experience, although similar narratives of engagement abound in Thoreau's Journal; each new encounter with the natural world offers a new opportunity to make contact with what Giles Gunn would call "other worlds," an opportunity tensed with the potential for danger and surprise. As Thoreau expresses it, "Something may take hold my fingers." In this particular example the natural creature Thoreau encounters is a rather docile one; in fact, when he touches the small owl, achieving even closer contact with it than his usual visual contact, the effect actually seems to be pacification rather than animosity. Still, the narrator's eyes (including his mind's eye as he recollects the experience) remain wide open, stimulated by this encounter with otherness and by the act of recording it.

Rossi quotes the following lines from Coleridge's *The Friend* in describing the emotional component of the process of discovery;

Coleridge refers to "the exhilarating surprise and the pleasurable sting of curiosity, which accompany the propounding and solving of an Enigma . . . the sense of a principle of connection given by the mind, and sanctioned by the correspondency of nature" (1:471; Rossi, 149–50). The naturalist's anticipation of certain natural phenomena, when born out in the observation of actual instances, constitutes another form of correspondence – and the recognition of this attunement of the mind to external reality results in a sudden emotional charge, a confirmation of awareness. H. Daniel Peck points out a passage from Thoreau's August 24, 1858 entry, in which, after describing a specific natural scene, Thoreau exclaims, "If that place is real, then . . . the places of my imagination are real" (11:122). "This passage," writes Peck, "expresses the fullest meaning of 'correspondence' for [Thoreau]. In their 'imaginative,' or 'phenomenal' quality, scenes of this kind correspond to inner life, so that in confirming the reality of phenomena, Thoreau is also confirming the reality (and authenticity) of the imagination" (*Morning Work*, 77). This process of empirically investigating the external world simultaneously serves the believer in correspondence as a pathway to the confirmation and understanding of the mind itself.

On other occasions Thoreau's journal entries, rather than expanding into detailed psychological dramas of exploration, slim down mostly to bare visual notes, lyrical in their spareness. Take, for instance, the following sequence of entries from the final days of June, 1855:

> *June 20.* A catbird's nest eight feet high on a pitch pine in Emerson's heater piece, partly of paper. A summer yellowbird's, saddled on an apple, of cotton-wool, lined with hair and feathers, three eggs, white with flesh-colored tinge and purplish-brown and black spots. Two hair-bird's nests fifteen feet high on apple trees at R.W.E.'s (one with two eggs). A robin's nest with young, which was lately, in the great wind, blown down and somehow lodged on the lower part of an evergreen by arbor, – without spilling the young!
>
> *June 21.* Saw a white lily in Everett's Pond.
> Sparrow's nest, four eggs, deep in the moist bank beyond cherry-bird's nest (have three), of peculiar color. She deserted the nest after one was taken. Outside of stubble, scantily lined with fibrous roots.

Clams abundant within three feet of shore, and bream-nests. The early grass is ripe or browned, and clover is drying. Peetweets make quite a noise calling to their young with alarm.

On an apple at R.W.E.'s a small pewee's nest, on a horizontal branch, seven feet high, almost wholly of hair, cotton without, not incurved at edge; four eggs, pale cream-color.

June 22. At 6 p.m. the temperature of the air is 77°, of river one rod from shore 72°. Warmest day yet.

June 23. Probably a redstart's nest (?) on a white oak sapling, twelve feet up, on forks against stem. Have it. See young redstarts about. Hear of flying squirrels now grown.

June 25. Under E. Wood's barn, a phoebe's nest, with two birds ready to fly; also barn swallow's nest lined with feathers, hemisphere or cone against side of sleeper; five eggs, delicate, as well as white-bellied swallow's.

June 26. C. has found a wood pewee's nest on a horizontal limb of a small swamp white oak, ten feet high, with three fresh eggs, cream-colored with spots of two shades in a ring about large end. Have nest and an egg.

June 28. On river.

Two red-wing's nests, four eggs and three—one without any black marks. Hear and see young golden robins which have left the nest, now peeping with a peculiar tone. Shoals of minnows a half-inch long. Eelgrass washed up.

June 30. 2 p.m.—Thermometer north side of house, 95°; in river where one foot deep, one rod from shore, 82°. (7:429–30)

Even in the absence of the first-person singular pronoun there is a distinctive personality dictating the content and language of these entries, a characteristic tone which identifies the origin of these bits of observation as a specific human inspector of nature. At first glance, these journal passages may seem to record a scattered miscellany of meaninglessly specific fact; but, when viewed together (and particularly when viewed along with entries from the same season during different years), the individual observations fall into a pattern. For this reason, I think Miller is correct in his claim that "More than almost any other comparable journal, Thoreau's has to be read as a whole" (*Consciousness*, 28–29). To illustrate this, it might be useful to present a few excerpts from the entries Thoreau made a year later, in 1856:

> *June 1*. Horse-radish in yard, to-morrow. . . .
> P.M. – To Walden.
> Somewhat warmer at last, after several very cold, as well as windy and rainy, days. Was soothed and cheered by I knew not what at first, but soon detected the now more general creak of crickets. A striped yellow bug in fields. Most of the leaves of the *Polygonatum pubescens* which I gathered yesterday at Island had been eaten up by some creature.
> A chewink's nest a rod and a half south of Walden road, opposite Goose Pond path, under a young oak, covered by overarching dry sedge; four eggs, *pretty* fresh. I am pretty sure the bird uttered the unusual hoarse and distressed note while I was looking for them.
> *Linaria Canadensis* on Emerson Cliff. Rock-rose, a day or two there. Whiteweed by railroad at pond to-morrow. Cotton-grass, several days before the 29th May. Heard a quail whistle May 30th. The late crataegus on hill, about May 31st.
> *June 2*. Carum, i.e. caraway, in garden. Saw most hummingbirds when cherries were in bloom, – on them.
> P.M. – With R.W.E. to Perez Blood's auction.
> Telescope sold for fifty-five dollars; cost ninety-five plus ten. See Camilla on rye, undulating light and shade; not 19th of April [grass and grain were already waving in the wind on April 19, 1775 – the day of the "Concord Fight"]. Returned by bridle-road. *Myrica cerifera*, possibly yesterday. Very few buds shed pollen yet; more, probably, to-day. Leaves nearly an inch long, and shoot and all no more. English hawthorn will open apparently in two days.
> Agassiz tells his class that the intestinal worms in the mouse are not developed except in the stomach of the cat. (8:361–62)

As one reads through the entries year after year, the writer's patterns of observation become predictable, habitual – much like the progression of the natural seasons. There is just enough variation and surprise to prevent tedium, or mechanical repetition. And even when Thoreau effaces his own presence in the described scenes, his emotional investment usually comes through, infecting even his deskbound reader with keen interest in whether the *myrica cerifera*, the buds of which "shed" no pollen the day before, might develop one step further today. Thoreau's intense, if not entirely systematic, monitoring of seasonal development provides him with a constant source of emotional stimulation. The changes of nature are expected, but subtly unpredictable – the human observer never knows exactly when the various changes will occur. Just as Annie Dillard seeks the sensation of awareness by exposing herself to the sudden changes in nature, Thoreau seeks and achieves similar stimulation in his ceaseless, unofficial role as "seasonal lookout." On June 5, he observes: "Pitch pine out, the first noticed on low land, *maybe* a day or two. Froth on pitch pine" (8:366). Four days later, in the evening: "Again, about seven, the ephemerae came out, in numbers as many as last night, now many of them coupled, even tripled; and the fishes leap as before. A young robin abroad" (8:373). The next day he notices: "Getting lily pads opposite Badger's. . . . The yellow lily and kalmiana are abundantly out" (8:373). On June 11, Thoreau visits Flint's Pond, noticing on the way that "The locust in graveyard shows but few blossoms yet. It is very hot this afternoon, and that peculiar stillness of summer noons now reigns in the woods. I observe and appreciate the shade, as it were the shadow of each particular leaf on the ground" (8:375-76). This process of monitoring seasonal changes becomes particularly active during the mounting fecundity of spring and the wrenching degeneration of autumn, but it is still a year-round feature of the Journal. There is also a similarity in the June 2 comment about the mouse's intestinal worms to Dillard's appreciation of the jarringly grotesque.

Nature itself provides subtle clues to its intricacies, and these are afforded only to the experienced observer. Waiting for the first hint of spring in February of 1852, Thoreau writes: "A mild, thawy day. The needles of the pine are the touchstone for the air; any change in that element is revealed to the practiced eye by their livelier green or increased motion" (3:276-77). The "practiced eye" is what Thoreau had acquired after fourteen and a half years of watching the seasons and journalizing about them. By so refining his attunement to nature, Thoreau seems actually to develop his initial "voluntary attention" (to use William James's term) into an almost effortless "involuntary attention" (*Psychology*, 195) – he sees subtleties in nature without having to look for them.

Natural phenomena seem to "register" themselves simultaneously in the book of nature and Thoreau's Journal:

> Here is self-registered the flutterings of a leaf in this twisted, knotted, and braided twine. So fickle and unpredictable, not to say insignificant, a motion does yet get permanently recorded in some sort. Not a leaf flutters, summer or winter, but its variation and dip and intensity are registered in THE BOOK. (7:140–41)

The final words of this passage seem to synthesize nature's own natural history and Thoreau's meticulous record of occurrences in nature, as if the Journal had become strangely coextensive with the universe. Thoreau's readers develop a similarly heightened alertness, not just to the seasonal progressions he describes, but to the quirks and passions of the writer himself.

Birds' nests (their locations, components, and contents), air and water temperatures, and newly emerged flora ("Saw a white lily")—these features of nature, which are emphasized in the June 1855 and 1856 entries quoted above, indicate to the observer the arrival of summer, the passage of time. The duration of one's own life is a very difficult thing to confirm, to know with any certainty, so it helps to obtain external corroboration. This seems to be one of Thoreau's goals in the Journal, not merely the witnessing of seasonal transitions in order to test the possibility of correspondence between nature and man, but the act of taking in concrete evidence of temporality for its own sake. When he tersely observes on June 22 that it's "Warmest day yet" (omitting the article), the emphasis is not on the perception of warmth, but on the more abstract implication of the word "yet," the suggestion that the temperature reading and the measurer himself are immersed in a continuing sweep of time.

These particular journal entries elide not only occasional articles ("beyond cherry-bird's nest") and verbs ("Outside of stubble"), but even leave out the narrator's self-referential pronoun, "I." Why would Thoreau choose to leave this out when only a month and a half earlier, in the passage about the discovery of the drowsing owl, the self's own process of investigation assumes such an important role in the text? There may, of course, be circumstances beyond the writing itself which determine the absence of self-referents in these end-of-June inspections of tree branches and pond shores — this is, after all, a private notebook which the author kept steadily even as his own life changed, so that sometimes he could lavish attention on his prose and his ideas, while at other times he must have written entries on the fly. But perhaps it's possible to view even these spare and apparently selfless entries as experiments in perspective. The author in these is not as conspicuous a participant in the scenes being described as he was in the earlier entry; in a sense, the earlier entry was written from a more detached point of view, one distant enough from the actual scene to encompass both nature and the self, to show the whole interaction. In these sparer entries, the self becomes either a transparent observer or merely an implied participant in the scenes. Almost never do the verbs in the eight entries from 1855 refer to the actions of the viewer, and on the three occasions when they do, they merely indicate perception — "saw," "see," and "hear and see" — nothing more active. Instead, motion, indeed physical existence altogether, is virtually identified with the external world, is made alien to the human viewer. The viewer's own physicality is merely implied, and only in a few brief instances, such as when the "peetweets" cry to their young with alarm (presumably because of Thoreau's approach), and later when he records "On river," apparently meaning his own location.

"A True Sauntering of the Eye": The Dawning of a Journal Aesthetic

The significance of this apparent experimentation with nearly transparent selfhood probably goes beyond the mere extension of the earlier suggestion that Thoreau used his Journal and his encounters with nature as a forum for testing perspective (and, implicitly, for determining the subtle boundaries of self and nonself). This evaporation of self also bears upon Thoreau's notion of the proper way to approach the natural world, his critique of objective science; for although this selfless stance misses the emotional, holistic element which the writer elsewhere advocates, it nonetheless demonstrates another valued tendency: utter, noncontrolling openness to the perceptible universe. This is, of course, merely an illusion. Although I have earlier suggested that Thoreau's own persistent interests and procedures are identifiable in these sightings of temporal landmarks, this is not to negate altogether the value of this curious deviation from the explicitly active process of scientific investigation.

Even though Thoreau occasionally presented Humboldtian lists of information (see, for instance, his list of "the *latest* trees and shrubs . . . in order of leafing" in May of 1860, [13:319–20]; or his tables of snow measurements and list of bird's-nest materials in January of 1856, [8:106–7, 113–14]), he remained forever committed to the fresh (even visionary) and palpably human apprehension of nature. It's evident that the Journal tends to function as a narrative of Thoreau's seasonal monitorings, but it is important to acknowledge its unsystematic, almost unguided form. "The charm of the journal must consist," Thoreau claims in one of his most famous sentences, "in a certain greenness, though freshness, and not in maturity" (8:134). This idea suggests a dawning "journal aesthetic," a sense that the journal might have a literary value of its own, one distinct from that of more polished (or ripened) public genres. Perhaps Thoreau's early aspirations did aim towards more public lectures and essays, but it seems that he eventually came to love his journalizing, to consider it far more than a prelude to publication or a consolation for meager recognition from his readers.

In *Emerson and the Art of the Diary* (1988), Lawrence Rosenwald raises significant doubts concerning our understanding of the "characteristic Transcendentalist pattern of composition" which Lawrence Buell defined in 1973 as "a threefold process of revision from journal to lecture to essay" (*Literary Transcendentalism*, 280). Rosenwald identifies the following "beliefs regarding the Emersonian corpus":

> Thinking that the essays are wholes, we have conceived of the journals as fragments; thinking of the essays as finished products, as ends, we have regarded the journals as raw material, as means. Accordingly, we have been reluctant to regard as a literary work what we have understood as essentially *ancillary* to literary work. (*Emerson and the Art of the Diary*, 65)

But Rosenwald's various arguments in favor of Emerson's diaristic art do not work as well in Thoreau's case. The consciously eloquent and cannibalizable (to adapt one of Rosenwald's terms) passages in Thoreau's Journal and the "cooked" material—the infrequent journal passages for which "other books are cannibalized," (68)—represent, I think, the least artistic aspects of Thoreau's journalizing. By the time he began to develop his journal aesthetic, the writing process had ceased to be intrusively self-conscious. Rosenwald argues that Emerson's journal, "being at every individual moment the creation of [the author's] will, becomes cumulatively the book of Emerson's character, represented imperfectly in each of his works, but revealed in their accumulation in its full truth" (104). This is true for Thoreau, too. However, the writer's "habit of attention"—which is so close to the core of his character—emerges even in individual journal entries. Accumulation merely sharpens the image.

One of the main reasons Thoreau so valued the Journal was its suitability to his consciously unsystematic approach to nature. After noting with surprise that he knew "most of the flowers" and all but "half a dozen shrubs" when he toured various local "swamp[s]" in 1856, he explains:

> I little thought that in a year or two I should have attained to that knowledge without all that labor. Still I never studied botany, and do not to-day systematically, the most natural system is still so artificial. I wanted to know my neighbors, if possible,—to get a little nearer to them. I soon found myself observing when plants first blossomed and leafed, and I followed it up early and late, far and near, several years in succession, running to different sides of the town and into the neighboring towns, often between twenty and thirty miles in a day. I often visited a particular plant four or five miles distant, half a dozen times within a fortnight, that I might know exactly when it opened, beside attending to a great many others in different directions and some of them equally distant, at the same time. At the same time I had an eye for birds and whatever else might offer. (9:158-59)

In this summary of his method of seasonal observation, Thoreau emphasizes his energy and enthusiasm rather than the orderliness of the enterprise. "I am abroad viewing the works of Nature and not loafing" (4:166), he writes defensively in a July 1, 1852, entry;

indeed, this passage describing his routine of inspection—not to mention the Journal's copious notations themselves—makes it plain that Thoreau was a model of industry, and yet his own industry was a sort that most of his human neighbors easily mistook for idleness. He is not a systematic student of botany, he claims; and yet his knowledge is expansive and he devotes much of his time (virtually all of it, it sometimes seems) to his private errands here and there in the Concord area, walking miles to visit specific plants, just "get[ting] a little nearer to [his 'neighbors']."

Throughout the Journal, Thoreau's primary criticism of formal science concerns its tendency to reduce the natural world to systems of knowledge; such systems, in their artificiality, strike him as inherently devoid of experiential fullness. As part of his own project to seek awareness and avoid the dullness which might result from excessively rigid methodology, Thoreau frequently exhorts himself in the Journal to see better, more subtly—even to avoid being turned to stone by staring too directly, too impetuously, at nature like the typical scientist. He writes: "To perceive freshly, with fresh senses, is to be inspired" (8:44). This suggests that he not only approached the examination of nature with the embracing spirit of the mystic, but that his philosophical inspiration took its vitality from the process of alert observation. Thoreau's method of achieving this visual alertness differs greatly from the usual volitional process of science, resembling more closely James's notion of "involuntary attention." In 1852, Thoreau exhorts himself to "walk with more free senses." He states:

It is as bad to *study* stars and clouds as flowers and stones. I must let my senses wander as my thoughts, my eyes see without looking. Carlyle said that how to observe was to look, but I say that it is rather to see, and the more you look the less you will observe. I have the habit of attention to such excess that my senses get no rest, but suffer from a constant strain. Be not preoccupied with looking. Go not to the object; let it come to you. When I have found myself ever looking down and confining my gaze to the flowers, I have thought it might be well to get into the habit of observing the clouds as a corrective; but no! that study would be just as bad. What I need is not to look at all, but a true sauntering of the eye. (4:351)

Of course, Thoreau could never teach himself always to see and never to look. In fact, the strenuous routine of seasonal inspection seems quite at odds with this idea of "sauntering," both with the feet and with the eyes. Instead, this elevated, involuntary mode of perceiving the world is merely intermittent; equally necessary for someone who has "the habit of attention" is the more mundane and active form of seeing external objects. Admittedly, this idea of visual "sauntering" does contradict Thoreau's many other comments about how we tend to see only what we already expect to see; still, I think this passage indicates his desired approach to nature and, to a considerable extent, describes the form, the cadences, of the original notebooks – or at least the version of the Journal published in 1906. Howarth suggests that by the early 1850s Thoreau's "pleasure in writing the Journal increased, but his publications often lagged behind its current level of ideas and style. A book like *Walden* could emulate those principles, but not embody them with the same vitality or apparent ease" (*Book of Concord*, 10). And "vitality" and "ease" – or aliveness and unsystematic sauntering of thought – have by this time become two of Thoreau's most prized literary qualities.

Thoreau's ideal mode of experiencing and perceiving nature entailed a mixture of active movement through natural settings and passive reception of sensory impressions (as well as subsequent active interpretation of these impressions in many cases, depending on whether he was in a purely observational phase or a more reflective one). The original version of the Journal, which shows yearly cycles of observation, is particularly faithful to the sauntering, erratic rhythms of the initial experience of the author. As early as 1837, he proposes, "If one would reflect, let him embark on some placid stream, and float with the current . . . " (1:8). By presenting the Journal in its natural chronology, the 1906 editors, Bradford Torrey and Francis H. Allen, allow readers to float along with the current of Thoreau's life, to saunter (virtually looking through his eyes) amid the placid scenes of Concord and nearby locales. Thoreau repeatedly complains that the lover of books and scientific systems knows nature only secondhand (3:271) and that the good writer must spend time in nature personally (3:276). The Journal in its original form comes especially close to the author's own immediate experience of the natural world—it is not a substitute for primary experience, but is better than artificial systematizing, particularly for the reader who wishes to observe the meanderings of the poet-naturalist's own mind.

Although he makes no grand pronouncements about it, Thoreau himself seems well aware of the value of active investigation—thus his long walks just to see "a particular plant," his climbing of trees to inspect birds' nests and to count eggs, and even his occasional use of an instrument such as a microscope to pry into the reality of nature. But, for Thoreau, it was important to keep in mind the ultimate goal of such acts of discovery, which was not enlargement of knowledge, but rather depth of awareness. It was for this reason that he declined to travel more than he did, preferring instead to get closer to his native surroundings. "It matters not where or how far you travel,—the farther commonly the worse,—" he writes, "but how much alive you are" (6:236). The primary indicator of this aliveness is intensity of emotion—nothing external or precisely quantifiable. The means of achieving this emotion, however, is profoundly connected with the act of brushing up against the external world. When Thoreau exclaims, after excessive time spent with other humans, "Ah! I need solitude . . . to behold something grander than man . . . " (6:439), his need is not merely for a respite from socializing, but for a deeper type of "intercourse," for the contact with nature which he finds vital to the "preservation of moral and intellectual health" (2:193). Indeed, in identifying one of the central facets of mental life as the task of self-discovery, he suggests that the teasing elusiveness of understanding is what enables heightened appreciation: "Let me forever go in search of myself; never for a moment think that I have found myself; be as a stranger to myself, never a familiar, seeking acquaintance still. . . . I love and worship myself with a love which absorbs my love for the world" (2:314–15).

The very act of keeping a journal also contributes to the writer's feeling of being alive. Unlike other modes of literary expression in which the emphasis is frequently on coherence and control, the very nature of the private journal prevents pristine stasis. In the midst of an 1852 entry, Thoreau notes simply: "Thoughts of different dates will not cohere" (3:288). Indeed, this very line juts out of the entry—strikingly coherent in itself, but not assimilated into the other rambling paragraphs. But the patterns of the Journal, much like the patterns of a life, emerge when viewed collectively; Thoreau intimates his own understanding of this when he suggests that "Time will make the most discordant materials harmonize" (4:134). Thoreau's Journal becomes an extension of his life, not only because of its existence as a record of experience, but because its very form emerges from the writer's pulse. The journal keeper observes:

> We cannot write well or truly but what we write with gusto. The body, the senses, must conspire with the mind. Expression is the act of the whole man, that our speech may be vascular. The intellect is powerless to express thought without the aid of the heart and liver and of every member. Often I feel that my head stands out too dry, when it should be immersed. A writer, a man writing, is the scribe of all nature; he is the corn and the grass and the atmosphere writing. It is always essential that we love to do what we are doing, do it with a heart. (2:441)

Thoreau repeatedly reminds himself in the Journal of this need to write and live with heartfelt intensity. Part of the value of this work is that it is cast within the searing forge of daily life, rather than undergoing successive refinements and burnishings long after the feeling of the original experience has gone cold. "Write while the heat is in you," Thoreau exclaims. "The writer who postpones the recording of his thoughts uses an iron which has cooled to burn a hole with. He cannot inflame the minds of his readers" (3:293). Nor can he inflame himself—or live up to the heat of the moment of insight—when he delays expression too long after an actual incident. An extension of this problem is the fallacy of believing it possible to write meaningfully without ever having experienced anything worth writing about. As Thoreau puts it, "How vain it is to sit down to write when you have not stood up to live! Methinks that the moment my legs begin to move, my thoughts begin to flow. . . . Only while we are in action is the circulation perfect" (2:404–5). Thus the Journal has value in allowing both spontaneous and immediate expression; the writer may not always make his journal entries while out in the field, but the medium nonetheless encourages a direct relationship with lived-through occurrences. Furthermore, the account seems to accord with Thoreau's fundamental notion that "The art of life, of a poet's life, is, not having anything to do, to do something" (3:480). There is, ultimately, no worldly reason for keeping a truly personal journal, no hope of fame or wealth or social reform. The Journal became the art of Thoreau's life when he ceased to view it as a prelude, but rather as an end in itself; hints of this dawning realization appeared years before he began writing *Walden*.

Thoreau's attitude toward science mirrors his attitude toward excessively polished and impersonal modes of literary expression. While disparaging modern science, Thoreau tended to admire the old-fashioned naturalists (such as the author of Gerard's *Herbal*, 13:29–30) who often wrote with childlike delight, revealing feelings and sensations rather than dry, numerical information. In fact, Thoreau once stated, the "inhumanity of science concerns me" (6:311). He found it inexcusable to kill for the sake of science (an attitude reminiscent of Wordsworth's critique of rational science in "The Tables Turned"); and after committing such a murder himself, Thoreau writes, "I pray that I may walk more innocently and serenely through nature" (6:452). Still, he displayed few qualms about inspecting, even bringing home, all kinds of corpses he encountered around Concord (in this way he gathered his furniture when he went to live at Walden Pond).

The writer's own scientific method was neither purely inductive nor purely intuitive—it was rather a kind of intuitive empiricism, an effort to observe as much as possible, often at odd hours, and then release his imagination when he sat down to record his observations. Rossi makes an illuminating comparison between Thoreau's intuitive approach to scientific investigation and Michael Polanyi's "description of the roles of 'subsidiary' and 'focal' awareness in perception, and the relation of scientific knowing to what he called the 'tacit dimension'" (137–38). Rather than detaching himself from the natural phenomena he examined and achieving objective, "focal" awareness of them, Thoreau relied upon his immersion in the entire experience of engagement with nature, upon personal involvement or what Polanyi calls "indwelling" (Polanyi and Prosch, *Meaning*, 37), in order to know the intricacies of nature and himself. Sometimes it's not even clear that the notes in the Journal are produced by the imagination because they appear so plain and factual, but the imaginative element becomes apparent if you reflect on the minute earthiness of the language or on the way even the plain sightings of newly blooming plants fit into the larger scheme of the Journal, the vast project of converging and diverging with the rhythms of nature.

As early as 1840, Thoreau realized that it would be impossible to discover immutable truths in nature: "The universe will not wait to be explained. Whoever seriously attempts a theory of it is already behind his age" (1:133–34). And yet he proceeded with the project of his Journal, perhaps because this form of writing, above all others, seemed attached to the life at hand, and was thus as organic and changeable as life itself. Did the Journal itself, after the writer had spent years accumulating observations and speculations, become Thoreau's clandestine natural history of Concord? It was, in fact, such a work, but I doubt that Thoreau ever intended to publish an encyclopedic study of nature in his home region. He must have had little faith in the potential of a popular audience to accept his rough-hewn Journal as a finished work. The Journal, thus, was truly a private workbook—it was not primed and worried over as it would have been, even by the coarse-talking Thoreau, in preparation for publication.

Still, it would be an exaggeration to say that the Journal is "modelled on a formless nature, with mindless seasonal repetition" (St. Armand, 2). In the first place, nature was not formless for Thoreau, not even during its seasons of rampant luxuriance. It is true that the precisely chronological structure of the Journal somehow imitates the author's own sauntering through the years, but I do not think that Thoreau really intended to imitate the seasonal movement or the formlessness of nature. "A journal is a record of experiences and growth, not a preserve of things well done or said" (8:134), the author claims, suggesting a distinctly Wordsworthian enterprise. And yet it is harder to trace Thoreau's process of personal development in the Journal than that of Wordsworth in *The Prelude*—there is no conspicuous and consistent change in vision, in language, or even in location. Of course, the opening volumes are more self-conscious and stiltedly rhetorical than the later ones, but eventually the process of journalizing becomes a steady routine and the linguistic kinks get worked out.

As various scholars have observed, there seems to be a gradual peaking of Thoreau's empirical tendencies in the early 1850s. He writes in 1852, "This is my year of observation" (4:174); and indeed the entries for that year are unusually full of observational detail. But the later years do not differ very noticeably, except for occasional bursts of predominant philosophizing (sometimes lasting for a month's worth of entries) or speechifying (as in 1859, when Thoreau was clearly using the Journal to prepare public remarks about the execution of John Brown). But in general the growth, the sudden shifts and reversions, that one finds in the Journal, seems more artless than artful. If there is art in the Journal, it appears in the individual insights and phrases or in the entire immense project, not in the predictable development of the writer's own character.

After years of keeping the Journal, Thoreau refers to himself routinely as a poet rather than as a scientist or a naturalist, and he observes one day that the poet's main job is to be an autobiographer, to keep a journal of "how he, the actual hero, lived from day to day" (10:115). There is a certain ritualistic component in the Journal. He says at one point, "I love to celebrate nature" (9:209), and even the plainer descriptions are celebratory in their mere devotion to what he has seen and in their implication of his own alert presence in nature. But the real celebration was his actual life in nature, not the later recollection and recording of it. Thus the Journal is not merely a document preparatory to communion or indicative of the trials and persistence of Thoreau's "faith" in nature. Nor is it strictly a Romantic project, an effort to work out and give voice to the intricacies of his own soul. Rather, the Journal itself becomes a life-act for the earnest Thoreau—if he is posturing, merely posing as a writer, then he is doing so only to deceive himself, and after a few years of daily journalizing the deception is so complete that he honestly conceives of himself, first and foremost, as a writer, as a person whose primary activity (along with roaming about Concord) is writing. He writes in the Journal not to initiate any kind of communion, and not merely to analyze and justify and assuage the angst of being a prickly, nature-loving, idealistic, exceedingly self-critical hermit and believer in the beauty of love and friendship, but because he is a writer, because he feels the words pulsing within him and within his surroundings. His devotion to the Journal indicates his determination to "drain the cup of inspiration to its last dregs" (3:221)—or, as he puts it ironically in the less vibrant *Walden*, "to live deep and suck out all the marrow of life" (91).

CHAPTER 3

Sudden Feelings:
Annie Dillard's Psychology

It's about waking up. A child wakes up over and over again, and notices that she's living. She dreams along, loving the exuberant life of the senses, in love with beauty and power, oblivious of herself—and then suddenly, bingo, she wakes up and feels herself alive. She notices her own awareness. . . .

    So the book is about two things: a child's interior life—vivid, superstitious and timeless—and a child's growing awareness of the world.
                                    —Dillard, "To Fashion a Text" (1987, 56)

"What could I contribute to the 'literature on the psychological present?' "

The final sentence of this epigraph reveals the specific text Annie Dillard was in the midst of fashioning when she delivered the talk from which the above epigraph comes. *An American Childhood*, Dillard's most openly self-conscious study of her own mind's maneuverings in and out of awareness, appeared in 1987, thirteen years after the publication of *Pilgrim at Tinker Creek* (hereafter abbreviated as *Pilgrim*) catapulted her to prominence among contemporary American nonfiction writers—particularly among nature writers—and stimulated a wealth of reviews and a steadily accumulating body of criticism.

In her talk at the New York Public Library Dillard suggests that the psychological phenomenon of awareness, "the vertical motion of consciousness, from inside to outside and back," was new territory for her—"I've written about it once before, in an essay about a solar eclipse, and I wanted to do more with it" ("Fashion," 57). However, the subject matter of the recent autobiography of childhood, described in the epigraph above, is hardly unique to *An American Childhood*; nor is it true that she had previously written about the subject of consciousness only in "Total Eclipse" (eventually collected in *Teaching a Stone to Talk*, 1982). Although critical attention has thus far focused on the spiritual patterns in the early works such as *Pilgrim* or on their implications for the contemplation of nature, Dillard's fascination with the mysterious workings of the mind is evident in all of her books, no less in *Pilgrim* than in *An American Childhood* or in her newly published reflections on writing (*The Writing Life*, 1989).

"The interior life is in constant vertical motion," Dillard observes. "It dreams down below; it notices up above; and it notices itself, too, and its own alertness" ("Fashion," 57). Inevitably, during the incessant tide-like undulation of consciousness, the writer will "notice" herself—if only temporarily—during the act of writing, and this brief consciousness of her own thinking, sensing self will solidify in the text she composes. Such moments of self-attentiveness not only dictate Dillard's approach to her external subject matter, but they themselves become objects of analysis; for instance, in such chapters as "Seeing" and "The Present" in *Pilgrim*. Certain critics such as Mary Davidson McConahay do discuss, at least in passing, Dillard's Thoreauvian "commitment to awareness" ("Into the Bladelike Arms of God," 106). More common, however, are the approaches of critics who respond to Dillard's critique of self-consciousness in *Pilgrim* by categorizing the work, as Margaret McFadden-Gerber does, as a "nonautobiographical" form of "literary ecology" ("The I in Nature," 5), devoted more to divine and natural speculations and observations than to self-exploration. David L. Lavery's article, "Noticer: The Visionary Art of Annie Dillard," demonstrates this approach, helpfully explaining Dillard's interest in "noticing," her "passion for vision," but emphasizing her Stevens-like alertness to "major weather" ("Noticer," 257) rather than her accompanying devotion to the drifts and dartings of her own "interior life." John Elder, in the brief section of *Imagining the Earth* devoted to Dillard and Peter Matthiessen, addresses Dillard's psychological concerns, noting her depiction of "the ironic *shifts* of human consciousness" and suggesting that, for her, "Revelation is housed in a moving human sphere of impression, expression, distraction, and recollection" (178). But this marks only a first step toward an exploration of her contribution as a literary psychologist.

Ever since the appearance of *Pilgrim at Tinker Creek*, Dillard has been lauded for her rejuvenation of the mystical tradition in literature. In a letter to Eleanor B. Wymard, excerpted in Wymard's

1975 review of *Pilgrim*, Dillard defined her own aims by saying, "Art is my interest, mysticism my message, Christian mysticism" ("A New Existential Voice," 496). David Lavery observes that Dillard quotes Thoreau's "unfathomable question" in two different works – "With all your science can you tell how it is and when it is, that light comes into the soul?" – and suggests that "the search for an answer to this question constitutes nothing less than the intrinsic movement of her books" ("Noticer," 256). The overwhelming inclination of critics responding to Dillard's work since the mid-seventies has been to analyze the nuances of her mystical methodology (for instance, Robert Paul Dunn's "The Artist as Nun: Theme, Tone and Vision in the Writings of Annie Dillard" and Joseph Keller's "The Function of Paradox in Mystical Discourse") or to locate her in the tradition of visionary literature (as McConahay does in " 'Into the Bladelike Arms of God': The Quest for Meaning Through Symbolic Language in Thoreau and Annie Dillard"). But few critics have yet grappled sustainedly with the paradox of self-consciousness in her work, with the fact that, in nearly the same breath, she deplores the intrusion of self-reflexive consciousness and yet still manages to describe potently what appear to be her own authentic mystical experiences.

The investigation of her own mental processes is an important and abiding feature of Dillard's work, though it is less prominent in the mystical prose poem *Holy the Firm*, which displays too sustained a roar of ecstatic consciousness to allow the narrator many moments of self-scrutiny. By studying the way Dillard uses the process of writing and coming in contact with the natural world in order to boost her own awareness, I will respond to the rhetorical question she herself asks in *Pilgrim*: "What could I contribute to the 'literature on the psychological present'?" (93).

Obstructive Self-Consciousness

"Process is nothing; erase your tracks," Dillard advises in *The Writing Life* (4). But what exactly is Dillard's perspective when she writes this? Is it that of a writer reflecting retrospectively on work already completed or that of a writer thick in the throes of composition? Such an utterance could easily apply to both her earlier

work and *The Writing Life*. The reason I raise this issue, the significance of which may at first glance seem minimal, is that Dillard
herself suggests on numerous occasions that the process of writing,
much like the process of mystical contemplation, must be per-
formed in fragile oblivion of the present self. You stymie yourself
by dwelling on the internal workings of your own mind or even on
the planned product of your efforts—to do so is to suffer the
obstruction of self-consciousness. Instead, as in splitting wood,
"You aim at the chopping block. . . . You cannot do the job
cleanly unless you treat the wood as the transparent means to an
end, by aiming past it" (*Writing Life*, 43). The wood, in the case of
Dillard's writing, is her mind. She seeks not a fixed view of nature
and her observant self at a specific moment in time, but rather an
understanding of her general process of engagement with the
world, of stoking awareness; and thus she "aims" her writing consciousness at the chopping block of the world in order to dissect
her kindling mind.

Consciousness of the present self interferes with both mystical vision and artistic creation. At the exact moment of composition or attunement to the outer world, Dillard aspires to a state
of self-transparency which she labels "innocence" in *Pilgrim*:
"What I call innocence is the spirit's unself-conscious state at any
moment of pure devotion to any object. It is at once a receptiveness and total concentration" (82). The visionary explorer of
"the neighborhood" is not a learned, preconditioned scientist, but
"an infant who has just learned to hold his head up [and] has a
frank and forthright way of gazing about him in bewilderment"
(*Pilgrim*, 11). This romantic idealization of childlike innocence as
the proper way to bear (or, even better, *bare*) oneself when
attempting to fathom the natural world finds similar expression in
Kathleen Raine's statement that "rather than understanding
nature better by learning more, we have to unlearn, to un-know, if
we hope to recapture a glimpse of that paradisal vision. Nature is
vision—epiphany—indeed theophany" ("Nature," 252). In what
way, then, does the visionary understand nature, if not through
rational knowing? The profound contact with nature Dillard
describes in works such as *Pilgrim* is evidenced by intensity of
emotion, the feeling of being fully alive, rather than by the con-

scious knowledge of biological systems or by the formal detection of theological design; the very emotions of heightened vitality which emerge periodically in *Pilgrim* appear likewise in *An American Childhood* as Dillard recollects her childhood dawning of awareness. Yet, even more than rationality per se, it is attentiveness to the present self which Dillard finds obstructive to mystical consciousness.

Dillard also asserts that the process of literary composition occurs, ideally, in trancelike freedom from the self-conscious mind. In *The Writing Life* she enumerates the various settings where she has done her writing, stressing her own unawareness of them during the actual writing process—stressing that "appealing workplaces are to be avoided. One wants a room with no view, so imagination can meet memory in the dark" (26). A room *with* a view would too insistently tug the writer's mind into awareness of its present location. This is actually a surprising assertion in view of the sense Dillard's writing so frequently conveys of the tangible presence of the external world, the sense of physical awareness so pronounced that it enables her, as she relates in *Pilgrim*, to discern the breathing of a grasshopper (64). "[I]t should surprise no one," she claims, "that the life of the writer—such as it is—is colorless to the point of sensory deprivation. Many writers do little else but sit in small rooms recalling the real world" (*Writing Life*, 44). Dillard explains, however, that she wrote her most intensely poetic book, *Holy the Firm*, not in a dark room, but in an extremely appealing workplace with a view of "Puget Sound, and all the sky over it and all the other wild islands in the distance under the sky. It was very grand. But you get used to it. I don't much care where I work. I don't notice things. The door used to blow open and startle me witless" (*Writing Life*, 42). The anesthesia of routineness takes the place of darkness, of windowlessness.

If Dillard's primary goal in writing is to achieve awareness—or, more specifically, awareness of the phenomenon of awareness itself—then it is paradoxical that she should require such a condition of "sensory deprivation," of unawareness, in order to carry out her literary examinations of this phenomenon. Suzanne Clark, in her study "Annie Dillard: The Woman in Nature and the Subject of Nonfiction," finds that what subverts the coherent character presented as a speaker, what undoes the convention and makes the nonfiction literary, is the unspoken "she," a recurring strangeness or estrangement, which acts as a counterpoint to the traditional and literary authority of the (male) observer—the naturalists, adventurers, and other writers whom Dillard cites. (111)

Thus, Clark explains the peculiar evasiveness of Dillard-the-author, the fact that "when we read Annie Dillard, we don't know who is writing. There is a silence in the place where there might be an image of the social self—of personality, character, or ego" ("Woman in Nature," 107). This is an intriguing suggestion, reminiscent, for instance, of recent feminist responses to Anne Bradstreet's well-known adaptations of the modesty topos (see Caldwell, "Why Our First Poet Was a Woman," 3, 30). However, it seems to me that Dillard's effacement of authorial identity—her tendency to avoid self-description, particularly of the moment of composition—is also explainable according to her own notions of the psychology of awareness. The author's apparent detachment from her own identity, her implication that, as Clark puts it, "she is not so much the subject of knowing, as subjected to it" (112), could well result from her need to achieve psychological distance from the object of investigation, not merely from her sense of "estrangement" from the male-dominated literary tradition in which she is participating.

Retrospection and Metaphor: Evading Self-Consciousness

Some critics, such as Charles Deemer, have actually found Dillard herself all too present in *Pilgrim*. Probably because he felt that "our age is crying out for a Thoreau—someone with a vision that would reunite man with the natural environment and get us off the macadam to possible extinction," Deemer resents the work's anthropocentrism, its emphasis on the individual's encounters with nature ("Up the Creek," 19–20). Because his expectations and desires are raised by the book's title and by the publisher's cue on the cover of the early Bantam edition that *Pilgrim* be a redemptive work of "visionary naturalism," and "a mystical excursion into the natural world," Deemer feels betrayed, and parodies Dillard's sincere characterization of her book by calling it "a meteorological journal of an egomaniac" (19). This cranky description of Dillard as an "egomaniac" overlooks the actual elusiveness of the author's presence in Pilgrim, and applies to her only if she's expected to be paying attention solely to external matters. However, as a circumspect investigator of the "interior life," it seems fitting that she look inward. It is important to distinguish whether the author herself or the phenomenon of human awareness in general is the true subject of the work. Dillard recalls in "To Fashion a Text" that she initially planned to write Pilgrim in the third person, about a man; and then in the first person, but from the perspective of a man. "I wasn't out to deceive people," she explained. "I just didn't like the idea of writing about myself. I knew I wasn't the subject" (57). She simply uses her own experiences, scrutinized in retrospect or through other distancing techniques, as ways of getting at the phenomenon of awareness.

"It is hard writing about the life one is actually living," Robert Finch notes in his journal about his stint of solitude on the west shore of North Beach on Cape Cod. "I came out here to put some distance between it and me, but I find I carry it around with me, unfinished" ("North Beach Journal," 107). Writing about ongoing experiences does not seem to be Dillard's particular problem. Hers, rather, is the distracting, distorting intrusion of self-consciousness during the process of writing. Like other practitioners of what John Elder calls "the genre of naturalist autobiography," Dillard bestows fundamental importance on the representation of "particularity" and "immediate experience" ("John Muir," 375, 377). And yet, in order to avoid weakening her focus on the general phenomenon of awareness, she must find techniques of representing her own particular experience obliquely. In her latest books of nonfiction, An American Childhood and The Writing Life, she dwells on remembered events from the near and remote past, the reanimation and analysis of safely distant memories enabling an acuity of insight impossible in reflection on the present self.

Sara Maitland, in an ambivalent review of The Writing Life, criticizes Dillard for her retrospective investigation of her own experiences as a writer, claiming that the book "is full of joys [which] are clearest to me when she comes at her subject tangen-

tially, talking not of herself at her desk but of other parallel cases"
("Spend It All," 15). I would argue, though, that even the apparently self-descriptive passages in *The Writing Life* treat the self as an
other. "The writing life" per se has become only gradually a man-
ageable topic for Dillard, not only because of her limited experience at the time when she composed her earlier books, but because
of her initial proximity to this experience. She recalls that during
the writing of *Holy the Firm*, particularly such high-pitched scenes
as the vision of Christ's baptism, she "mostly shut [her] eyes . . .
trancelike" (*Writing Life*, 76). The baptismal scene begins with a
kind of Dickinsonian awareness, a sensitivity so intense that the
very senses become paradoxically occluded:

> Here is a bottle of wine with a label, Christ with a cork. I bear
> holiness splintered into a vessel, very God of very God, the sem-
> piternal silence personal and brooding, bright on the back of my
> ribs. I start up the hill.
>   The world is changing. The landscape begins to respond as a
> current upswells. It is starting to clack with itself, though nothing
> moves in space and there's no wind. It is starting to utter its infinite
> particulars, each overlapping and lone, like a hundred hills of
> hounds all giving tongue. The hedgerows are blackberry brambles,
> white snowberries, red rose hips, gaunt and clattering broom. Their
> leafless stems are starting to live visibly deep in their centers, as hid-
> den as banked fires live, and as clearly as recognition, mute, shines
> forth from eyes. Above me the mountains are raw nerves, sensible
> and exultant; the trees, the grass, and the asphalt below me are living
> petals of mind, each sharp and invisible, help in a greeting or glance
> full perfectly formed. There is something stretched or jostling about
> the sky which, when I study it, vanishes. Why are there all these
> apples in the world, and why so wet and transparent? Through all
> my clothing, through the pack on my back and through the bottle's
> glass I feel the wine. Walking faster and faster, weightless, I feel the
> wine. It sheds light in slats through my rib cage, and fills the but-
> tressed vaults of my ribs with light pooled and buoyant. I am moth; I
> am light. I am prayer and I can hardly see. (64–65)

Not only does the external world shift and vanish when the narrator attempts to study it, but the character herself becomes less and
less substantial as she undergoes the experience of awareness; her

very senses ("raw nerves") are transferred to the nonhuman surroundings, where she becomes "weightless," translucent—an ab-
straction, a "prayer." It seems that only after completing the book
itself has the author contemplated (or at least written about) the
actual process of composing it. "And I have remembered it often,
later," she writes,

> waking up in that cabin to windows steamed blue and the sun gone
> around the island; remembered putting down those queer stark sen-
> tences half blind on yellow paper; remembered walking ensorcerized,
> tethered, down the gray cobble beach like an aisle. (*Writing Life*, 77)

Looking back, she can comment upon, even analyze, experiences
of which she was only dimly aware at the time—or, rather, in
which she was almost too engaged to notice her own involvement
for more than a few ecstatic moments. This reliance upon retro-
spection as a mode of self-inspection is extremely important, for it
enables Dillard to avoid the freezing glare of self-consciousness,
"the glimpse of oneself in a storefront window" (*Pilgrim*, 81) which
paralyzes one and interferes with living and experiencing the
world. When you write about the past self you are writing about
another self, not the same self doing the remembering, despite the
use of the pronoun "I." The philosopher G. E. M. Anscombe, in an
essay entitled "The First Person," sums up the Lockean notion of
indirect self-consciousness this way:

> [M]ight not the thinking substance which thought the thought "I did
> it"—the genuine thought of agent-memory—nevertheless be a dif-
> ferent thinking substance from the one that could have had the
> thought: "I am doing it" when the act was done? Thus [Locke] de-
> tached the identity of the self or 'person' from the identity even of the
> thinking being which does the actual thinking of the I-thoughts. (52)

Anscombe's "thinking substance" that thinks about the "I" in the
past tense represents Dillard-the-writer, who, like Thoreau peering
through "the side of his eye" in order to escape the Medusa-stare of
nature (*Journal*, 5:45), achieves penetrating circumspection by not
being wholly conscious of the present self. Absolute unconscious-
ness of the present self would, of course, result in a lack of memory,
so it seems that this utter unself-consciousness is not what Dillard

has really achieved in either the mystical experiences she records in her books or in her actual state of mind while writing. Sometimes, but not always, Dillard writes about the visionary self in the present tense—this is a rhetorical ploy, a means of vitalizing the scene and perhaps even transfusing some of the original emotion to the reader, but it does not mean she is, at the very moment of writing, undergoing the described experience. To believe so is to commit the written-in-the-field fallacy: to imagine the deskbound writer composing in the woods, with one eye on the trees and the other on the page, having just "strip[ped] off a piece of birch bark for paper" (Thoreau's Journal, 11:111).

In further effort to avoid the paralysis of self-consciousness and yet still perform her studies of the self's compelling maneuvers of thought, Dillard also relies on the traditional autobiographical technique of metaphor. (See James Olney's *Metaphors of Self: The Meaning of Autobiography*, 1972). Readers of *Pilgrim* will never forget many of the extraordinary metaphors and similes used to describe the natural world: "He was a monster in a Mason jar. Those huge wings stuck on his back in a torture of random pleats and folds, wrinkled as a dirty tissue, rigid as leather" (61). Such figurative language serves primarily as a "startler," as a tool for prompting strong emotion, the indicator of awakeness. The type of metaphor that interests me, however, is that which the writer uses to encapsulate and make scrutable her own cogitating self. A splendid example of this occurs in the final chapter of *The Writing Life*, in which Dillard leaves off contemplating her own previous writing experiences and the writing process in general, and turns instead to study the harrowing artistry of a stunt pilot named Dave Rahm, who constitutes an implicit metaphor for herself. To reveal the association explicitly would not only spoil the subtle relevance of the chapter to the rest of the book, but would make the writer *self-conscious*, undercutting the psychological advantage of metaphor.

The chapter begins nonchalantly, preparing the reader, it would seem, for a simple biographical sketch:

> Dave Rahm lived in Bellingham, Washington, north of Seattle. Bellingham, a harbor town, lies between the San Juan Islands in Haro Strait and the alpine North Cascade Mountains. I lived there

between stints on the island. Dave Rahm was a stunt pilot, the air's own genius. (93)

"The air's own genius," this phrase bursts the initial matter-of-factness, exerting a light tug on the reader's own anticipation, but then the prose relapses into plainness. (It was only in thinking back or upon rereading that I noticed the haunting use of the past tense to connect Rahm with what he did and where he lived. Dillard writes of herself, too, in the past tense in this passage – and her obvious presence among the living makes it difficult, initially, to sense what has become of the pilot.)

Dillard portrays herself as an observer, and, initially, a rather disinterested one at that. When she arrives at an air show in 1975 "with a newcomer's willingness to try anything once" (93), she has little idea what to expect from the event in the program titled simply "DAVE RAHM":

> Idly, paying scant attention, I saw a medium-sized, rugged man dressed in brown leather, all begoggled, climb in a black biplane's open cockpit. . . . He was off; he climbed high over the airport in his biplane, very high until he was barely visible as a mote, and then seemed to fall down the air, diving headlong, and streaming beauty in spirals behind him.
>
> The black plane dropped spinning, and flattened out spinning the other way; it began to carve the air into forms that built wildly and musically on each other and never ended. Reluctantly, I started paying attention. Rahm drew high above the world an inexhaustibly glorious line; it piled over our heads in loops and arabesques. It was like a Saul Steinberg fantasy; the plane was the pen. Like Steinberg's contracting and billowing pen line, the line Rahm spun moved to form new, punning shapes from the edges of the old. Like a Klee line, it smattered the sky with landscapes and systems. (94–95)

Rahm's role as artist, hinted at earlier in the word "genius" becomes full-blown as Dillard's description of the air performance piles metaphor upon artistic metaphor – "carve the air into forms," "musically," "drew," "arabesques" – before concluding with a brief string of similes, explicitly associating Rahm's work in the sky with that of literary and visual artists. This figurative language merely bolsters the overarching metaphorical relationship between

Dillard herself, the referent, and Rahm, the externalized symbol. Even the description of his flight as the drawing of a "line" connects his artistry to the writing process, described in the opening sentence of the book: "When you write, you lay out a line of words" (3).

At this point, though, Dillard herself remains purely a spectator—she has not yet asserted her specific experiential kinship with Rahm. There is not yet a clear sense of how she might be using this essay in order to glance circumspectly at herself. However, her spectatorship itself evolves, from "scant attention" to genuine aesthetic rapture:

> Like any fine artist, he controlled the tension of the audience's longing. You desired, unwittingly, a certain kind of roll or climb, or a return to a certain portion of the air, and he fulfilled your hope slantingly, like a poet, or evaded it until you thought you would burst, and fulfilled it surprisingly, so you gasped and cried out. (96)

As Dillard's interest—her "longing"—intensifies, her description of the artistry becomes subtly more applicable to her own work. The slanting, prolonging fulfillment, the incessance of Rahm's work, is reminiscent of *Holy the Firm* with its constant intensity. "[T]he poetry's beautiful sentence never ended" (97), she writes of Rahm's flying. The jolting, unexpected moments of Rahm's routine bring *Pilgrim* to mind with its pattern of lapses and intensifications. But finally, after drawing the observer's attention to its climax, Rahm lands his plane and Dillard sees him climb down, "an ordinary man"—this idea of the artist's ordinariness brings him yet another step closer to the observer. The potential for metaphorical connection becomes even more real when Dillard proceeds to describe the imitative antics of a bird near the runway: "It was a swallow, a blue-green swallow, having its own air show, apparently inspired by Rahm" (97).

The process of identification continues as Dillard returns home to reflect on the aesthetic marvels she has just observed in the air. Earlier in *The Writing Life*, she had proposed that "Writing every book, the writer must solve two problems: Can it be done? and, Can I do it?" (72). After watching Rahm, her sense of what is achievable undergoes revision: "Nothing on earth is more gladdening than knowing we must roll up our sleeves and move back the boundaries of the humanly possible once more" (98). Her notion of human possibility, not just the possibilities of airborne artistry but of verbal artistry as well, expands in the aftermath of such an inspiring performance. As the realization of what one has witnessed settles in, it brings along a transference of possibility to the observer's own field of endeavor—in Dillard's case, to her writing. Of course, this indirect contemplation of possibility is not quite the same as weighing the viability of a specific project at hand, but it is a similar experience, and an emboldening experience.

Next, Dillard relates how she actually flew with Rahm—the union of herself and the once-distant aeronautical "poet" becomes manifest. At first, though, Dillard remains a passive, if absolutely proximate observer (they see the same images from the small plane's windows—they share eyes): "I gave up on everything, the way you do in airplanes; it was out of my hands" (99). But gradually she begins to participate more actively in the experience; when the plane takes a dive at the side of Mount Baker, she realizes, "If I forced myself to hold my heavy head up against the g's, and to raise my eyelids, heavy as barbells, and to notice what I saw, I could see the wrinkled green crevasses cracking the glacier's snow" (100). Dillard is now forcing herself to see, no longer merely waiting for experiences to be provided for her.

But there are certain things you cannot fully fathom through direct, active inspection. You can force yourself to peer at crevasse-ridden mountain slopes, but not so easily at your own mental patterns of insight and creativity. This is where the implicitly metaphorical portrait of Rahm serves its main purpose. As Rahm talks about flying, curt though his comments are, Dillard picks up on traits which seem to correspond to her own processes of thought, even though she doesn't make this connection explicitly. Rahm's main comment about his craft is: "I get a rhythm and stick with it" (102). This suggestion of minimally self-conscious improvisation perfectly describes the selfless writing condition Dillard so often ascribes to herself elsewhere, but when she externalizes this observation, using metaphor in lieu of more direct self-analysis, it impinges upon her awareness in a way that open explanation could not manage.

Dillard-the-passenger takes a progressively more active role in Rahm's flight. At one point, she asks if they could "do a barrel roll" (103) and then a second, and Rahm obliges, enabling Dillard to feel her "eyeballs . . . newly spherical and full of heartbeats" (104), to know the basic sensation of stunt flying, from which she can extrapolate the sensation of Rahm's endless, body-wrenching routines. But there are certain aspects of Rahm's flying—and of her own work—that she cannot easily confront. The physical sensation is one thing. The vague, ominous danger of the activity is another. How does the pilot know when he will "keep twirling until he [runs] out of sky room or luck" (104)? How does the writer know when she will enter a mental tailspin and never straighten out? Eventually, Dillard gets word that Rahm has been killed doing an air show in Jordan for King Hussein, confirming the ominous note in the introductory paragraph of the chapter. Dillard's response is to think back to her previous innocence, to a time when it appeared that "The air was a fluid, and Rahm was an eel" (108), when "danger was the safest thing in the world, if you went about it right" (107). She says she didn't really know him, merely "admired his flying" and went "up" with him once; but her "filling eyes" suggest that she knew him more deeply than this, that perhaps she even shuddered at her own jeopardy upon hearing of Rahm's fate.

The ultimate self-discovery Dillard makes in her contemplation of Dave Rahm's art and death is that we never do quite understand what we're doing in life, neither the processes nor the risks. Having devoted an entire book to studying her own writing life, Dillard defers to mystery, ignorance, and selfless oblivion on the next-to-last page:

> Sitting invisible at the controls of a distant airplane, he became the agent and the instrument of art and invention. He did not tell me how he felt, when we spoke of his performance flying; he told me instead that he paid attention to how his plane and its line looked to the audience against the lighted sky. If he had noticed how he felt, he could not have done the work. (110)

Likewise, Dillard could not do *her* work if she noticed how it felt. She must be attentive to her "controls," to pen and yellow paper, and to how her "line of words" will appear to her audience on the ground. As for the actual generation of language, she conceives of herself, like Rahm, as the simultaneous "agent" and "instrument" of "art and invention." To a certain extent she is in control of the composition process; she states to Mike Major, "You're writing consciously, off of hundreds of index cards, often distorting the literal truth to achieve an artistic one" (Major, "Annie Dillard," 363). But there remains always a lingering ineffability which makes the artist feel like a tool in other hands.

In his discussion of the role of metaphors in autobiography, James Olney proposes:

> Metaphor is essentially a way of knowing. . . . To a wholly new sensational or emotional experience, one can give sufficient organization only by relating it to the already known. . . . This is the psychological basis of the metaphorizing process: to grasp the unknown and thereby fit that into an organized, patterned body of experiential knowledge. A metaphor, then, through which we stamp our own image on the face of nature, allows us to connect the known of ourselves to the unknown of the world, and, making available new relational patterns, it simultaneously organizes the self into a new and richer entity; so that the old known self is joined to and transformed into the new, the hitherto unknown, self. (*Metaphors of Self*, 31–32)

However, Dillard's use of an implicit metaphor of self (the life and art of Dave Rahm) is not really a way for her to use "the old known self" to understand a new phenomenon, nor is she precisely establishing a "new relational pattern" between herself and the world in order to merge known and unknown facets of the self. Instead, given her sense of the obstructive potential of self-consciousness, she needs implicit metaphor as a mode of circumspection, as a way of seeing herself as if she were a stranger. Rahm makes the perfect vehicle for such indirect self-examination, because in most respects he is very different from Dillard ("He was in shirtsleeves, tanned, strong-wristed. I could not imagine loving him under any circumstances; he was alien to me, unfazed. He looked like G.I. Joe," [105]), but in the specific features of their artistry they are mirror images. For Dillard, implicit metaphor is less a way of knowing— for she surely understands rationally how much of what she says about Rahm applies to herself as an artist—than a way of extra-rational seeing, a way of heightening her emotional awareness of certain personal traits that interest her without facing the brick wall of self-consciousness.

Two Kinds of "Seeing": *Pilgrim at Tinker Creek* as a Psychological Document

Rather than thinking of *Pilgrim* as a spiritual document, as a kind of exemplary confession of faith, I would classify it as an informal, experiential work of psychology, the specific themes of which—because of their relevance at one extreme to religious experience—often appear more supernatural than natural. To me, *Pilgrim* fits readily into the tradition of William James's *The Varieties of Religious Experience* (1902), though Dillard's text is more fully experiential than James's. In his introduction to James's book Reinhold Niebuhr calls it "non-dogmatic and thoroughly empirical" (5). While Dillard's study of her own psychological processes may not be exactly thorough or systematic, it is both learned and empirical. Like James, she is undogmatic in that she espouses, at least in *Pilgrim*, no conspicuously sectarian beliefs, no formal theological systems, but rather tries to show the varieties of heightened natural awareness. Even James, after enumerating the basic attributes of mystical experience (ineffability, noetic quality, transiency, and passivity—all of which seem to fit the experiences Dillard describes in *Pilgrim*), voices in his "scientific" text what sounds like a personal argument for the acceptance of the mystical as an important mode of apprehending reality. He writes in *The Varieties of Religious Experience*:

> Some years ago I myself made some observations on this aspect of nitrous oxide intoxication [as a stimulant of "the mystical consciousness"], and reported them in print. One conclusion was forced upon my mind at that time, and my impression of its truth has ever since remained unshaken. It is that our normal waking consciousness, rational consciousness as we call it, is but one special type of consciousness, whilst all about it, parted from it by the filmiest of screens, there lie potential forms of consciousness entirely different. We may go through life without suspecting their existence; but apply

the requisite stimulus, and at a touch they are there in all their completeness, definite types of mentality which probably somewhere have their field of application and adaptation. No account of the universe in its totality can be complete which leaves these other forms of consciousness quite disregarded. How to regard them is the question—for they are so discontinuous with ordinary consciousness. Yet they may determine attitudes though they cannot furnish formulas, and open a region though they fail to give a map. At any rate, they forbid a premature closing of our accounts with reality. (305)

This passage resembles Dillard's *Pilgrim at Tinker Creek* in its mixture of advocacy and analysis, though Dillard is more dramatic (James's use of testimonial evidence notwithstanding) and flamboyant. But my point is that *Pilgrim*, which is often read almost exclusively as a religious or mystical text, as an attempt to answer Thoreau's "unfathomable question" concerning the mechanism of divine illumination, is also, at its core, a psychological document.

Patricia Ward, in her brief article on *Pilgrim* and *Holy the Firm*, "Annie Dillard's Way of Seeing" (1978), quickly sums up the form and the nonspiritual subject matter of *Pilgrim*:

> Tinker Creek and the cycle of the seasons during one year in Virginia make up the framework of a nature diary in the first book. She also deals with the process of her own consciousness as she moves between observation and poetic vision. Moments of insight into the mystery of nature lead Dillard to a new understanding of what writing is. . . . To see is to perceive connections between everything in this world and thus is a metaphoric act. (30)

I believe that "the process of [Dillard's] own consciousness," far from being an incidental subtopic of her first book, is actually the primary object of study in this work, and in the rest of her writings. Nearly every scholar and reviewer who has written on *Pilgrim* has quoted Dillard's description of her own work that she provides near the end of the opening chapter:

> I propose to keep here what Thoreau called "a meteorological journal of the mind," telling some tales and describing some of the sights of this rather tamed valley, and exploring in fear and trembling, some of the unmapped dim reaches and unholy fastnesses to which those tales and sights so dizzyingly lead. (11)

Just what is a "meteorological journal of the mind"? This phrase, often cited and seldom explicated, implies a correspondence between astronomical phenomena and the mind of the journal writer (see Thoreau's journal entry for August 19, 1851 [2:403]). Thoreau himself, as noted in the previous chapter, devotedly studies this precise correspondence in his own journal. The specific aspects of himself which Thoreau found attuned to the rhythms of nature were his moods and feelings. His journal functions as a simultaneous record, explanatory medium, and investigatory process, in which he examines both himself and his environment. The journal format itself is vital to this process. In its ideal form, its entries are chronological, frequent, and intimate. Above all, the journal implies the repeated scrutiny of the author's own experience as well as observations on external phenomena.

So when Dillard announces with the hyperbole of a sideshow barker—or an earnest mystic—"the unmapped dim reaches and unholy fastnesses" to which her ensuing "journal of the mind" will lead, she is referring to the inner depths of the mysterious mind. Of course her rambles through the countryside near Tinker Creek lead to rather strange and unsettling discoveries in nature also, but the emphasis of the book seems to be on her own psychological responses to these discoveries. Other times she focuses not so much on response to nature as on the advantages or disadvantages of two states of consciousness. I refer to the closed/material and the open/mystical ways of perceiving the world which are studied informally in the chapter "Seeing." The first kind of seeing, which critics of *Pilgrim* tend to disparage in their enthusiasm for the metaphysical alternative, is what enables her to attend to the details of experience. "Seeing is of course very much a matter of verbalization," she formulates. "Unless I call my attention to what passes before my eyes, I simply won't see it" (30). Language, whether spoken, written, or muttered inaudibly, serves as an attention-provoking agent; it imbues the object of contemplation with a concreteness.

Yet language, which provokes this awareness in the viewing self, prevents the self from ascending to the metarational plane of consciousness to which Dillard's persona in *Pilgrim* often aspires. In fact, the apparently instinctive attempt to use language as a way of preserving and vivifying experience results in the dissolution of the cosmic gas station vision, occurring in the chapter entitled "The Present." Dillard says:

> This is it, I think, this is it, right now, the present, this empty gas station, here, this western wind, this tang of coffee on the tongue, and I am patting the puppy, I am watching the mountain. And the second I verbalize this awareness in my brain, I cease to see the mountain or feel the puppy. I am opaque, so much black asphalt. (78–79)

And in mock annoyance, using a parodic cliché from the realm of advertising that pokes fun at the profundity of her realization, she continues, "Thanks. For the memories." But is she genuinely distressed at this diminishment of awareness? She realizes, "[A] certain amount of interior verbalization is helpful to enforce the memory of whatever it is that is taking place" (81). And this preservative role is rather important, given the intrinsic brevity of the visionary experience. To support this thought, Dillard quotes Arthur Koestler who cites the findings of a scientist named Woodrow that "the psychological present" has a "maximum span . . . estimated to lie between 2.3 and 12 seconds" (92). It is a commonplace of Saussurian linguistics, echoed even in such writing texts as James E. Miller's *Word, Self, Reality: The Rhetoric of Imagination* (1973), that any sort of ratiocination, indeed even the maintenance or communication of emotive or aesthetic thought, could not occur without language. Saussure himself writes, "Philosophers and linguists have always agreed in recognizing that without the help of signs we would be unable to make a clear-cut, consistent distinction between two ideas. Without language, thought is a vague, uncharted nebula" (*Course in General Linguistics*, 111–12).

The first kind of seeing discussed in *Pilgrim* is wholly active and volitional. "When I see this way," Dillard writes, "I analyze and pry. I hurl over logs and roll away stones; I study the bank a square foot at a time, probing and tilting my head." By contrast, the second kind of seeing implies "letting go": "When I see this way I sway transfixed and emptied" (31). This mystical, selfless type of seeing often seems to take priority for Dillard: "When I see this way I see truly. As Thoreau says, I return to my senses" (32). But it is neither a prolonged nor a complete mode of apprehending the world. The two states of awareness described in the chapter "Stalking"—seeking versus waiting—echo precisely the Jamesian distinction between voluntary and involuntary attention, outlined in James's *Psychology: Briefer Course* (195). The bulk of the writing in *Pilgrim* describes experiences of nonvisionary consciousness. Unlike Dillard's second book of prose, *Holy the Firm*, which tumbles from the outset at a mystical, lyrical tilt, *Pilgrim* consists to a great degree of mundane natural observations or analyses of various modes of personal consciousness. When visions do occur, they occur by surprise, unbidden: "I can't go out and try to see this way. I'll fail, I'll go mad. All I can do is try to gag the commentator, to hush the noise of useless interior babble that keeps me from seeing just as surely as a newspaper dangled before my eyes" (32). Only when the mind's inner noise is silenced, when expectation and habits of thought have been temporarily stilled, is the mystical experience liable to occur.

Toward the beginning of "Seeing," Dillard adopts the phrase "the artificial obvious" from Stewart Edward White to describe what exists in the world in defiance of our normal sense of what is "natural" (18)—and she implies that attunement to the subtler aspects of nature, such as a camouflaged deer or, by extension, a "tree with lights on it" (33), requires that we be devoid of expectation, open to surprise. The first visionary episode Dillard records in *Pilgrim* occurs after she reads Marius von Senden's study of "newly sighted" people in *Space and Sight* and is herself imitating, not intentionally but simply because of intense identification with the patients described in von Senden's book, the observation of "color-patches" (29), of raw, unconstrued images. But these minor "visions" do not last: "Form is condemned to an eternal danse macabre with meaning: I couldn't unpeach the peaches" (29). After reading von Senden's book, having searched actively for years for a special lit-up tree, she finally does see it, only by accident, while walking along Tinker Creek one day "thinking of nothing at all" (33). This is her first full-scale vision.

Likewise, the full awareness of "the present" described in the chapter by that name occurs following a phase of mental emptiness: "I am dazed from a long day of interstate driving homeward" (77). But various stimuli–the proximity of home, "cheerful human conversation" with the boy working at the gas station, and a "free cup of coffee"–bring the narrator "not to a normal consciousness, but to a kind of energetic readiness," followed by the vision itself:

> I am absolutely alone. There are no other customers. The road is vacant. . . . I have hazarded into a new corner of the world, an unknown spot, a Brigadoon. Before me extends a low hill trembling in yellow brome, and behind the hill, filling the sky, rises an enor- mous mountain ridge, forested, alive and awesome with brilliant blown lights. I have never seen anything so tremulous and live. Overhead, great strips and chunks of cloud dash to the northwest in a gold rush. At my back the sun is setting–how can I not have noticed before that the sun is setting? My mind has been a blank slab of black asphalt for hours, but that doesn't stop the sun's wild wheel. I set my coffee beside me on the curb; I smell loam on the wind; I pat the puppy; I watch the mountain. (78)

There is, of course, something wrong with this passage, and with all other visionary narratives as well. Dillard herself shows on the next page how language and the speaker's incumbent self-consciousness destroy transcendental consciousness. The mystical text here is an illusion, an effort to reconjure for the reader–and probably for the author herself–the thrill of vital feeling, the intense rush of awareness which was actually experienced in a lin-guistic vacuum. The repeated emphasis on solitude, the use of the present tense, and the almost complete reliance upon sensory (mainly visual) imagery make this a compelling, believable descrip-tion of an experience which, by definition, must defy full verbal communication; but the apparent awareness of the mind's recent laxity–"My mind has been a blank slab . . . "–indicates an intru-sion of self-consciousness and chips away at the text's spell.

Another interesting study of the visionary process appears in "Stalking" when the narrator recalls observing a muskrat, which she manages to watch undetected for forty minutes: "The wonder-ful thing about muskrats in my book is that they cannot see very well, and are rather dim, to boot" (194). Here, as Dillard notes else-where with regard to her unattentiveness to writing locations, it is the phenomenon of habit which frees the experiencer from the obstructive awareness of self:

> I never knew I was there, either. For that forty minutes last night I was as purely sensitive and mute as a photographic plate; I received impressions, but I did not print out captions [i.e., *no language*]. My own self-awareness had disappeared; it seems now almost as though, had I been wired with electrodes, my EEG would have been flat. I have done this sort of thing so often that I have lost self-consciousness about moving slowly and halting suddenly; it is second nature to me now. And I have often noticed that even a few minutes of this self-forgetfulness is tremendously invigorating. I wonder if we do not waste most of our energy just by spending every waking minute saying hello to ourselves. (198)

In this passage, and even in a passage preceding it describing the foraging muskrat, there is little pretense of mystical urgency or journal-like immediacy. Instead, what it amounts to is a psychological study of the sensation of mystical awareness and selflessness. Even as Dillard wonders if self-consciousness ("saying hello to ourselves") is a waste of energy, she is in the midst of greeting her own past self and scrutinizing her ongoing tendencies of thought.

Experiences such as the mystical episodes recounted in *Pilgrim* show how "invigorating" it can be to leave behind the cumbersome awareness of the self. In another essay, "Living Like Weasels," Dillard muses that she might learn from wild animals "something of mindlessness, something of the purity of living in the physical senses and the dignity of living without bias or motive" (15). However, she cannot truly "live like a weasel." Her own artistic medium, despite its intermittent mystical episodes, is highly discursive: not only demonstrative, but analytical. Although the subject matter in such books as *Pilgrim* is often suggestive of spirituality, or, at least, of secular mysticism, her goal seems more explanatory than persuasive. It is difficult for me to read *Pilgrim* as an evangelical appeal to the hearts and minds of agnostic late-twentieth-century American readers. Dillard's essential project actually seems to be directed at improving understanding of the polar vacillations of her own mind, the gradations of consciousness from not seeing, to seeing, to Seeing.

"Oh yes, the world":
Chafing against the Natural "Other"

Perhaps it is the form of *Pilgrim* (for instance, its reliance upon first-person narrative) that leads readers often to associate it with spiritual rather than psychological traditions in literature. Readers also seem to have difficulty reading *Pilgrim* as a kind of psychological autobiography – specifically, as a "journal of the mind" – because of the author's castigation of the condition of self-consciousness. "Consciousness itself," she writes, "does not hinder living in the present. . . . *Self*-consciousness, however, does hinder the experience of the present. . . . It dams, stills, stagnates" (81). She seems to desire mystical awareness of the present moment of life so much that she leads us to believe she could not bear to settle for anything less: but this is not so. In fact, her way of explaining human apprehension of the present is to depict her own mental processes: "I want to come at the subject of the present by showing how consciousness dashes and ambles around the labyrinthine tracks of the mind, returning again and again, however briefly, to the senses" (87). What do we make, then, of Dillard's occasional claims of disinterest in the self? For instance, she wrote the following in an *Esquire* article a few years ago:

> I distrust the forest, or any wilderness, as a place to live. Living in the wilderness, you may well fall asleep on your feet, or go mad. Without the stimulus of other thinkers, you handle your own thoughts on their worn paths in your skull till you've worn them smooth. The contents of your mind are so familiar you can forget about them. You glide through your days even calmer; when you talk, you whisper. This is the torpor of deprivation. Soon your famished brain will start to eat you.
>
> Many of the people I know who live as hermits among other hermits far from cities honestly find the self an object worthy of study. They are more interesting than I am. When I study myself, I fall asleep. I am a social animal, alive in a gang, like a walrus, or a howler monkey, or a bee. ("Why I Live Where I Live," 92)

The self in isolation is not what Dillard studies in her investigations of human consciousness, but rather the self in friction with external phenomena, sometimes human (for instance, in the form of texts by other writers), but more often natural. Eudora Welty once complained with regard to *Pilgrim* that "Annie Dillard is the only person in her book, substantially the only one in her world. . . . Her own book might have taken in more of human life without losing a bit of the wonder she was after" ("Meditation on Seeing," 5). But what *Pilgrim* lacks in human confrontation it makes up for in encounters with the broader organic community around Tinker Creek. James Aton suggests that Dillard "rarely entertains the concept that [Edward] Abbey develops: man and nature are distinct and separate from each other" ("Sons and Daughters," 78). Yet even in the mystical episodes, when the narrator feels as if something of the true essence of nature is being revealed to her, she remains detached from nature, observant of it and attuned to it, but still essentially separate. If she were truly part of nature, she would miss the vital, energizing tension of opposition, the element of unexpectedness which plays such an important role even in her visions of correspondence, of connection. Think, for instance, of the moment of encounter in "Living Like Weasels": "The weasel was stunned into stillness as he was emerging from beneath an enormous shaggy wild rose bush four feet away. I was stunned into stillness twisted backward on the tree trunk. Our eyes locked, and someone threw away the key" (*Teaching a Stone*, 13–14). The two share only each other's eyes and, the author surmises, the emotion of stunned stillness, but otherwise they are wholly alien to one another; in fact, it is this very strangeness that snaps them awake, for their mental images of the other species have not yet been worn smooth. Throughout *Pilgrim*, too, we can see that Dillard requires the "otherness" of nature to stimulate the prized emotions of surprise and uncertainty, the feeling of looking mystery in the eye.

David Lavery argues that the narrator's encounters with the grotesque in *Pilgrim* result in her undesired fall into Cartesian dualism:

> Though she lost no appendage in the incident, she was nevertheless dismembered: there [where she observed the giant water bug consuming the melted innards of a frog] she had lost the unity of eye and world she had once possessed; there had begun a rift between them

and her own estrangement from the natural. Yet from this scene she does not, will not, flee. The grotesque is to her an "oracle" in which she hopes to find the means of revelation to enact her "re-membrance" as well. ("Noticer," 263)

What this interpretation implies is that only visionary unity is desirable to Dillard—or, at least, to her narrator in this particular book. I disagree. Just as the bugs and animals of the natural world feast on each other, the observing writer feasts on the excitement derived from witnessing strange, inexplicable, and even abhorrent phenomena in nature. What she desires, not only in *Pilgrim* but in all of her work, is maximal awareness—not simply joyous, eternal convergence with nature or with any human individual or community. And such awareness arises from change, from the dialectical tension between self and other, and between her opposing states of consciousness as well. Prior to discovering the sucked-out frogskin she had been stalking along the edge of the island in the creek, confident in her increasing ability "to recognize, slowing down, the difference in texture of light reflected from mudbank, water, grass, or frog" (5)—this resembles the state of harmony in the scene later in the book when she watches the muskrat. But in the case of the frog, what passes for awareness is actually complacency, an inadequate appreciation of "what is." So when what appears to be a frog suddenly collapses "like a deflating football [into] a monstrous and terrifying thing," the narrator is thrust into a new state of awareness. True, "[she] gaped bewildered, appalled" and "couldn't catch [her] breath" (6), but this did not mean that she immediately yearned to "re-member" her monistic universe, or restore predictability and a sense of order to her world. It is not continued calm, but rather calamity, that is the appropriate stimulus of consciousness during periods of relative harmony.

"You know you're alive": Thrills, Chills, and the Language of Feeling

Throughout *Pilgrim* there are instances where both great beauty and great grotesqueness excite the awareness of the viewer. The instances of beauty generally prompt visions of mystical union, while the more disturbing phenomena prompt feelings of alienation—but both represent important and alternatingly desirable states of consciousness. When, on a partly cloudy January day, "light chooses an unexpected part of the landscape to trick out in gilt, and then shadow sweeps it away," there is no remorse on the part of the viewer. Light and dark in this scheme are not equivalent simply to good and evil, the beautiful and the grotesque. Even when "shadow sweeps [the gilt] away," "you know you're alive" (3), thanks to the suddenness, the unexpectedness, the sheer thrill of change. It is not change or even violent discovery that is truly horrifying; rather, "it is the fixed that horrifies us, the fixed that assails us with the tremendous force of its mindlessness" (67). As Dillard writes in "Total Eclipse," having witnessed an astonishing, cataclysmic natural blackout, eventually "enough is enough. One turns at last even from glory itself with a sigh of relief" (103). Change is relief, refreshing—a kind of awakening even when it means descending to "the workaday senses" (99).

The antidote to the experience of mind-dulling fixity is the encounter with something startling, reinvigorating. In the chapter called "The Fixed," in *Pilgrim*, the narrator mopes along Tinker Creek in winter, despairing because of its excessive tameness and predictability: "Where was the old exhilaration? This dumb dead drop over rocks was a hideous parody of real natural life, warm and willful. It was senseless and horrifying; I turned away." What finally snaps the narrator out of her torpor is a startling and rather grotesque bit of information: "I'm tired of reading; I pick up a book and learn that 'pieces of the leech's body can also swim.' Take a deep breath, Elijah: light your pile," (69). Relief—sensation. It doesn't matter that the image is grotesque; the important thing is that the feeling of consciousness is being stirred. And it is this excitation of consciousness, it seems, rather than conventional definitions, that determines what is truly beautiful. A few lines after Dillard reports that leech parts can swim, the narrator asserts that "shadow itself may resolve into beauty" (69).

Often, for Dillard, the tiniest encounter with something fey and new—usually a visual event or a tidbit stumbled across while reading—sparks the richest feeling of being alive. Her contribution to the Autumn 1988 issue of *Antaeus*, devoted to journals, diaries, and notebooks, is a four-page collection of gemlike definitions and quotations, entitled simply "Notebook." One item reads: "serein: 'a very fine rain falling after sunset from a sky in which no clouds are visible' " (84). Another one: "Emerson thought he wrote best in sentences; he called his paragraphs collections of 'infinitely repellent particles' " (86); this statement, which evidently caught Dillard's eye, is certainly descriptive of the paradoxical element in her own writing, not so much because of repellence between sentences, but because of the competing, contradicting currents which run throughout her work.

Dillard teases and provokes herself and her reader into new awareness by tossing forth ideas which "repel" or contradict one another. In *The Writing Life*, she asks, "Is it pertinent, is it courteous, for us to learn what it cost the writer personally?" (7). This is a way of reinforcing her earlier assertion that a writer should jettison his or her earlier jottings and retain only the truly "finished" portion of a project, for it's not necessary to show the "groundwork" (6). But how can we, as readers of Dillard's work, *avoid* learning "what it cost" her? Dillard suggests in one breath that writing is a blind, impersonal process—like that of an inchworm wandering crazily out on a blade of grass (*Writing Life*, 7–8), and then a few breaths later, she issues a statement which suggests the utter essentiality of personal experience to the writing process:

> The line of words fingers your own heart. It invades arteries, and enters the heart on a flood of breath; it presses the moving rims of thick valves; it palpates the dark muscle strong as horses, feeling for something, it knows not what. A queer picture beds in the muscle like a worm encysted—some film of feeling, some song forgotten, a scene in a dark bedroom, a corner of the woodlot, a terrible dining room, that exalting sidewalk; these fragments are heavy with meaning. The line of words peels them back, dissects them out. Will the bared tissue burn? Do you want to expose these scenes to the light? You may locate them and leave them, or poke the spot hard till the sore bleeds on your finger, and write with that blood. If the sore spot is not fatal, if it does not grow and block something, you can use its power for many years, until the heart resorbs it. (20)

How can we fail to discern what the writing has cost the writer? How, for that matter, can the "queer picture" thus "dissect[ed]" from the writer's own flesh in the process of becoming language fail, in a more figurative sense, to embody something of the author's intrinsic being? And so the reader of Dillard's work finds it rife with Emersonian paradox, with assertions, then equally ardent and eloquent counterassertions and reassertions of previously undermined premises. Immediately after explaining so impressively that writing is a process of self-mutilation, Dillard pivots and offers, deadpan: "The line of words feels for cracks in the firmament"—in other words, it rockets towards the stars with the "single-minded, rapt" unself-consciousness of Dave Rahm whirling through the air (20). Thus paradox, like simple quirkiness and the jarring metaphorical pairing of incompatibles, spurs the reader's imagination, prompting not placid wisdom but a biting sense of life's mystery.

This awareness—does it hurt? Do we feel it at all or does it simply sweep over us and transport us out to sea, like a breaking wave that's caught us with our backs turned, before we have time to fear its approach, to know what hit us, or even to call for help? For Dillard, although certain experiences of full consciousness do occur, if only transiently, on an exalted plane where the self is nothing, there is nearly always an emotion of intense vitality associated with each new shudder of awareness. It's difficult to categorize this sensation—akin to what Albert Einstein must have meant when he wrote, as quoted by Kathleen Raine, "The most beautiful and profound emotion we can experience is the sensation of the mystical" ("Nature," 252). For Dillard, the sensation of intense awareness does not fit the usual notions of positive and negative experience—it simply *is*. Dillard's texts abound with gasps, screams ("Total Eclipse" is full of these), and exclamations of surprise and wonder. Unlike Barry Lopez's *Arctic Dreams* (1986), in which there is a gradual, meditative ascent to the narrator's final epiphanous experience of the earth's beauty and the glimpse of his own "desire" (371), the awarenesses in Dillard's works are invariably sudden and brief, leaving the experiencer struggling to catch her breath.

The roller coaster of awareness, built and tested by the author herself, is enjoyed by the readers, too. Though at times she doubts the efficacy, the communicative force, of writing—"This writing that you do, that so thrills you, that so rocks and exhila-

rates you, as if you were dancing next to the band, is barely audible to anyone else," *Writing Life*, 17—she ultimately does seem to
believe in the capability of literature to transmit vitalizing voltage
to its readers. Drawing no doubt upon her own experience as a
reader, she writes:

> Why are we reading, if not in hope of beauty laid bare, life height-
> ened and its deepest mystery probed? Can the writer isolate and viv-
> ify all in experience that most deeply engages our intellects and our
> hearts? Can the writer renew our hope for literary forms? Why are we
> reading if not in hope that the writer will magnify and dramatize our
> days, will illuminate and inspire us with wisdom, courage, and the
> possibility of meaningfulness, and will press upon our minds the
> deepest mysteries, so we may feel again their majesty and power?
> What do we ever know that is higher than that power which, from
> time to time, seizes our lives, and reveals us startlingly to ourselves as
> creatures set down here bewildered? Why does death so catch us by
> surprise, and why love? We still and always want waking. We should
> amass half dressed in long lines like tribesmen and shake gourds at
> each other, to wake up. . . . (*Writing Life*, 72–73)

But what Dillard knows—in fact, what her entire literary output
demonstrates—is that we do not need to go out of our way "to
wake up." We do not need to drive five hours to a special hill for
the best view of a natural wonder. If we do go out of our way, it is
merely because we desire awareness so strongly. But awakening
will seek us out anyway, unsolicited. Take, for instance, the words
of the college student speaking to Dillard after the 1979 eclipse of
the sun: "Did you see that little white ring? It looked like a Life
Saver. It looked like a Life Saver up in the sky." The world is full of
such "walking alarm clock[s]" (*Teaching a Stone*, 98).

An American Childhood: Universalizing the Study of Awareness

Dillard shows similarly in *An American Childhood* that the
stimulation of awareness is an inevitable process, that it occurs
naturally even when one is too young to understand the very

phenomenon of awareness. While *Pilgrim* portrays the vacillation of the adult consciousness between various degrees of awareness, *An American Childhood* emphasizes child development as a more steady accumulation of specific awarenesses which, once achieved, become secure facets of our world knowledge. A striking instance of this occurs early in the autobiography when the five-year-old Annie Doak, suffering from the visitations of a "transparent, luminous oblong" on her bedroom wall at night—"It was a swift spirit; it was an awareness"—finally figures out that its source "was a passing car whose windshield reflected the corner streetlight outside" (21). The young girl's true breakthrough into awareness happens not when she simply notices the mysterious image and feels her pulse quicken fearfully in response, but when she realizes, by way of reason, what it really is. For a while, she "threw [her] own switches for pleasure. It's coming after me; it's a car outside. It's coming after me. It's a car. It raced over the wall, lighting it blue wherever it ran; it bumped over Amy's maple headboard in a rush, paused, slithered elongate over the corner, shrank, flew my way, and vanished into itself with a wail." But the game finally ends. The child's consciousness "matures" to a new plateau. "It" could not be after her. "It was a car," the vignette concludes (23). This scene does, in a sense, represent the loss of wonder, but Dillard does not portray this as defeat. Rather, she emphasizes the triumph of external discovery, of "a child's growing awareness of the world," as she puts it in the epigraph to this chapter.

A related event occurs much later in the autobiography when the child rushes to invite her parents to come and see the amoeba she has finally located in a drop of pond water under her microscope lens: "I told them, bursting, that he was all set up, that they should hurry before his water dried. It was the chance of a lifetime" (148). But when her parents react "warmly" and yet display no interest in this "chance of a lifetime," it is not an occasion for despair. Instead, it boosts the child to a new, unrelinquishable realization: "She did not say, but I understood at once, that they had their pursuits (coffee?) and I had mine. She did not say, but I began to understand then, that you do what you do out of your private passion for the thing itself. I had essentially been handed my own life" (148–49). This rational form of awakening—the devel-

opmental variant of the adult discoveries represented in *Pilgrim* as
the products of active "seeing," seeing with a lower-case "s" — is demonstrated to be a linear process in *An American Childhood.* Children learn certain things and cannot unlearn them. They can
throw their "switches" for a little while, teasing themselves with
mystery-like ignorance, but eventually they settle into knowledge.

This may, at first, seem a violation of the visionary yearnings
expressed so frequently elsewhere in Dillard's writing. But it is not.
The two principal modes of apprehending the world — studied initially in *Pilgrim* as "seeing" and "Seeing" (my use of capitalization to
distinguish between the rational and the metarational), as "analyz-
ing and prying" versus "letting go" — are complementary, neither
being sufficient on its own to allow for complete human experience. The second type of seeing arises in *An American Childhood* as
well, though it is portrayed wholly in emotional terms, devoid of
supernatural implications. Perhaps the most memorable scene of
this kind is when Annie, seven years old at the time, and several
older boys are passing a winter morning in Pittsburgh by bombard-
ing moving cars with snowballs. The cars make perfect, passive tar-
gets — until the kids hit a black Buick in the windshield, and "a
man got out of it, running." "All of a sudden," Dillard writes, "we
were running for our lives" (46). The chase works its way through
intricate backyards, and all the while the object of pursuit "was
cherishing [her] excitement." When the man finally catches Annie
and one of her small cohorts, all he can say is, "You stupid kids."
The writer recalls that "the point was that he had chased us pas-
sionately without giving up, and so he had caught us. . . . I wanted
the glory to last forever" (48). The glory doesn't last, of course, but
it is the sort of sensation which the wide-eyed individual can relive
intermittently throughout his or her lifetime.

An American Childhood makes conspicuous, accessible, and
secular the varieties of consciousness so often couched in mystical,
distancing jargon in *Pilgrim at Tinker Creek,* a book which many
readers, despite its impressive prose, may find remote from their
own experience of the natural world specifically, and of the world
at large. What Dillard reveals in *An American Childhood* is that the
visions and realizations which occur on an adult level in her first
book — which occur at an age when many people's minds, like the

"hideous crumpled wings" (*Pilgrim*, 61) of the Polyphemous moth in "The Fixed," have hardened into solemnity—are mere extensions of more universal childhood experiences. Thus *An American Childhood* not only demonstrates the persistence of Dillard's interest in the psychology of awareness, but universalizes the subject matter, lifting it out of the rarefied domain of the mystic, or even that of the amateur naturalist. Her most recent book of nonfiction, *The Writing Life*, continues with both the psychological themes and the universalizing process, suggesting that the reader participates in the writer's quest for awareness—or, rather, performs in the very act of reading a separate but similarly passionate prompting of awareness.

CHAPTER 4

"Rudolf the Red knows rain, dear": The Aestheticism of Edward Abbey

[W]ith five published novels and three volumes, including this one, of personal history to my credit – or discredit if you prefer – why am I still classified by librarians and tagged by reviewers as a "nature writer"?
— Abbey, Abbey's Road (1979, xviii)

"A voice crying in the wilderness, for the wilderness"?

For Edward Abbey, the literary description of nature was not simply an effort to explain and demystify his subject matter, to familiarize his readers with it. Much of what he wrote before his death in March of 1989 was intended to alarm and disorient his readers – precisely the opposite of what a tour guide or an ordinary rhapsodic publicist would try to do. Now and then in *Desert Solitaire* (1968) Abbey pauses to comment explicitly on "how the mind sees nature," noting at one point "the power of the odd and unexpected to startle the senses and surprise the mind out of their ruts of habit, to compel us into a reawakened awareness of the wonderful – that which is full of wonder" (41). As we read *Desert Solitaire*, we come to realize that the book itself imitates the startling effect of nature; it "remind[s] us – like rock and sunlight and wind and wilderness – that *out there* is a different world, older and greater and deeper by far than ours, a world which surrounds and sustains the little world of men as sea and sky surround and sustain a ship" (41–42). Our encounters with the otherness of nature, and by extension with the unruliness of Abbey's text, result in what the author calls "The shock of the real" (42) – a condition of elevated, though not altogether comfortable, awareness.

Desert Solitaire contains many examples of the harshness and unfamiliarity of the desert landscape. Even features of the desert which most of us would consider predictable and commonplace, such as the general lack of water, and the occasional, sudden, deadly, and nourishing return of water in the form of deluges and flash floods, are presented hyperbolically, sometimes nightmar-ishly, so that they become defamiliarized, alien. Near the end of *Desert Solitaire*, Abbey recalls in the chapter called "Havasu" his own initial stay in the desert. I would liken this extravagantly wrought narrative about getting lost in a side canyon off Havasu Canyon to the book as a whole in its bewildering conjunction of rapturous language and disconcerting subject matter. The final chapter, "Terra Incognita," leads us into a region called "The Maze," which is actually, in a sense, where we've been since open-ing the book. The emotions of fear, disorientation, and surprise are thus central to the heightening of environmental awareness which results from our reading of *Desert Solitaire* and many of Abbey's other books.

Jim Aton suggests that "Abbey's most intimate connection with Thoreau [in *Desert Solitaire*] lies in his use of a half-year natu-ral cycle—April to October—to frame his narrative experience" ("Sons and Daughters of Thoreau," 6). The book is, in a sense, an account of Abbey's "season" as a novice park ranger in Arches National Monument, Utah, during the late 1950s. And, as in *Walden*, there is no consistently explicit seasonal progression in *Desert Solitaire*. The book mixes digressions about the desert or about Abbey's own earlier experiences in the region with chapters on his stint as a ranger, which constitutes the overarching narra-tive frame of the book. When the author does portray himself in the present, he is often sitting at a table next to his ranger's trailer, simultaneously observing the desert landscape and writing about it. Sometimes, as in the chapter recounting his first morning in res-idence at Arches, we get the sense that he is simply observing—but this impression is repeatedly disrupted when the narrator shifts from description of the actual scene into subtly generalized rumi-nations on the appearance and natural processes of the region:

> What are the Arches? From my place in front of the housetrailer I can see several of the hundred or more of them which have been dis-covered in the park. These are natural arches, holes in the rock, win-dows in stone, no two alike, as varied in form as in dimension. They range in size from holes just big enough to walk through to openings large enough to contain the dome of the Capitol building in Wash-ington, D.C. Some resemble jug handles or flying buttresses, others

natural bridges but with this technical distinction: a natural bridge spans a watercourse—a natural arch does not. The arches were formed through hundreds of years by the weathering of the huge sandstone walls, or fins, in which they are found. Not the work of a cosmic hand, nor sculptured by sand-bearing winds, as many people prefer to believe, the arches came into being and continue to come into being through the modest wedging action of rainwater, melting snow, frost, and ice, aided by gravity. In color they shade from off-white through buff, pink, brown and red, tones which also change with the time of day and the moods of the light, the weather, the sky. (5-6)

Our link to the present scene is strained, then restored, then effaced again. We picture the narrator taking in the scene with his own eyes, but soon find him presenting visual images (as well as more abstract observations) that are not immediately present before him. This particular chapter, "The First Morning," meanders back and forth between the concrete present and the abstract, frequently trying to pass off the latter as the former. "That's the way it was this morning" (7), the chapter ends. And our response, if we have paid attention to the actual narrative detail of the text, must be: "So, what happened?" Yes, the sun, "the flaming globe," has, after much anticipation, made its sudden appearance. But otherwise the concrete experience of the morning has been permeated with the internalized musings of the narrator. The "bedrock" of experience, of conscious perception, shivers inevitably into the uncertain quicksand of imagination and speculation.

Even a precise physical observation—"Near the first group of arches, looming over a bend in the road, is a balanced rock about fifty feet high, mounted on a pedestal of equal height"—is immediately transformed into a creation of the author's own mind. "It looks like a head from Easter Island, a stone god or a petrified ogre," Abbey says. But the narrator, aware of his own mental tendencies, quickly scrambles to correct himself:

Like a god, like an ogre? The personification of the natural is precisely the tendency I wish to suppress in myself, to eliminate for good. I am here not only to evade for a while the clamor and filth and confusion of the cultural apparatus but also to confront, imme-

diately and directly if it's possible, the bare bones of existence, the
elemental and fundamental, the bedrock which sustains us. (6)

This "bedrock" proves more difficult to experience "immediately
and directly" than the narrator, at once knowledgeable and naive,
initially believes. His desire, as he "gap[es] at this monstrous and
inhuman spectacle of rock and cloud and sky and space, . . . to
know it all, possess it all, embrace the entire scene intimately, as a
man desires a beautiful woman" (6), is quickly revealed as the silli-
ness of the uninitiated. But the yearning simultaneously to control
and to surrender (or belong) to something beyond the self becomes the essential tension of the book. And just as the narrator
vacillates ceaselessly between apparent conjunction and disjunction with his natural surroundings, the reader feels alternatingly
"at home" with the text and alienated by it. Thus Abbey clearly
inherits the correspondence/otherness dialectic from Thoreau,
and passes on this tension, in the manner of Dillard, to the reader.

Abbey's desert is a conglomeration of opposing qualities. Its
apotheosis is the flower of the desert cactus: "[F]rom this nest of
thorns, this snare of hooks and fiery spines, is born once each year
a splendid flower. It is unpluckable and except to an insect almost
unapproachable, yet soft, lovely, sweet, desirable, exemplifying
better than the rose among thorns the unity of opposites" (28).
Abbey's book itself demonstrates this paradoxical unity; it is alter-
nately, sometimes simultaneously, moralistic and aesthetically
playful, sympathetic and antagonistic. One of the more memorable and intractable passages depicts the narrator, "taken by the
notion to experiment" (37), braining a wild rabbit with a stone. He
writes,

> He crumples, there's the usual gushing of blood, etc., a brief spasm
> and then no more. The wicked rabbit is dead. For a moment I am
> shocked by my deed. But the shock is succeeded by a mild ela-
> tion. . . . I continue my walk with a new, augmented cheerfulness
> which is hard to understand but unmistakable. What the rabbit has
> lost in energy and spirit seems added to my own soul. I try but can-
> not feel any sense of guilt. I examine my soul: white as snow. Check
> my hands: not a trace of blood. No longer do I feel so isolated from
> the sparse and furtive life around me, a stranger from another world.
> I have entered into this one. We are kindred all of us, killer and

victim, predator and prey, me and the sly coyote, the soaring buz-
zard, the elegant gopher snake, the trembling cottontail, the foul
worms that feed on our entrails, all of them, all of us. Long live diversity, long live the earth! (38–39)

"We are kindred all of us," except that Abbey's killing of the rabbit
is motivated only by the desire to experience what it feels like to
kill something, and to know whether he could survive in the desert
if he "were ever out here hungry, starving, no weapon but [his]
bare hands" (37). Unlike Thoreau who, though "strongly tempted
to seize and devour [a woodchuck] raw," confines the act to the
realm of thought (*Walden*, 210), Abbey kills the rabbit but leaves
its body to the vultures and maggots, rationalizing that "the flesh is
probably infected with tularemia," (38). Even as he revels in his
unity with the "sparse and furtive life around [him]," his very self-
consciousness, his intellectualization of the event, and his rational
decisions to kill and then not to eat the rabbit betray a schism
between self and world. He is rejoicing in unity but depicting
actual disunity; there is discordance between the deed itself and
the language of the account, between the destruction of an animal
carefully chosen for its very benignity and the whimsically parodic
prose: "The wicked rabbit is dead." Though the scene concludes
with the sentiment, "The experiment was a complete success; it will
never be necessary to perform it again" (39), this does little to
reverse the provocation. Indeed, it makes us even less certain how
to perceive the narrator.

The rabbit scene is calculatedly repellent, but ultimately
more disorienting than upsetting. It is immediately preceded by a
tranquil encounter with a doe and her fawn. When the deer
depart, Abbey considers following them, but doesn't: "[W]hy
should I disturb them further? Even if I found them and succeeded
in demonstrating my friendship and good will, why should I lead
them to believe that anything manlike can be trusted?" (36). The
abrupt change in the narrator's behavior from quiescent restraint
to violent engagement indicates the unreliability, the unfathom-
ability, of the narrator himself. Just when we think we have him
figured out, he perplexes us anew. Another example of this is
when, after enumerating a few of the peculiarities of desert water

(its poisonousness and scarcity), he describes with lavish grotesqueness and simultaneous adoration the sight of a flash flood:

> A wall of water. A poor image. For the flash flood of the desert
> poorly resembles water. It looks rather like a loose pudding or a thick
> dense soup, thick as gravy, dense with mud and sand, lathered with
> scuds of bloody froth, loaded on its crest with a tangle of weeds and
> shrubs and small trees ripped from their roots.
>
> Surprised by delight, I stood there in the heat, the bright sun,
> the quiet afternoon, and watched the monster roll and roar toward
> me. It advanced in crescent shapes with a sort of forelip about a foot
> high streaming in front, making hissing noises like a giant amoeba,
> nosing to the right and to the left as if on the spoor of something
> good to eat. Red as tomato soup or blood it came down on me about
> as fast as a man could run. I moved aside and watched it go by.
> (137–38)

The effect of this passage on the reader is likely to be as jarring as
the actual sight of the flood apparently was — and was *not* — for the
writer. Though "surprised by delight," the narrator uses descriptive
language which is strangely calm and ornately figurative, the flood
itself seeming more static than violent and threatening. My own
impression is of a bullfight in slow motion, the matador regally
moving aside to watch the bull, hideous in its aggravated fury, go
by. Abbey does everything in his power to estrange his language
from the predictable desert landscape; he gives us a torrent of
unsettling metaphors rather than "words from the land," to borrow Stephen Trimble's phrase. It is difficult to feel genuine horror
in response to this or any other such scene in *Desert Solitaire*.
Instead, we may feel ourselves nervously suspended between the
incompatible realms of life and art, of down-to-earth advice and
moral urgings and the rarefied play of hyperaesthetic language.

The chapter called "Water" exemplifies the primary, Dillard-
esque emotion of awakening or surprise which occurs intermittently throughout the book. In fact, this emotional response to the
unpredictability of the desert landscape becomes a prominent
motif in this chapter. After an initial encounter between Abbey's
park-ranger persona and a tourist from Cleveland who thinks the
desert would be a nice place if it had a little more water (a splendid
example of what Barry Lopez would call "prejudice"), the narrator

begins to introduce the element of human experience, the hard-
ship of living in such a place. "The desert is a land of surprises," he
tells us, "some of them terrible surprises. Terrible as derived from
terror" (132). Unlike Wendell Berry who suggests that through
careful "watchfulness" it is possible to "belong" to a particular piece
of land, and unlike Lopez who asserts that a receptive, "tolerant"
approach even to a wholly exotic landscape makes "intimacy" possible, Abbey seems to discredit the very idea of anyone ever feeling
calm and comfortable in the desert. And among all the surprises
in the canyon lands, few are as "terrible" as the unpredictability of
water, its erratic paucity and overabundance. Abbey, strangely,
seems unbothered by quicksand, poisoned springs, and flash
floods—but he is stimulated ("surprised by delight") when he
encounters something unexpected. He realizes that prolonged hab-
itation in such country is for spadefoot toads and coyotes, not for
human beings. But the desert landscape is suitable, Abbey suggests, for "thirst-crazed wanderers . . . seeking visions" (145–46),
and the desert's mere existence provides a powerful symbol of the
disjunction between the mind and nature.

What can we make of a text which is one moment entirely
self-enclosed, more imaginative than naturalistic, and the next
anchored in the semisolid earth of environmental philosophy?
Somehow we must make the adjustment from floodwaters "red
as tomato soup or blood" to the passionate conviction that "We
need wilderness whether or not we ever set foot in it. We need a
refuge even though we may never need to go there. . . . We need
the possibility of escape as surely as we need hope; without it the
life of the cities would drive all men into crime or drugs or
psychoanalysis" (148–49). It is difficult, if not impossible, to distill
a coherent moral argument from *Desert Solitaire*, an argument
which could translate into new attitudes and new behavior—
this, despite the fact that Abbey tells Judy Nolte Lensink in an
interview, "I think that poets and writers, essayists and novelists,
have a moral obligation to be the conscience of their society. I
think it's the duty of a writer, as Samuel Johnson said, to try to
make the world better, however futile that effort might be"
(Trimble, *Words from the Land*, 28). However, Abbey also tells
Lensink in the same interview:

> I write in a deliberately outrageous or provocative manner be-
> cause I like to startle people. I hope to wake up people. I have no
> desire to simply soothe or please. I would rather risk making people
> angry than putting them to sleep. And I try to write in a style that's
> entertaining as well as provocative. It's hard for me to stay serious for
> more than half a page at a time. (27)

Herein lies the key to Abbey's participation in the Thoreauvian
tradition of consciousness-raising. It is precisely this unwillingness
to smooth his beliefs into a neat package, to allow his readers to
passively consume even his ideology, which tends to stimulate the
readers' attentiveness to specific natural phenomena, and to the
more abstract concepts (such as freedom and individualism)
which Abbey considers important. During the mid-1980s, Diane
Wakoski wrote that "Abbey, like his Desert, presents riddles which
have no answers." However, she finds "his lack of doctrine or
dogma . . . reassuring in itself when we are aware of a very probably approaching nuclear holocaust" ("Visionary 'Inhumanists,'"
106-7). Even Wendell Berry states in "A Few Words in Favor of
Edward Abbey":

> I read him . . . for consolation, for the comfort of being told the
> truth. There is no longer any honest way to deny that a way of living
> that our leaders continue to praise is destroying all that our country
> is and all the best that it means. . . . For those who know this,
> Edward Abbey's books will remain an indispensable solace. (47)

But it seems uncharacteristic for Abbey to be "reassuring," for his
works to provide "consolation," "comfort," and "solace." Berry criticizes "some of [Abbey's] defenders, who have an uncontrollable
itch to apologize for him: 'Well, he did *say* that. But we mustn't
take him altogether seriously. He is only trying to shock us into
paying attention'" (36). The point of my own argument is not to
apologize for Abbey or to demean the truthfulness of his works,
but rather to *explain* his strategies for provoking attention, for this
does seem to be an important goal of his writings. It is by way of
such provocation that he compels his readers not to think a certain way, but to think *period*, to abandon secure mental ruts.

The *Lolita* of Environmental Literature

Is provoking the reader to think the goal of Abbey's fiction, too? To evoke in us some sort of fundamental disorientation which will pass for awareness—awareness, at least, of the difficulty of knowing the world? I believe this is precisely the aim of Abbey's best-known novel, *The Monkey Wrench Gang* (1975). In fact, I think this book, far from being overtly ideological, calls into question the very notion of allowing a static ideology, whether pro-environment or pro-development, to govern our behavior in the wilderness. The world Abbey depicts in *The Monkey Wrench Gang* is a pliant, elusive one, alternatingly secure and deceptive; as we read, we find our attention shifting incessantly from the real-world issues of wilderness use to the conspicuously artificial realm of Abbey's adventure story. The language frequently shifts from the purely aesthetic level of lavish description and exuberant word-play to the expression of clashing ideologies.

Abbey, it seems, delights in luring us to make a commitment to one ideology or another, to one mode of reading or another, only to suddenly pull the rug out from under our feet. Suckered into the novel by the fast-moving narrative of environmental sabotage, we find ourselves unable to halt the roller coaster until the ride comes to its scheduled end. Reading *The Monkey Wrench Gang* is like attempting a controlled "friction descent" down a thirty-foot rock wall with George Washington Hayduke. Abbey tells us:

> Hayduke holsters his revolver and slides on his stomach over the edge, facing the wall, feeling the cool unyielding bulge of the stone against his chest and thighs. He hangs for a moment to the last possible handhold. Friction descent, he thinks, what they call a friction fucking descent. He looks below, sees only shadows, no bottom at all.
>
> "I change my mind," he says desperately, inaudibly (losing his grip), speaking to nobody in particular—and who is listening?—"I'm not going to do this, this is insane." But his sweaty hands know better. They release him.
>
> *Falling*, he yells, *falling*. Thinks he yells. The words never get past his teeth. (324)

Both the world and self are deceptive to Hayduke—and he, it turns out at the conclusion of the novel, is the grandest deceiver of all. He commits himself to the firm, cool contours of the wall, only to realize too late that the cliff has no visible bottom, and offers no real friction. He cannot prevent his hands from releasing their grip, nor does he know whether or not he has uttered an audible cry. He is, in other words, in a situation beyond his control, subject to the frictionlessness of the rock, the pull of gravity, and the solidity of the ground where he'll eventually land, where he'll experience the full "shock of the real." We don't actually see Hayduke hit the ground—Abbey cuts to a later scene as Hayduke and his three fellow saboteurs, Doc Sarvis, Bonnie Abbzug, and Seldom Seen Smith, continue their escape through the desert with Bishop Love's posse on their trail—but we do learn that he survives the fall, albeit with "bruised limbs and abraded hide [and] lacerated palms" (326).

We, too, are never quite sure what is real as we free-fall through the narrative, expecting one thing and often getting another. Just what is the ideological bedrock of the novel? Abbey, perhaps more so than any other recent nature writer, has been cursed by some readers and exalted by others as a left-wing ideologue, as a cantankerous gadfly of the military-industrial complex. Edwin Way Teale called *Desert Solitaire* "a voice crying in the wilderness, *for* the wilderness" ("Wild Scene," 7). And Grace Lichtenstein, reviewing *The Monkey Wrench Gang* for the *New York Times*, notes that Abbey "has been the most eloquent spokeman for angry nature-lovers. . . . His message, that only a radical change in the American life-style or even more radical action will preserve the land for future generations—has become a watchword among the growing minority of those who call themselves 'eco-freaks' " (24). Indeed, *The Monkey Wrench Gang* inspired the formation of Earth First!, the country's most visible radical preservationist group. But what some readers have found to be the direct espousal of an extremist ideology has proven to be a more perplexing text for other readers—and rightly so.

Ann Ronald points out in *The New West of Edward Abbey* that this work "has more ambition than an ordinary propaganda novel of eco-raiders and environmental protest and speaks more profoundly than a vulgar little fairy tale," and it "broaden[s] the dimensions of romance" in order to "project Abbey's increasingly complex vision of what man can do to stop the twentieth century from cannibalizing its land and its humanity" (183). Ronald also observes, as I mentioned in my introductory chapter, that Abbey uses "his sense of humor to pronounce a sobering message" (200). But I would suggest that the purely aesthetic element (including wordplay and other types of humor) in virtually all of Abbey's works is there not only to be entertaining, not only to make serious material more palatable, but chiefly to *conflict* with the moral strata of the texts. Rather than merging together to "pronounce" Abbey's "sobering message" about the environment, the aesthetic and moral currents in *The Monkey Wrench Gang* strain to become separate, like oil and water; they produce a tense disjunction which forces us to stay on our toes.

After calling *The Monkey Wrench Gang* a "violently . . . revolutionary novel" and a "long, extravagant, finely written tale of ecological sabotage in the American Southwest" in a 1976 *New York Times* review, Jim Harrison observes the irony that

> Edward Abbey wrote the book in an atmosphere of political vacuum as a sort of soldier of the void when the only possible audience the book could truly resonate against, the New Left, had largely turned to more refined dope, natural foods, weird exercises, mail order consciousness programs, boutiques and Indians (jewelry). Surely a base of warhorses is left, a core of politically astute veterans who have changed their pace but not their intentions, but the sense of mass movement is deader than Janis Joplin. (59)

It seems to me, however, that *The Monkey Wrench Gang* is not really designed to launch a mass movement or to strike home merely with a base of stalwart warhorses, such as the Earth First! activists who have come to bear out the author's mock disclaimer on the copyright page of the novel: "This book, though fictional in form, is based strictly on historical fact. Everything in it is real and actually happened. And it all happened just one year from today" (vi). I think the goal of this novel is far more universal than either Harrison or Lichtenstein suggest in their early reviews—that is, instead of merely presenting an environmental ideology or even a group of fictional role models for would-be activists, Abbey is trying to prompt a more basic kind of consciousness among his readers, to provoke not a singleminded political movement but rather an awareness on the individual level of the need to question moral and aesthetic assumptions. *The Monkey Wrench Gang* is less a clear-cut call to action than a call to feeling.

To the extent that the novel does bear a political message, it does so in the manner of Raymond Barrio's postmodern protest novel *The Plum Plum Pickers*, which first appeared in 1969. Rather than engaging us in individual migrant workers' frustrated quests for self-realization or merely day-to-day security, Barrio presents a series of disjunctive vignettes, skipping from scene to scene with scant narrative continuity, describing even the foulest situations with incongruously lush prose, as if to emphasize tacitly the gap between the characters' dreams and their actual predicaments. In one scene, for instance, a group of rowdy farm workers, after leaving a bar, winds up in a garbage dump to enjoy "a good long heartfelt piss": "They were floating in the midst of a sea of garbage," Barrio writes, "all lit up by the light of the romantic moon, lovingly delineating every scrap, every crump of used paper, every bent straw, every spent can of lucky, every piece of string, every spawn of stinking, decaying, moldy, barnacled banana peel. Mounds and mounds of pure useless garbage gently degenerating in the warm moonlight" (51).

Abbey, too, beginning in the initial scene of his novel, the ceremonial opening of a bridge over the Colorado River between Utah and Arizona which becomes the opportunity for flamboyant monkey-wrenchery, makes a point of depicting morally charged situations in lovingly amoral language. After several tedious speeches, fireworks are exploded and the crowd at the bridge cheers, "thinking this the high point of the ceremonies." Abbey goes on to say:

> But it was not. Not the highest high point. Suddenly the center of the bridge rose up, as if punched from beneath, and broke in two along a jagged zigzag line. Through this absurd fissure, crooked as lightning, a sheet of red flame streamed skyward, followed at once by the sound of a great cough, a thunderous shuddering high-explosive cough that shook the monolithic sandstone of the canyon walls. The bridge parted like a flower, its separate divisions no longer joined by any physical bond. Fragments and sections began to fold, sag, sink

and fall, relaxing into the abyss. Loose objects—gilded scissors, a monkey wrench, a couple of empty Cadillacs—slid down the appalling gradient of the depressed roadway and launched themselves, turning slowly, into space. They took a long time going down and when they finally smashed on the rock and river far below, the sound of the impact, arriving much later, was barely heard by even the most attentive.

The bridge was gone. The wrinkled fragments at either end still clinging to their foundations in the bedrock dangled toward each other like pendant fingers, suggesting the thought but lacking the will to touch. As the compact plume of dust resulting from the catastrophe expanded upward over the rimrock, slabs of asphalt and cement and shreds and shards of steel and rebar continued to fall, in contrary motion from the sky, splashing seven hundred feet below into the stained but unhurried river. (5–6)

The description of this event defines it as neither heroic nor criminal. The morally neutral language beguiles us into forgetting what this final explosion means to the human observers, those who want the new bridge and those who don't. Despite the use of the word "catastrophe" in the midst of this descriptive passage, we are not made to feel that we are witnessing a genuine catastrophe. In fact, after reading these exquisitely violent and seemingly nonhuman paragraphs, it shocks us when the narrative perspective returns suddenly to the petty human level and we overhear various public officials plotting to catch the saboteurs once and for all. The effect is more comical than moving. Then, in the next breath, we return to the cosmic perspective, to the "ultimate farthest eye" of the vulture high above in the sky, "so far beyond all consequence of dust and blue [of land and water]," who "contemplat[es] the peaceful scene below" and derives no meaning from it (6–7). But this shifting perspective does not instill the narrative with a discernible moral imperative, either in this first scene or elsewhere in the novel. We feel a constant tension between the passions of the human characters and passionless gaze of the cosmos, represented intermittently by a circling vulture.

Abbey's novel, though I believe it does not attach us firmly to a single perspective on the environment, helps us to become aware of the interplay (and frequently the opposition) between morality and the amoral perception of phenomena, including the perception of beautiful objects and beautiful language. In this respect, *The Monkey Wrench Gang* reminds me of Vladimir Nabokov's *Lolita*. As a graduate student at Brown University, I occasionally taught them together in undergraduate courses to demonstrate this connection. In his 1980 interview with *The Bloomsbury Review* Abbey mentions his respect for Nabokov, "chiefly as a stylist, a master of the language" (Solheim and Levin, "The *Bloomsbury Review* Interview," 83). But I think *The Monkey Wrench Gang* actually betrays Abbey's deeper affinity with Nabokov's project in his Rousseauvian novel about the wayward passion resulting from the narrator's obsessive yearning to recapture the innocence and beauty of childhood, particularly with the disjunctive use of lavish, punning language to tell such a violent and, to most readers, perverse story. In an early scene, the middle-aged Humbert Humbert recalls the "nymphet" Lolita sprawling innocently across his lap:

> She was musical and apple-sweet. Her legs twitched a little as they lay across my live lap; I stroked them; there she lolled in the right-hand corner, almost asprawl, Lola the bobby-soxer, devouring her immemorial fruit, singing through its juice, losing her slipper, rubbing the heel of her slipperless foot in its sloppy anklet, against the pile of old magazines heaped on my left on the sofa—and every movement she made, every shuffle and ripple, helped me to conceal and to improve the secret system of tactile correspondence between beast and beauty—between my gagged, bursting beast and the beauty of her dimpled body in its innocent cotton frock. (56–57)

When *Lolita* first appeared in 1955, American readers recoiled from it, crying "Pornography!" In response, the author attached a few notes to the end of the book in which he explained that he was "neither a reader nor a writer of didactic fiction," that "*Lolita* has no moral in tow," and that for him "a work of fiction exists only insofar as it affords . . . aesthetic bliss" (286). But do most readers believe this? I've found that it requires considerable coaching to get student readers beyond the sexual surface of *Lolita*, to help them appreciate the tension between the playful language and the narrative of desire and remorse. Abbey himself refers similarly to "the sheer ecstasy of the creative moment" in his introduction to

Abbey's Road: "It is this transient moment of bliss," he writes, "which is for the artist, as it is for other lovers, the one ultimate, indescribable, perfectly sufficient justification for the sweat and pain and misery and humiliation and doubt that lead, if lucky, to the consummation we desire" (xxiii). It may seem out of character for Abbey, whom many readers came to view as a rather traditional storyteller and environmental advocate in the wake of *Desert Solitaire*, to voice this postmodern devotion to rarefied "aesthetic bliss" — a few years ago, at a conference on Postmodernism, I heard John Hawkes state that *his* goal as a writer is to enjoy the eroticism of language, to seek the never-quite-attainable aesthetic bliss of crafting the perfect sentence. But Abbey claims in a 1977 interview at the University of Arizona Poetry Center, and again in the introduction to *Abbey's Road* (note the explicit Beatles' pun in the title) that he "never wanted to be an environmental crusader, an environmental journalist. I wanted to be a fiction writer, a novelist" (Hepworth, "Poetry Center Interview," 39).

Indeed, in *The Monkey Wrench Gang*, Abbey creates a highly aestheticized fictional world, but it's a world in constant tension with the real American Southwest that his readers know, or at least know about. Ann Ronald calls the novel "simply another Edward Abbey romance," a book which "projects a fictive version of Edward Abbey's wildest nonfiction dreams. The Western formula circumscribes his exuberant imagination, inducing him to impose a nineteenth-century brand of frontier justice on the modern atrocities he sees everywhere" (183–84). But beyond the evocation of anachronistic "frontier justice" in response to twentieth-century environmental problems, *The Monkey Wrench Gang* is a novel which never lets us forget, at least not for long, that it is an artifact, a work of the imagination. Abbey seems to take advantage of his readers' perception of him as "an environmental crusader" to defy facile wish fulfillment. Abbey's artifice is evident at nearly every level of the novel, and the seams are intentionally left showing. Paul Bryant in his study of *Hayduke Lives!*, Abbey's sequel to *The Monkey Wrench Gang*, remarks that the novel's precise echoing of such disparate works as *The Grapes of Wrath* and Kipling's poem "The Betrothed" "is text calling attention to the literary nature of its own textuality" ("Echoes," 317).

The first four chapters of *The Monkey Wrench Gang* sketch the characters who will soon become the infamous gang of marauders, and while the characterizations are lively and, as Jim Harrison said, "convincing," they are nonetheless caricatures, exaggerated character types. "A. K. Sarvis, M.D.," the pollution-hating Albuquerque surgeon who underwrites the group's adventures, is immediately ascribed grotesque physical characteristics and a whimsical scholarly interest in the environment; Sarvis's "bald mottled dome and savage visage, grim and noble as Sibelius," his "tall and ponderous [frame], shaggy as a bear" (9), contrast strangely with his playful intellect and his actual inexperience in wild places. The first thing we learn about George Washington Hayduke is that he is an ex-Green Beret with a "grudge," for he returned after three years in Vietnam "to the American Southwest he had been remembering only to find it no longer what he remembered, no longer the clear and classical desert, the pellucid sky he roamed in dreams" (15); Hayduke, "a short, broad, burly fellow, well-muscled, built like a wrestler" whose "face is hairy, very hairy, with a wide mouth and good teeth, big cheekbones and a thick shock of blue-black hair" (17), represents the brawn of the Monkey Wrench Gang, and its animal aspects in his ceaseless swearing, beer-swilling, pissing, sexual impulses, and love of guns and violence (later in the novel he is called an "anthropoid ape," 179). Seldom Seen Smith, a maverick Mormon who makes his living as a river runner, is the gang's closest thing to a traditional environmentalist, but his earnest love of the Utah landscape is generally concealed beneath his eccentricities, which include his physical appearance; Abbey tells us early on that "Smith was a lanky man, lean as a rake, awkward to handle. His arms were long and wiry, his hands large, his feet big, flat and solid. He had a nose like a beak, a big Adam's apple, ears like the handles on a jug, sun-bleached hair like a rat's nest, and a wide and generous grin" (35). The fourth caricature is of "Ms. B. Abbzug (Bonnie)," the New Age secretary and lover of Doc Sarvis (and later of Hayduke), whose witty feminism and splendid sexuality become her trademarks. The physical, verbal, and philosophical traits of these four characters become prominent motifs in the novel, but they are at once convincingly consistent and exaggeratedly stylized.

The structure of the work is neatly symmetrical, the bulk of the narrative framed between a prologue subtitled "The Aftermath" (the bridge scene) and an epilogue called "The New Beginning." This conspicuously clever framing contributes to the reader's awareness of the work's fictionality. So, too, do the narrative's many premonitory moments—scenes such as Hayduke's "friction descent" and his later escape from Bishop Love's Search & Rescue Team by winching himself and his jeep down a cliff foreshadow Hayduke's mysterious disappearance and presumed death at the edge of yet another cliff in the penultimate chapter of the book. The epilogue, of course, reveals semimysteriously that Hayduke has survived once again; indeed, the title of the sequel confirms it.

But perhaps the most prominent feature of Abbey's aestheticism in this novel, a feature in which the author indulges so freely as to obscure the real-life political issues of wilderness use and to jeopardize the plausibility of his narrative and the credibility of his characters, is the ubiquitous, often outrageous, use of puns and other affectionate forms of language. Both the narrator and the characters demonstrate this love of language; sometimes the narrator actually puns on behalf of individual characters. Even the description of a cocktail waitress becomes an occasion for the narrator to indulge in homophones: "[She] came between [Bonnie and Doc], wearing only her barely there see-through flimsy, her barely anywhere expression. She was too weary of it all" (132). The only purpose of the words "anywhere" and "weary" is to play upon the sound of "wearing," a word which fits more naturally into the context of the scene.

One of the more vulgar features of the novel is Hayduke's fecal obsession, a motif which becomes a gauge of his fear. Everything is "structurally perfect" (93) when he's safe and "structurally imperfect" (370) when it looks like the law finally has him pinned down near the end of the book; but even this motif becomes fodder for the narrator's punning mentality when, during one episode, he reads Hayduke's fearful mind and asks, "Will the sphincter hold until I get out of here and free and clear? The riddle of the sphincter. That was the question" (265). Bonnie's consciousness of language is evident first in her critique of Hayduke's constant cursing: "That's a brilliant retort you've worked out, Hayduke. . . . Really brilliant. A real flash of wit for all occasions" (110), and later, after she and Hayduke have become lovers, in her subtle adoption of his speech "It's time to get fucking back to work!" she exclaims (137). In the final line of the novel, Doc Sarvis hints similarly at Hayduke's survival by winking at Bonnie and Smith during a card game and saying, "Deal me in . . . and don't forget to cut the fucking deck" (387). Hayduke, of course, is typically characterized as behemothic, and yet he too shows his own kind of love of language, shouting at one point when he and Bonnie have captured a guard and a helicopter pilot, "Stay that way, please, or I'll blast both you cocksuckers into eternity." The narrator then tells us that "Hayduke liked that majestic phrase so much he repeated it" (245).

Seldom Seen Smith, whose earnest love of the canyon lands most closely resembles Abbey's attitude in *Desert Solitaire*, gazes at the landscape at one point in the narrative and savors the convergence of places and their names. The narrator tells us,

> He could see for a hundred miles. Though the sky was lidded with heavy clouds there was no wind. The air was clear. The stillness was impressive. Filtered sunlight lay on the strange land, and waves of heat, shimmering like water, floated above the canyons. Must be a hundred ten in the shade down there. He could see Shiprock, Ute Mountain, Monument Valley, Navajo Mountain, Kaiparowits, the red walls of Narrow Canyon, the dark gorge of the Dirty Devil River. He could see the five peaks of the Henrys—Ellsworth, Holmes, Hillers, Pennell and Ellen—rising behind the maze of canyons, beyond the sandstone domes and pinnacles of Glen Canyon.
> Hell of a place to lose a cow. Hell of a place to lose your heart. Hell of a place, thought Seldom Seen, to lose. Period. (285)

Similarly, in the "Tukuhnikivats" chapter of *Desert Solitaire*," Abbey himself relishes the names of desert places, which he calls "the folk poetry of the pioneers" (255). Strangely, the learned doctor's rebellious vulgarity, if not his precise taste in language, is more in line with Hayduke's: "Used to do this all night," he says to Bonnie after spending the night with her, "Now it takes me all night to do it" (48). Another time, after Doc Sarvis charges a hated district attorney $500 for a ten-minute hemorrhoid operation, the narrator quips, "Prosecutors will be violated" (213). The language of the novel, not only the punning but the extravagant dialogue and the lush rhapsodies, is part of what makes this such an engaging book, despite its occasional interference with the credibility of the narrative, the instances where the language seems to exist for its own sake.

It seems to me that the multiple layers of the work are particularly evident in the scene from which I've taken my title for this chapter. While lying with Bonnie near a campfire, Hayduke (alias "Rudolf the Red") is awakened by raindrops falling on his face. " 'What's the matter, Rudolf?' " Bonnie asks.

> "It's raining."
> "You're nuts. It's not raining. Go to sleep."
> "It is. I felt it."
> She poked her head out of the hood of the bag. "Dark all right . . . but it's not raining."
> "Well it was a minute ago. I know it was."
> "You were dreaming."
> "Am I Rudolf the Red or ain't I?"
> "So?"
> "Well goddammit, Rudolf the Red knows rain, dear."
> "Say that again?" (282–83)

End of scene. On one level, of course, this dialogue fits into the larger context of the narrative: the two characters are out in the wilderness and it starts to rain. But the main purpose of this scene is simply to set up the reindeer pun, which Hayduke supposedly utters unconsciously but which Bonnie, in her half-sleep, catches. Is Abbey merely having fun with language here? Is this why the novelist intrudes elsewhere with more or less explicit references to himself? In one scene, for instance, a ranger named "Edwin P. Abbot Jr." (190) inspects a box of Bonnie's belongings and finds, among other things, a "personally autographed extremely valuable first-edition copy of *Desert Solipsism*" (196), an allusive echo of Abbey's original title for the work *Desert Solecism*, which became *Desert Solitaire*. It seems that Abbey had a great deal of fun in writing this novel, but I don't think this is the only reason for the work's many conspicuous aesthetic games and extravagances. All of this, I believe, is related to Abbey's exploration of the way our minds work, and his discovery that we frequently become alert to things (including ourselves) not through harmony but through opposition, even antagonism.

Awareness and Dissonance: Abbey's Literary Anarchism

In his 1990 book *Nature Writing and America: Essays upon a Cultural Type*, Peter Fritzell argues that "Witting or unwitting, paradoxes are the essence of American nature writing" (287). Commenting on the early passage in *Desert Solitaire* when the narrator "dream[s] of a hard and brutal mysticism in which the naked self merges with the nonhuman world and yet somehow survives still intact, individual, separate" (6), Fritzell observes that

> the figure here in the approaching sunrise is no civil reformer, finally – no clear-minded, programmatic renovator of the world's ways – lamenting in some public and political forum the discord between nature and culture in the modern world. . . . No, this is a figure – a prototypical figure in American nature writing – who finds the discord between nature and culture very much, too much, within himself. (289)

However, rather than reading Abbey's "lonely cries into the canyons against society" as "cries against himself, his human language, and his inherited dreams" (289), as Fritzell suggests, I would argue that Abbey actually appreciated the value of such dissonance in prompting his own awareness, such stimulation being an end in itself. And I believe the playfulness and ornateness of the prose in such works as *The Monkey Wrench Gang*, which often seem to detract from narrative coherence and ideological dissemination, are actually part of an attempt to create textual paradoxes or incongruities which force readers to intensify their own attentiveness.

The epistemologist Michael Polanyi suggests in his essay "The Structure of Consciousness" (1965) that there are "*two levels of awareness*: the lower one for the clues, the parts or other subsidiary elements and the higher one for the focally apprehended comprehensive entity to which these elements point." He goes on to explain that "The way we know a comprehensive entity by relying

on our awareness of its parts for attending to its whole is the way
we are aware of our body for attending to an external event. We
may say therefore that we know a comprehensive entity by *interi-
orizing* its parts or by making ourselves *dwell in them . . .* " (214).
The strain of trying to interiorize disparate elements—such as the
self and nature or, perhaps, the divergent moral and aesthetic
strata of a novel such as *The Monkey Wrench Gang*—vaults us to
higher levels of awareness.

Edward Abbey was made into an environmental guru during
his lifetime, although he once said "it would be a fate worse than
death to become a cult figure, especially among undergraduates"
(Lichtenstein, "Edward Abbey," 24). A fuller sense of his "message"
requires that we come to terms with the incongruities, the paradoxes, and apparent rough edges of his writings, and that we not
be too quick to ascribe an ideology to Abbey which we desire for
ourselves, as if to give it legitimacy by attributing it to a prophet, to
"a voice crying in the wilderness, *for* the wilderness." Abbey ended
up writing his master's thesis in philosophy at the University of
New Mexico on the ethics of violence, but he told his interviewers
from *The Bloomsbury Review* that he had originally planned to
write a thesis called "General Theory of Anarchism" (Solheim and
Levin, 86). Indeed, a study of the conflicting "subsidiary elements"
in *The Monkey Wrench Gang* (to use one of Polanyi's phrases) suggests that the author's overarching message is closer to anarchism
than environmentalism. As Hayduke tells himself, "Freedom . . . is
the highest good" (26).

Abbey's goal is not to imbue his readers with a shared, plac-
idly adopted ideology of environmental protection, but to alert us
to our essential wildness, to stir us out of the complacency which
allows us to give up our own freedom. The wilderness of southern
Utah is only one kind of useful wilderness, he suggests in his brief
article called "On the Need for a Wilderness to Get Lost In," published in the *New York Times* in 1972:

> The reason we need wilderness is because we are wild animals.
> Every man needs a place where he can go crazy in peace. Every Boy
> Scout troop deserves a forest to get lost, miserable and starving in.
> Even the foulest murderer of the sweetest wife should get a chance

for a run to the sanctuary of the hills. If only for the sport of it. For freedom and delirium.

Only then can we return to man's other life, to the other way, to the order and sanity and beauty of what will somewhere be, unless all visions are false, the human community. (29)

The giddy aestheticism of *The Monkey Wrench Gang*, like the "decaying piers and abandoned warehouses" (29) of Hoboken and the remote canyons of the Southwest, is just such a wilderness. And in attempting to appreciate this aspect of the novel, we get a little closer to appreciating and respecting not only the wild side of our own humanity, but the wildness of the nonhuman world.

CHAPTER 5

Coming Home to "the Camp": Wendell Berry's Watchfulness

He had known no other place. From babyhood he had moved in the openings and foldings of the old farm as familiarly as he moved inside his clothes. Before he bought it he had farmed it for five years as the tenant of other heirs. But after the full responsibility of it fell to him, he saw it with a new clarity. He had simply relied on it before. Now when he walked his fields and pastures and woodlands he was tramping into his mind the shape of his land, his thought becoming indistinguishable from it, so that when he came to die his intelligence would subside into it like its own spirit.

— Berry, The Memory of Old Jack *(1974, 38)*

Stunt Pilots and Plowhorses

Thoreau's statement of purpose in the second chapter of *Walden* could be taken as the rallying cry of virtually all the subsequent nature writers in this country. "We must learn to re-awaken and keep ourselves awake," he wrote, "not by mechanical aids, but by an infinite expectation of the dawn, which does not forsake us in our soundest sleep." This state of "infinite expectation of the dawn," a condition of maximal alertness to the aesthetics of landscape, to the patterns of natural history, and, in our own post–*Silent Spring* era, to the moral and political imperatives of ecology, is what has driven many of our finest writers to devote themselves to the literary pondering and exposition of nature. But how can language best be used not only to depict specific American landscapes (both wilderness and non-wilderness), but to instill in readers an urgent awareness of the environment? This is by no means a simple question, and it has resulted in a striking diversity of wilderness voices.

Wendell Berry's "The Long-Legged House" (1969) demonstrates more graphically than many of his other essays the notion that people must learn to perceive and respect the "what is" of

115

nature rather than manufacturing too much human significance. To invest too much imagination in understanding or describing the natural world would, Berry implies, amount to an attempt to possess it, to make nature the imaginative property of the human observer. The essay itself, far from being a static, polished artifact of this ideology of humility, demonstrates a process of growing and learning, as if in remembering the course of his association with a special place, the author discovers anew what it means to be truly indigenous.

Berry's writing, particularly in "The Long-Legged House" and in the less self-conscious essays such as "A Country of Edges," is strikingly unflamboyant and unelaborate, in keeping with his goal of showing "how a person can come to belong to a place, for places really belong to nobody" ("Long-Legged House," 145). Humble, patient watchfulness, rather than bold, aggressive inter-pretation, is what Berry learns to rely upon in coming to know, and thus belonging to, his native place along the Kentucky River, which he calls "the Camp." The place will reveal its secrets to the human observer, but it takes prolonged contact and an attitude of nonintrusive attentiveness: "The only condition," he writes, "is your being there and being watchful" (169). The very language of "The Long-Legged House," though intensely detailed and morally emphatic, is devoid of the garish, manipulative phrases and the jolting metaphors that often animate the works of other nature writers, such as Annie Dillard and Edward Abbey. So intent is Berry upon giving himself over to the actuality of the place and perceiving its genuine significance in his own life that he keeps a tight rein on his own use of language, carefully measuring the interpretive movements of his mind, allowing interaction with the observed and remembered landscape, but trying not to dominate or act upon what he sees.

I have already explained in my introduction, William James's theory of perception, which is encapsulated in the statement: "Per-ception is of probable and definite things." Dillard and Abbey seem well aware of this tendency of the human mind; they toy with our uncritical expectations, frequently startling us into aware-ness. Far from living in "infinite expectation" of the wholly regular "dawn," they capitalize in their work upon the harsh, chilling, and surprising features of their favorite landscapes. They delight in upsetting our notions of what is probable and definite.

Fear, disorientation, surprise—these emotions are central to the heightening of environmental awareness which results from our reading of the works of Dillard and Abbey, and not only the books I've singled out in this study. Equally central is what Ron Powers calls in a 1989 essay on literary nonfiction "the inflected voice," the harnessing of passion to idea, so that "[w]e know instantly that we've been plunged inside a private vision, a vision like no one else's, and that vision, that voice, is going to be our vehicle into unknown territory" (145). Such writing, Powers says, "is by turns outraged, obsessive, lyrical, extreme, overwrought, exquisite, minutely pictorial, self-mocking, glorious—and poetic in the Emersonian sense of that word" (147)—this description of James Agee's *Let Us Now Praise Famous Men* could, I think, apply directly to *Desert Solitaire* and, with the deletion of the word "outraged," to *Pilgrim at Tinker Creek*. The goal of the highly inflected eloquence of Dillard and Abbey, as I've been emphasizing, is to awaken themselves and their readers by depicting nature as strange and inhuman, by highlighting the *uncertainty* of their chosen landscapes. Through Dillard's imagination, even the rolling hills of Virginia become wilderness, become a realm of "unmapped dim reaches and unholy fastnesses" (*Pilgrim*, 11).

When I read these two writers, I think not only of their inheritance from the Romantic tradition of reverence and rapture, but of their roots in the Gothic depiction of unpleasant, repulsive, frightening landscapes. In his 1919 essay on "The Uncanny," Freud reveals the intriguing etymological connection between *das Unheimlich* and *das Heimisch*, between the uncanny and that which is " 'familiar,' 'native,' 'belonging to the home' " (21). The uncanny, he observes, "is in reality nothing new or foreign, but something familiar and old-established in the mind that has been estranged only by the process of repression" (47). Dillard and Abbey count on our expectation of reading about benign, bucolic landscapes, about safely aestheticized and perhaps somehow innocent wildernesses—and our repression (or simply our ignorance) of the destructive realities of the natural world lays us open to the experience of startling *Unheimlichkeit*.

By contrast, what we experience in reading Wendell Berry's essays about Kentucky is the steady intensification of *Heimischkeit*, or the feeling of being at home. He begins with the assumption of widespread homelessness in our modern age—what Freud might refer to as *Heimatlosigkeit*. Dillard and Abbey assume that we're comfortable and proceed to disorient us in quest of deeper awareness, but Berry starts with the opposite premise and takes us back home. "[W]hereas most American writers—and even most Americans—of my time are displaced persons, I am a placed person," he writes in "The Long-Legged House."

> For longer than they remember, both sides of my family have lived within five or six miles of this riverbank where the old Camp stood and where I sit writing now. And so my connection with this place comes not only from the intimate familiarity that began in babyhood, but also from the even more profound and mysterious knowledge that is inherited, handed down in memories and names and gestures and feelings, and in tones and inflections of voice. I never . . . lost affection for this place, as American writers have almost traditionally lost affection for their rural birthplaces. (141)

The persistence of his affection notwithstanding, Berry must still work at the process of truly belonging to the Camp—and we, as readers, learn vicariously what it means to become "placed persons." His approach to the Thoreauvian project is to immerse us ever more securely in a specific place, not to awaken us by splashing our faces with the cold water of defamiliarization. Dillard and Abbey make us conscious of our own bewilderment by playing on our expectations and then, suddenly, either letting all the air out of the frog-tent-football-balloon or losing us in The Maze; Berry, on the other hand, steadily increases our level of consciousness through the opposite strategy of repetition and reassurance, always intensifying descriptive detail or adding layer upon layer of perception.

The prose of Dillard and Abbey is acrobatic, while Berry's is steady, subtly modulated, more like plowing a field or floating downriver with the current than like Dillard's metaphor of heaving and whirling through the air like a stunt pilot. Berry's writing is certainly not inflected in the manner of Dillard's or Abbey's, nor does it resemble the "content-free, value-free, disinflected" language that Ron Powers calls "The Disinvolved Stare" ("Don't Think of It as Art," 143). Whatever inflection or "individual voice" there is in Berry's essays resides in the plain, uninflated statement of experience and conviction. A few years ago, Scott Russell Sanders wrote, "Once you have heard [Wendell Berry's] stately, moralizing, cherishing voice, laced through with references to the land, you will not mistake it for anyone else's. Berry's themes are profound and arresting ones. But it is his voice, more than anything he speaks about, that either seizes us or drives us away" ("The Singular First Person," 669).

Proximate Wildness

I do not mean to suggest that, for Berry, wild nature is something that ought to be civilized or flooded with the light of the human intellect—in a word, domesticated. "The Long-Legged House" actually shows the gradual evolution of Berry's own understanding of how to know and accept a natural place for what it is. His initial sweaty clearing of the physical and psychological landscape gives way eventually to a less invasive and more attentive reception of what the place offers. But, as he argues in an essay titled "Getting Along with Nature," first published in 1982, the process involves both giving and taking, both making changes and also accepting what nature is:

> The survival of wilderness—of places we do not change, where we allow the existence even of creatures we perceive as dangerous—is necessary. Our sanity probably requires it. Whether we go to those places or not, we need to know that they exist. And I would argue that we do not need just the great public wildernesses, but millions of private or semiprivate ones. Every farm should have one; wildernesses can occupy corners of factory grounds and city lots—places where nature is given a free hand, where no human work is done, where people go only as guests. These places function, I think, whether we intend them to or not, as sacred groves—places we respect and leave alone, not because we understand well what goes on there, but because we do not. (17)

The echoes of John Muir and Wallace Stegner are unmistakable here, but Berry adds something new. These patches of wilderness—not just vast and remote ones, but also nearby corners of farmyards and city lots—help to give us perspective on our lives by showing that there are forces and processes, or "natural economies," as Berry calls them, beyond our own. Yet Berry's intention is not to deepen the apparent disjunction between man and nature, or to imply that we can go to the wilderness "to escape the ugliness and the dangers" of civilization. He writes: "The wild and the domestic now often seem isolated values, estranged from one another. And yet these are not exclusive polarities like good and evil. There can be continuity between them, and there must be" (18). What Berry advocates in our dealings with nature, and what I think his own writing effectively demonstrates, is the necessity of careful, limited impact.

The wholesale humanization of nature would be misguided on the part of either the farmer or the writer, but utter detachment and nonengagement is not the answer, either. Berry explains in "Getting Along with Nature":

> People cannot live apart from nature, that is the first principle of the conservationists. And yet, people cannot live in nature without changing it. But this is true of *all* creatures; they depend upon nature, and they change it. What we call nature is, in a sense, the sum of the changes made by all the various creatures and natural forces in their intricate actions and influences upon each other and upon their places. . . .
> . . . And so it can hardly be expected that humans would not change nature. Humans, like all other creatures, must make a difference; otherwise, they cannot live. But unlike other creatures, humans must make a choice as to the kind and scale of the difference they make. If they choose to make too small a difference, they diminish their humanity. If they choose to make too great a difference, they diminish nature, and narrow their subsequent choices; ultimately, they diminish or destroy themselves. Nature, then, is not only our source but also our limit and measure. (7–8)

One of Berry's first essays on precisely this kind of controlled, patient process of adaptation to a natural place is the piece called "A Country of Edges" (originally in the 1971 collection *The Unfore-*

seen Wilderness). This is actually a study of erosion. The writer wanders through Kentucky's Red River Gorge and observes so intensely and sustainedly how the river becomes "intimate with its banks" that he himself seems transparent, subsumed within the place (229). His imagination kicks in, but only in the attempt to perceive what the landscape itself implies, not to appropriate the place for himself: "[N]ot to the human eye, nor to the collective vision of human history, but within the long gaze of geologic time the Gorge is moving within itself, deepening, changing the outline of its slopes; the river is growing into it like a great tree, steadily incising its branches into the land" (224). The human observer perceives this with all of his senses. He sips water from a clear, cold pool among the rocks, but knows that "Looking and listening are as important as tasting. One drinks in the sense of being in a good place" (224). Such "drinking" takes time, and it takes what Berry calls "being watchful."

Absence and Return: "A Reclamation Project"

As stated in my introduction, Berry displays a relatively linear movement from estrangement to belonging/understanding — and this is one of the most interesting differences between both him and Barry Lopez and such nature writers as Thoreau, Dillard, and Abbey, who continually vacillate between correspondence and otherness and whose works are thus more conspicuously dialectical. Berry's return to his native Kentucky is a return after a sustained absence. This absence, this separation from the place he knew as "home," was a career move and yet it contributed profoundly to the process of his later reattachment. Berry notes at the beginning of the essay "The Making of a Marginal Farm" that his appreciation of the plot of land where he now lives began nearly a decade before he and his family actually returned from "exile" to live there. He recalls,

> One day in the summer of 1956, leaving home for school, I stopped on the side of the road directly above the house where I now live. From there you could see a mile or so across the Kentucky River Valley, and perhaps six miles along the length of it. The valley was a

green trough full of sunlight, blue in its distances. I often stopped
here in my comings and goings, just to look, for it was all familiar to
me from before the time my memory began: woodlands and pastures
on the hillsides; fields and croplands, wooded slew-edges and hollows
in the bottoms; and through the midst of it the tree-lined river passing down from its headwaters near the Virginia line toward its
mouth at Carrollton on the Ohio.

Standing there, I was looking at land where one of my great-great-
great-grandfathers settled in 1803, and at the scene of some of the
happiest times of my own life, where in my growing up years I
camped, hunted, fished, boated, swam, and wandered—where, in
short, I did whatever escaping I felt called upon to do. It was a place
where I had happily been, and where I always wanted to be. And I
remember gesturing toward the valley that day and saying to the
friend who was with me: "That's all I need." (329–30)

However, there are two essential differences between the level
of awareness indicated by the above statement "That's all I need"
and the awareness we see developing in the rest of this particular
essay, and in such pieces as "The Long-Legged House" and "Notes
from an Absence and a Return." The first difference results from
the special intensity of commitment one feels after actually working on the land, and the second is caused by the phenomenon of
separation and return.

The merely aesthetic appraisal of a landscape can be either
sensitive or somehow obstructed (perhaps by "prejudice," as Lopez
would say), but it can never equal in intensity the understanding
which derives from the direct contact necessitated by labor. Berry
makes this clear when he writes:

As a child I always intended to be a farmer. As a young man I
gave up that intention, assuming that I could not farm and do the
other things I wanted to do. And then I became a farmer almost
unintentionally and by a kind of necessity. That wayward and necessary becoming—along with my marriage, which has been intimately
a part of it—is the major event of my life. It has changed me profoundly from the man and the writer I would otherwise have been.

There was a time, after I had left home and before I came back,
when this place was my "subject matter." I meant that too, I think,
on the day in 1956 when I told my friend, "That's all I need." I was
regarding it, in a way too easy for a writer, as a mirror in which I saw

myself. There was obviously a sort of narcissism in that—and an inevitable superficiality, for only the surface can reflect.

> In coming home and settling on this place, I began to *live* in my subject. . . . One's relation to one's subject ceases to be merely emotional and esthetical, or even merely critical, and becomes problematical, practical, and responsible as well. Because it must. It is like marrying your sweetheart. ("Marginal Farm," 336–37)

The honeymoon may not last forever, but the marriage becomes more substantial, more deeply felt, after the onset of daily practicalities and responsibilities. So unlike Lopez's studies of the repeated process of achieving "intimacy" with various landscapes, Berry's concern is with how to make the most out of a sustained relationship with one particular place. The traveler does not stay long enough to feel permanent, daily, pragmatic responsibility toward any one place, though he or she may achieve a condition of generalized sensitivity to all landscapes, whether foreign or familiar, a sensitivity capable of becoming, momentarily, as intense as that of the Arctic hunter or the Kentucky farmer. Such sensitivity, such awareness, is idealized in this chapter's epigraph from Berry's novel *The Memory of Old Jack*.

Work and commitment, which combine in the form of devoted, hands-on attention to a place over a sustained period of time, produce a necessary convergence of the human mind and the place itself. Berry would not claim that this convergence is ever absolute, ever complete. But the connection becomes steadily more intense until perhaps, for all intents and purposes, if one lives to the age of ninety-two like Old Jack, the mind of the man does become "indistinguishable" from the place. Although Berry is more reluctant than Lopez to invent phrases for this idea of harmony, the idea itself is pervasive in his work. In describing the process of restoring or reclaiming his land after its earlier abuse by a developer, Berry affirms this connection:

> As we have continued to live on and from our place, we have slowly begun its restoration and healing. Most of the scars have now been mended and grassed over, most of the washes stopped, most of the buildings made sound; many loads of rocks have been hauled out of the fields and used to pave entrances or fill hollows; we have done perhaps half of the necessary fencing. A great deal of work is still left

to do, and some of it – the rebuilding of fertility in the depleted hillsides – will take longer than we will live. But in doing these things we
have begun a restoration and a healing in ourselves. ("Marginal
Farm," 334)

This process of caring for the land becomes essential to the
farmer/writer's sense of self, to his understanding of what it means
to be a "placed person." "In order to affirm the values most native
and necessary to me," he writes, " . . . indeed to affirm my own life
as a thing decent in possibility – I needed to know in my own experience that this place did not have to be abused in the past, and
that it can be kindly and conservingly used now" (336). What
Berry does here is more than simply recount his own experiences
as a farmer and a land-rehabilitator, and more than simply assert a
wholesome, proper way for other people to live on the land.
Instead, like the other writers examined in this book, Berry is
intrigued by and engaged with the workings of his own mind. He
studies what it means, emotionally, spiritually, and on a pragmatic
cognitive level, to maintain responsible contact with a patch of
land. And his favorite metaphor for such contact – that of a marriage between human beings – resonates with a sense not only of
affection, but of attentiveness.
    One of the main ways of establishing such contact is through
sustained labor – through the physical process of reclamation and
cultivation. But other important aspects of Berry's homecoming to
"the Camp" are the realities of absence, separation, and deprivation. It seems reasonable to compare these experiences to the
repeated minor disjunctions which occur routinely, if unpredict-
ably, in the works of Thoreau, Dillard, and Abbey. An even closer
analogue would be Lopez's process of visiting new and exotic places
in order to experience repeatedly, on a small scale, the psychological phenomenon of "intimacy," the overcoming of expectation.
However, Berry's approach differs in that, for him, there was just
one major disruption of his relationship with "the Camp": his
extended sojourn as a teacher and writer in such distant places as
California and New York City.
    In the essay "Notes from an Absence and a Return" (which
appeared in *A Continuous Harmony* in 1972, but actually consists of

journal entries from 1968 when Berry spent six months in California), Berry begins by describing, as explicitly as Dillard and Abbey do, the feeling of "alertness" caused by the uncertainty of a particular environment:

> Nov. 17
>   At dark yesterday I walked home through the golf course at the back of the campus. Enjoyed the marvelous alertness that comes with walking in the dark without a light. All the senses wake up. Hearing is more conscious and acute; peripheral vision becomes a necessary function; there is a complex, delicate *feeling* of the ground one is walking over. The body seems filled out to it limits with an intense consciousness of itself and of things around it. That was the first time I've walked in the dark, I think, since we left Kentucky. (37–38)

But midway through the entry, the focus changes—during the isolation of the night walk, a pivotal decision occurs and the writer realizes: "I have become, in a very cool, knowing way, hungry to be at home again. I want back the clear, exacting sense of myself that I only get from being at work there on my writing and on the place itself." But it is the condition of absence that enables Berry to reach this decision with such clarity and resolve, for in absence, he says, "I have come deep enough into this experience, sifted and sorted through enough of it, that my mind is quieter" (38).

The rest of the entries from California show the writer testing his decision to return by meditating on "the sense of oneness with the land" and on the hypothetical compatibility of the physical and mental work he plans to do after returning to Kentucky:

> I want, and I think in my farming poems I have been consciously working toward, a poetry that would not be incompatible with barns and gardens and fields and woodlands. The mind, carrying such poetry into such places, would be freed and eased in the presence of *what is there.* (39)

For this move back to rural Kentucky to be successful, he realizes the decision to return must be continually remade, or kept fresh. Once again he notices that it is the condition of absence which enables him to reach this understanding:

> What I get from the experience out here is the awareness that the life
> we want is not merely the one we have chosen and made; it is the
> one we must be choosing and making. To keep it alive we must be
> perpetually choosing it and making its differences from among all
> contrary and alternative possibilities. We must accept the pain and
> labor of that, or we lose its satisfactions and its joy. Only by risking
> it, offering it freely to its possibilities, can we keep it. (40)

The constant repetition of the decision to come home is precisely
what allows the decision to be effective, to satisfy the needs of the
person making it. Ironically, in order to consider the other possibilities, the farmer/writer must distance himself from his present
place after his relocation to the farm. He must *imagine* the feeling
of exile or absence in order to reinforce his desire for homecoming.

From this point on, the notes focus on the actual experience
of homecoming, paralleling the earlier homecoming process presented in "The Long-Legged House." Berry not only records his
physical activities after returning to "the Camp," but also studies
his feelings. The difference between homecoming as a process of
developing awareness and the wandering strategies demonstrated
by all of the other four writers mentioned is seen in Berry's replace-
ment of "surprise" with "familiarity":

> The redeeming aspect of the sense of involvement and responsibil-
> ity is that it does not stand alone, but is only part of a process, a way
> of life that includes joy. Not always or necessarily or even preferably
> the dramatic joy of surprise — though that is one of its possibilities —
> but the quiet persistent joy of familiarity. (44)

In the later pages of the essay, which skip from entry to entry
(sometimes weeks or even months apart) and cover a period from
March to October, we see the writer's familiarity with the place
intensify dramatically, simply by noting the increasing length and
detail of the specific entries. Unlike "The Making of a Marginal
Farm" which emphasizes work (that is, farming and repairing the
land) as an essential part of achieving familiarity, "Notes from an
Absence and a Return" dwells upon the value of watching, of paying attention to the land with one's senses. Berry gives the impression, as he recalls walking through the wildflowers of the nearby
woods, of being so eager to perceive his surroundings that he can-

not take it all in: "Walking among all these flowers, I cannot *see* enough. One is aware of the abundance of lovely things—forms, scents, colors—lavished on the earth beyond any human capacity to perceive or number or imitate" (48). And later, peering through a magnifying glass, he feels similarly unable to "plumb" nature: "On my walk I carried a 15x lens. Looked at through it, the blue-bells are depthless; you seem to be looking deep in or far out. Like looking down into clear, still, blue water, or off a mountaintop into the sky" (50). Closer and closer the writer examines his place, only to realize ever more powerfully that his senses alone will not complete his homecoming. What he must finally realize is that he and the inhuman inhabitants of the place are there together, participating together in the life of the place. As time passes, he begins to perceive not only the natural world as being distinct from himself, but its relationship to him, so that he concludes the essay implying continued movement and change, with the sentence: "We [the writer and an old sycamore] are moving in a relationship, a design, that is definite—though shadowy to me—like people in a dance" (55).

Homecoming: An Intensification of Sensitivity

"Notes from an Absence and a Return," as I have said, describes the process of homecoming, which echoes the process explained in "The Long-Legged House." While "Notes" focuses on the decision to return home which continues to be reinforced long after the physical journey home seems complete, "The Long-Legged House" describes in detail the subtle condition of being committed to a specific landscape by participating in it rather than simply owning and controlling it. Often we find ourselves, as readers, attracted to nature writing because of its explanatory, interpretive role—it helps to orient us in the world. But what is so interesting about the essay "The Long-Legged House" is the way Berry follows his ideology of humility and limited impact in avoiding conspicuous interpretation. To avoid interpretation altogether would be, of course, impossible for the writer. However, Berry manages to suggest that both the language and the ideas of his essay originate somehow in the natural place and in his family's long association with the place rather than in his own mind. Rather than making the land part of him, he and his essay grow out of the land. Similarly, the Red River, even as it erodes and changes the gorge through which it flows, is guided fundamentally by the contours, the "edges," of the gorge itself. Don Mitchell identifies three levels of engagement in nature writing, suggesting that the deeper the engagement, the better — the *truer* — the writing; the first level is "Mere Observation," the second "Appreciation of Nature," and the third "Involvement or Investment." He writes, "This happens when one engages nature as an actor, which usually means as a manager of one kind or another" ("Dancing with Nature," 192–93). What Berry demonstrates by being not only a farmer and a country dweller but also an increasingly nonintrusive observer is, to adapt Mitchell's terms, investment without appropriation, without excessive possessiveness.

"The Long-Legged House" begins sweepingly, covering many years of the author's association with the place where he later came to live, beginning actually before Berry's own birth, "Sometime in the twenties" when Curran Mathews, the bachelor brother of Berry's grandmother, built the old cabin which Berry would eventually dismantle and incorporate into his own long-legged house. Curran Mathews, Berry notes, was something of an eccentric and a carouser, and yet the place worked its magic even upon him. "It was a place," Berry writes, "where a man, staying by himself, could become deeply quiet. It would have been a quiet that grew deeper and wider as the days passed, and would have come to include many things, both familiar and unexpected" (113). Throughout this essay, the writer depicts himself, too, as a still and silent observer, a savorer of the quiet. "It is a place I like, and like to go to and sit down," he says of the lot where Curran's house originally stood (114). Much of Berry's writing — his poetry, works of fiction such as *The Memory of Old Jack*, and many of the agricultural essays — emphasizes the deep psychological bond between the farmer and his fields, the product of actual tactile engagement. "The Long-Legged House" begins by showing how such a connection arises from the physical activity of clearing a plot of land and building a place to live, but the essay comes to focus more and more on the moral and aesthetic bond between the writer and the place he watches and cares about—sometimes exploring, sometimes just sitting and seeing, and sometimes looking at nothing but the paper before him, simply *thinking* about the place which surrounds him.

The initial section of the essay proceeds rapidly. As the years pass, we learn of the author's deepening entrenchment in this place. We hear at length about a childhood visit during a flood in March, 1945. A few years later when Berry was "nearly fourteen," he went by himself to the Camp, which had "fallen into disuse and neglect" (121), and spent the night in a sleeping bag on the porch. His friend Pete stopped by, liked the place, and decided to stay. "The next morning," Berry recalls, "we began scraping out the dried mud that the last high water had deposited on the floors— and suddenly the place entered our imagination. We quit being campers and became settlers" (122). Over the years, Berry used the Camp as a place to retreat to and brood about the problems of growing up. He writes that the peace he received from his visits to the Camp "suggested to [him] the possibility of a greater, more substantial peace—a decent, open, generous relation between a man's life and the world." This condition, he then says, this "decent, open, generous" relationship, is something he has never fully achieved—rather, it "has come more and more to be, the hope and ruling idea of [his] life" (124). This supports the idea that the essay itself is not a depiction of an ideal relationship, but a representation of the process of learning to be quiet inside and watchful of what's outside, so as to gradually achieve the "greater, more substantial peace" of Thoreauvian awareness.

This awareness and openness occurred sporadically during Berry's teen-age years. He recalls one afternoon spent fishing from a boat, anchored to a snag in the middle of the river:

> There is some nearly mystical charm about a boat that I have always been keenly aware of, and tied there that afternoon in midstream, a sort of island, it made me intensely alive to the charm of it. It seemed so intact and dry in its boatness, and I so coherent and satisfied in my humanness. I fished and was happy for some time, until I became *conscious* of what a fine thing I was doing. It came to me that this was one of the grand possibilities of my life. And suddenly I became deeply uneasy. What I had been at ease with, in fact and without

thinking, had become, as a possibility, too large. I hadn't the thoughts for it. I hadn't the background for it. My cultural inheritance had prepared me to exert myself, work, move, "get someplace." To be idle, simply to live there in the sunlight in the middle of the river, was something I was not prepared to do deliberately. I tried to stay on, forcing myself to do what I now thought I ought to be doing, but the spell was broken. . . . I would have to live to twice that age before I could do consciously what I wanted so much then to do. And even now I can do it only occasionally. (124–25)

What came more easily, and what Berry proceeds to describe in the essay, is the active exertion of turning the Camp into a home for himself and, eventually, for his wife. By an intriguing paradox, Berry found himself attracted by the Camp's very wildness, even though he felt compelled to open up a place for himself within this wildness, to make certain changes necessary for him to feel at home there. Perhaps what initially attracted him was the sense of returning to a once-familiar place which had since become estranged, or wild. But whereas Dillard and Abbey alternate continually between bewilderment and familiarization, Berry, after displaying an initial inclination to make the bewildering into some place habitable, gradually opens himself to the wilderness, accepting it as his own native place.

Early in the essay, recollecting the days he spent clearing the lot and restoring the house while in college, Berry is preoccupied with his own inner life:

I would sit down now and again to rest and dry the sweat a little, and look at what I had done. I would meditate on the difference I had made, and my mind would be full of delight. It was some instinctive love of wildness that would always bring me back here, but it was by the instincts of a farmer that I established myself. The Camp itself was not imaginable until the weeds were cut around it; until that was done I could hardly bring myself to enter it. A house is not simply a building, it is also an enactment. That is the first law of domesticity, even the most meager. The mere fact must somehow be turned into meaning. Necessity must be made a little ceremonious. To ever arrive at what one would call home even for a few days, a decent, thoughtful approach must be made, a clarity, an opening. (128)

"The mere fact must somehow be turned into meaning" suggests just the kind of aggressive human manipulation of nature which I have been saying does not occur in Berry's work—and in this case the manipulation occurs not merely in the form of extravagant description, but in the depiction of rather drastic physical alteration of the landscape. However, this change is controlled, limited, and even, as Berry puts it, "a little ceremonious." It is an investment of meaning, never rampantly, meaninglessly destructive. Using language which recalls, ironically, the less careful, less caring labor of earlier settlers on this continent, Berry writes, "I would come down with ax and scythe . . . and drive back the wilderness" (128).

Before his wedding in 1957, Berry made final preparations, final changes. Through his prolonged contact with the place and through his active interaction with it, it was becoming for him more and more *heimisch*, literally "a home"—a far cry from the recurring *Unheimlichkeit* (strangeness) of the natural areas described in *Desert Solitaire* and *Pilgrim at Tinker Creek*. Still, the result for Berry was not a diminishment of feeling or awareness, but rather an intensification of sensitivity. "This was the place that was more my own than any other in the world," he writes. "And now I had changed it, to make it the place of my marriage. And a complex love went into those preparations—for Tanya, and for the place too" (130). The process of making changes seems to end with the wedding—this is a pivotal moment in the essay, a moment of quiet and stasis, of breathless awareness. Berry writes:

> Our marriage became then, and has remained, the center of our life. And it is particularly true that the Camp is at the center of our marriage, both as actuality and as symbol. . . .
> . . . In the life we lived that summer we represented to ourselves what we wanted—and it was *not* the headlong pilgrimage after money and comfort and prestige. We were spared that stress from the beginning. And there at the Camp we had around us the elemental world of water and light and earth and air. We felt the presence of the wild creatures, the river, the trees, the stars. Though we had our troubles, we had them in a true perspective. The universe, as we could see any night, is unimaginably large, and mostly empty, and mostly dark. We knew we needed to be together more than we needed to be apart. (132–33)

Here Berry's language slows to the point of utmost calm. Annie Dillard's most vibrant moments of awareness usually result from calamity, while Berry's concentration intensifies when his mind and words are suspended in stillness. His body, too, seems suspended, for at this point in the narrative, the process of clearing out overgrown nature ceases, and observation really begins: "I began that summer of my marriage the surprisingly long and difficult labor of *seeing* the country I had been born in and had lived my life in until then" (141). As yet, his visual descriptions of the environment remain vague and generalized, but particularity is in the offing.

Throughout the narrative, Berry's awareness of this place seems not to waver, or come and go—instead it stays fresh through a process of accumulation, through steady additions to previous insights. When, after college and marriage, Berry began to pursue his career as a writer, one of the first things he realized he needed to do was to jettison "the corrupt and crippling local colorism of the 'Kentucky' writers." He could not buy into the rural clichés of his region: "Kentucky is a sunny, beautiful land, full of happy country folks, whose very failures are quaint and delightful and to be found only here" (140). He writes: "I was so intricately dependent on this place that I did not begin in any meaningful sense to be a writer until I began to see the place clearly and for what it was" (142). This, at last, is the condition of watchful alertness toward which all of his earlier clearing and cleaning and house building have been leading. Watchfulness is the necessary condition of the writer.

Writing and Awareness

Shortly after Berry begins to recount the start of his career as a writer and teacher, the essay is interrupted by the insistent demands of the place upon the attention of the writer/farmer. Section two begins: "My work was interrupted by the spring weather, when gardening and other outside concerns took me away from writing again. But now it is winter again. . . . It is a morning for books and notebooks and the inviting blank pages of writing paper" (144). Berry resumes the history at the point where he and his wife have returned to the Camp after several years of academic wandering, and he has vowed to revitalize his roots there. He recalls that he began writing at that time "a sort of journal, keeping account of what [he] saw" (146). Immediately after he mentions this, the style of the essay changes – it becomes much more detailed and concrete, the pace of the narrative slowing to allow the presentation of specific natural descriptions.

One can imagine Berry reading from his journal as he works on the essay. He writes, for instance, "I first went back to the Camp that year on a rainy Monday, May 8. Heavy rains had begun the Saturday before, and the river was in flood" (146). Another page and a half of flood description ensue, then Berry remarks, "I resumed my connection with the Camp" (148). Not only resumed his connection, it seems, but pushed it to a new level, a level open to and appreciative of the "mere fact[s]" of the natural world. No longer must "the mere fact . . . somehow be turned into meaning," as he said earlier when describing his clearing of and establishing his presence at the Camp. Berry depicts himself working outside after his return to the Camp. He is supposedly writing, but mostly he seems to be taking in his surroundings: "I would pause in my writing and reading to watch [a pair of phoebes] fly out [of their nest], pick an insect out of the air, and return to the branch. Sometimes I could hear their beaks snap when they made a catch" (148). The observations accumulate, mainly recollections of bird sightings. The author's watchfulness is soon augmented with binoculars:

> But the binoculars not only give access to knowledge of lives that are usually elusive and distant; they make possible a peculiar imaginative association with those lives. While opening and clarifying the remote, they block out the immediate. Where one is is no longer apparent. . . . One sees not just the bird, but something of how it is to *be* the bird. One's imagination begins to reach and explore into the sense of how it would be to be without barriers, to fly over the river, to perch at the frailest, most outward branchings of the trees. (150)

Whereas in the earlier scenes it took his own lively participation, his physical act of changing the place, to spark his imagina-

tion, now it is simply the intense perception of the drama of life
surrounding the Camp that stimulates Berry's interest. The in-
wardness of his earlier relation to the place is gradually being
reversed. His clearing of the wilderness with ax and scythe had
been self-centered, self-accommodating. The essay which began as
a history of *self*-consciousness, recounting the process of clearing
out a space for the self within opposing nature, now reveals his
dawning "realization of the complexity of the life of this place."
Berry says,

> . . . that summer, I remember, I began to think of myself as living
> within rather than upon the life of the place. I began to think of my
> life as one among many, and one kind among many kinds. I began to
> see how little of the beauty and the richness of the world is of human
> origin, and how superficial and crude and destructive—even self-
> destructive—is man's conception of himself as the owner of the land
> and the master of nature and the center of the universe. (150)

Earlier in the essay, Berry attributes his understanding of the
importance of allowing his writing to grow out of the clear-eyed
apprehension of place to his reading of other writers: Andrew
Marvell, William Carlos Williams, Henry David Thoreau, Gilbert
White, Henri Fabre, Kenneth Rexroth. But his later revelations
derive directly from watching nature. Meaning, which he had previously imported to and constructed from the natural place, now is
turned inside out. "Seen as belonging there with other native
things," he writes, "my own nativeness began a renewal of meaning. The sense of belonging began to turn around. I saw that if I
belonged here, which I felt I did, it was not because anything here
belonged to me" (151).

Berry's journal keeping, it becomes increasingly clear, is an essential part of this devotion to the external natural world, and is
the writer's means of forcing himself to be attentive. It is, in
Thoreau's terms, a "mechanical aid" to awareness, but undeniably
a valuable one. Berry's knowledge of the place cannot be hastened,
and this important discovery validates the patient receptiveness of
the journal-writing process. Berry recalls in the final pages of
the essay:

> As soon as I felt a necessity to learn about the nonhuman world, I
> wished to learn about it in a hurry. And then I began to learn per-
> haps the most important lesson that nature had to teach me: that I
> could not learn about her in a hurry. The most important learning,
> that of experience, can be neither summoned nor sought out. . . . It
> comes of its own good time and in its own way to the man who will
> go where it lives, and wait, and be ready, and watch. Hurry is beside
> the point, useless, an obstruction. The thing is to be attentively
> present. To sit and wait is as important as to move. Patience is as
> valuable as industry. What is to be known is always there. When it
> reveals itself to you, or when you come upon it, it is by chance. The
> only condition is your being there and being watchful. (169)

"The Long-Legged House" evolves thus into a celebration of
watchfulness – and at the same time an enactment of it. What
began as a summary of personal history becomes history relived.
As he reads through his old journals and transfers observations
into new words, coupling images with passion and ideas, Berry
demonstrates the ongoing process of learning about the place to
which he belongs, knowledge of it being the only way, he says, to
belong fully to it. This knowledge resides ultimately not in abstrac-
tions, but in concrete observations. The very ability to make out
subtle features of the place is a way of gauging the degree of his
belonging: "It is only in the place that one belongs to, intimate and
familiar, long watched over, that the details rise up out of the
whole and become visible: the hawk stoops into the clearing before
one's eyes; the wood drake, aloof and serene in his glorious plum-
age, swims out of his hiding place" (161).

Berry seeks exactly the same sense of at-homeness in nature
that Dillard and Abbey hint at, but promptly, in order to prevent
dullness and complacency, dispel. By carrying out before our eyes
the continuation of his own quest to belong, to awaken himself to
the Camp, Berry exemplifies for us, in the best Thoreauvian tradition, the habits of watchfulness and humility. Echoing Thoreau –
who implied his imperfect awareness when he wrote, "I have never
yet met a man who was quite awake. How could I have looked him
in the face?" (*Walden*, 90) – Berry acknowledges the inchoateness of
his own watchfulness by recalling, near the end of "The Long-
Legged House":

On the last morning of October, waking, I looked out the window and saw a fisherman in a red jacket fishing alone in his boat tied against the far bank. He sat deeply quiet and still, unmoved as a tree by my rising and the other events that went on around him. There was something heron-like in his intent waiting upon what the day might bring him out of the dark. In his quietness and patience he might have been the incarnation of some river god, at home among all things, awake while I had slept. (162)

CHAPTER 6

"A More Particularized Understanding": Seeking Qualitative Awareness in Barry Lopez's *Arctic Dreams*

Albert Camus, as we know, has named absurdity *the impassable gulf which exists between man and the world, between the aspirations of the human mind and the world's incapacity to satisfy them. Absurdity is in neither man nor things, but in the impossibility of establishing between them any relation other than* strangeness.

—*Alain Robbe-Grillet, "Nature, Humanism, Tragedy" (1958, 62–63)*

Hibakusha **and the Need for Awareness**

To overcome the absurdity – the meaninglessness and destructiveness – of man's estrangement from the natural world is precisely the goal of Barry Lopez's *Arctic Dreams* (1986). From its inception, American nature writing has been not merely descriptive, but prescriptive. John Smith's account of life in Virginia during the early decades of the seventeenth century does more than merely expose the natural abundance of the region; it promotes a particular human attitude toward the land – one of plunder and exploitation. Farther north in New England, Smith's contemporaries emphasized the enmity between man and nature, drawing solace and a sense of purpose for their isolated existence in the New World by comparing themselves to the Israelites wandering in the hostile biblical wilderness. More recently, nature writers have often become less explicit in their espousal of one particular attitude toward nature, their goal being instead the empirical study of their own psychological responses to the world – or, in other words, objective scrutiny of subjective experience.

And yet, having said this, I would be remiss not to admit that there is, in the very concern for the human process of becoming alert to the nonhuman environment, an implicit belief that we need this awareness. Thoreau, although he has served well as the posthumous spokesman for numerous environmental organizations, seems to have been motivated in his musings about nature by an ingenuously philosophical impulse—a desire to know the "truth" about the world and himself. However, it is no coincidence that Annie Dillard, Edward Abbey, Wendell Berry and Barry Lopez produced their works during or just after the surge of environmental consciousness which occurred during the 1960s and 1970s. And these writers, although they may be elusive, nondirective, and even anti-ideological (as is the case with Dillard and Abbey, at least), are hardly as neutral as Thoreau. They may hedge in their pronouncement of why they and their readers ought to be more aware (not just of the environment, but of existence in general), but their advocacy of heightened attentiveness is difficult to miss. However, in Wendell Berry's work, and similarly in Barry Lopez's writings during the 1980s, there is a sense of timeliness, of urgency—a sense that awareness is not a mental game, but a condition which helps us to act responsibly and respectfully.

In the chapter "Epilogue" in *Arctic Dreams*, Lopez makes a rather shocking association in a curiously understated way—and this passage, I think, indicates as distinctly as any other that his concern about his readers' probable estrangement from the earth (and thus from people who have traditionally lived close to the earth) is more than passive. He writes:

> I think of the Eskimos compassionately as *hibakusha*—the Japanese word for "explosion-affected people," those who continue to suffer the effects of Hiroshima and Nagasaki. Eskimos are trapped in a long, slow detonation. What they know about a good way to live is disintegrating. The sophisticated, ironic voice of civilization insists that their insights are only trivial, but they are not.
>
> I remember looking into a herd of walrus that day and thinking: do human beings make the walrus more human to make it comprehensible or to assuage loneliness? What is it to be estranged in this land?
>
> It is in the land, I once thought, that one searches out and eventually finds what is beautiful. And an edge of this deep and rarefied beauty is the acceptance of complex paradox and the forgiveness of others. It means you will not die alone.

.   .   .

One of our long-lived cultural differences with the Eskimo has been over whether to accept the land as it is or to exert the will to change it into something else. The great task of life for the traditional Eskimo is still to achieve congruence with a reality that is already given. The given reality, the real landscape, is "horror within magnificence, absurdity within intelligibility, suffering within joy," in the words of Albert Schweitzer. We do not esteem as highly these lessons in paradox. We hold in higher regard the land's tractability, its alterability. We believe the conditions of the earth can be changed to ensure human happiness, to provide jobs and to create material wealth and ease. Each culture, then, finds a different sort of apotheosis, of epiphany, and comfort in the land.

Any latent wisdom there might be in the Eskimo position is overwhelmed for us by our ability to alter the land. The long pattern of purely biological evolution, however, suggests that a profound collision of human will with immutable aspects of the natural order is inevitable. This, by itself, seems reason enough to inquire among aboriginal cultures concerning the nature of time and space and other (invented) dichotomies; the relationship between hope and the exercise of will; the role of dreams and myths in human life; and the therapeutic aspects of long term intimacy with a landscape. (367-69)

The elements of admonishment, warning, and exhortation remain, for the most part, tacit in these paragraphs. And yet, couched within this simultaneously compassionate and detached summary of the distinctions between Eskimos and us (Lopez and his subarctic, urban readers), is the potent implication that we must pay closer attention to the real landscape (and the people who are a part of it) if we are even to fathom, let alone avert, the "profound collision of human will with immutable aspects of the natural order" which Lopez finds inevitable.

It is interesting to ask whether prose such as Lopez's is likely to draw as much attention to mankind's degradation of the natural world as, for instance, the direct action of Greenpeace or Earth First!, or even more prosaic journalistic reports. But what Lopez suggests in the very language of *Arctic Dreams* is that he respects not only the Arctic itself, but also his readers; he intimates the expectation that, although we may not traditionally "esteem [the] lessons in paradox" which come from the experience of intimacy with landscape, we have the potential to understand and adopt this "therapeutic" way of thinking. In his *New York Times* review of *Arctic Dreams*, Edward Hoagland writes, "Among contemporary nature writers Mr. Lopez is especially a rhapsodist, and what he has done in this passionate paean to the Arctic and its cycles of light and darkness, its species of ice, its creatures and waters, is to present a whole series of raptures and riffs on the subject of musk oxen, ivory gulls, white foxes, polar bears, icebergs and sea currents" (1). I would add that Lopez celebrates, at the same time, the hoped-for ability and willingness of his audience to achieve a more profound awareness of the world. He clearly shares Edward Abbey's aversion to rigid dogmatism, seeking instead to "create an environment in which thinking and reaction and wonder and awe and speculation can take place," as he explains it to Nicholas O'Connell in a 1985 interview. "What you are doing when you write nonfiction, the frame of mind you should have," he continues, "is to make a bow of respect toward the material and make a bow of respect toward the reader—that's what the piece is" ("Barry Lopez," 16). *Arctic Dreams*, therefore, is an optimistic work on many levels, a work reaching toward enlightened solutions rather than wallowing in despair, despite the fact that Lopez identifies the Arctic as a whole—not only the Eskimos—as *hibakusha*, a word which resonates apocalyptically.

If Lopez is more ideologically assertive (though antidogmatic) than the other writers I have been examining, he is still not the type of writer to propose an entirely concrete solution to the situations which worry him. In 1982, for instance, he published an article on the troubling effects of the 1972 Marine Mammal Protection Act upon both Eskimos and wildlife (an article which later evolved into the epilogue of *Arctic Dreams*), but, while this article succeeds in evoking the human and cosmic aspects of the issue, it concludes with a conundrum "that justice and compassion rival each other, and that laws are incomplete resolutions of these two impulses" ("Faint Light," 21). Nonetheless, Lopez proposes at the outset of *Arctic Dreams* that the purpose of his book is practical, not merely speculative or rhapsodic—in fact, he resembles Berry in his concern for pragmatism and responsibility. He writes:

> If we are to devise an enlightened plan for human activity in the Arctic, we need a more particularized understanding of the land itself—not a more refined mathematical knowledge, but a deeper understanding of its nature, as if it were, itself, another sort of civilization we had to reach some agreement with. I would draw you, therefore, back to the concrete dimensions of the land and to what they precipitate: simply to walk across the tundra; to watch the wind stirring a little in the leaves of dwarf birch and willows; to hear the hoof-clacket of migrating caribou. Imagine your ear against the loom of a kayak paddle in the Beaufort Sea, hearing the long, quivering tremolo voice of the bearded seal. Or feeling the surgical sharpness of an Eskimo's obsidian tool under the stroke of your finger. (11)

Lopez's point here and throughout *Arctic Dreams* is that we must change our habitual way of thinking about the Arctic in order to develop "an enlightened plan for human activity" there—and the specific change he calls for is the renewed reliance upon primary personal experience, in addition to the less subjective and more quantitative approaches which western civilization, at least since Francis Bacon, has come to esteem most highly. The idea of comprehensive awareness as a prerequisite for enlightened behavior seems appropriate as a guideline not only for human involvement in the Arctic, but for our presence in the natural world more generally. In the lines just quoted there is a distinct echo of Wendell Berry's moral concerns and his belief in patience, concrete attentiveness, and experience itself as the core of true knowledge. Similarly, these authors each display a primitivist impulse; they desire, as Lopez puts it, "to achieve a congruence with a reality that is already given" in much the way that pre-European natives of Kentucky must have desired that congruence, and traditional Eskimos still do.

"I am a writer who travels."

Barry Lopez's desire to achieve "particularized understanding" of a "Northern Landscape" (as opposed to merely "mathematical understanding") is the key to his place in the tradition of psychological nature writing. His self-conscious interest in the psychology of awareness is especially noticeable not only in "Prologue" and "Epilogue" in *Arctic Dreams*, but in such chapters as "The Country of the Mind" and "Ice and Light," as well as in the essay "Landscape and Narrative" (1984), the newly published travel parable *Crow and Weasel* (1990), and numerous interviews and public statements issued in the past half-decade. In response to the question, "What is it that distinguishes the human being?" Lopez tells Kay Bonetti: "There are several things, but certainly central is this passion for metaphor that we have. . . . This fascination with metaphor is what sets us apart" ("An Interview with Barry Lopez," 75). The idea of metaphor means many things for Lopez, including the capacity to accept and even incorporate other people's perspectives into his own worldview. But the term takes on a more specific meaning in connection with *Crow and Weasel*, the book which is itself an extended metaphor, an allegorical depiction of Lopez's travels to exotic places and his returning home to tell the story with care and deliberation. Storytelling, thus, is not only the process in which the author engages himself, but is frequently the subject of his comments and writing.

In interview after interview (see the citations under Aton, Bonetti, Gonzalez, Margolis, and O'Connell), Lopez abstractly discusses the necessary conditions and purposes of wholesome storytelling—and he theorizes similarly in the essay "Landscape and Narrative" about the relationships between the traditional storyteller, the landscape, and the audience. Don Scheese, in his review of *Crossing Open Ground*, criticizes this essay for being "a nebulous, incoherent piece that fails to deal intensively with the supposed basis of the piece—Alaskan narrative and Navaho tales—and instead delivers a panegyric on the importance of storytelling in all cultures" (208). Indeed, Lopez is generally at his best when he is being most specific and concrete, and when he couches his ideas in the form of actions and perceptions in precise surroundings. *Crow and Weasel*, however, demonstrates a new approach to Lopez's analysis of the craft of storytelling—it is an approach at once precise and oblique, and it adds new resonance to the ideas he has expressed more formally in his interviews.

The two central characters of *Crow and Weasel*, who take the names and forms of animals (as shown in Tom Pohrt's watercolor illustrations), undertake a long and frightening journey to the Far

North, and as they begin their laborious trip back to their home on the southern plains they encounter Badger, who invites them to stay the night in his lodge:

> Badger made up a good meal, and after they ate, Crow and Weasel offered the pipe. In the silence that followed, Crow and Weasel felt a strange obligation to speak of what they'd seen.
>
> "Now tell me, my friends, what did you see up north? I have always wanted to know what it is like up there."
>
> Weasel began to speak.
>
> "My friend," said Badger. "Stand up, stand up here so you can express more fully what you have seen."
>
> Weasel stood up, though he felt somewhat self-conscious in doing so. He began to speak about the people called Inuit and their habit of hunting an unusual white bear.
>
> "Wait, my friend," said Badger. "Where were you when this happened?"
>
> "We were in their camp. They told us."
>
> "Well, tell me something about their camp."
>
> Weasel described their camp, and then returned again to the story of hunting the bear.
>
> "But, my friend," interrupted Badger, "tell me a little first of who these people are. What did they look like?"
>
> Badger's words were beginning to annoy Weasel, but Crow could see what Badger was doing, and he smiled to himself. Weasel began again, but each time he would get only a little way in his story before Badger would ask for some point of clarification. Weasel was getting very irritated.
>
> Finally Crow spoke up.
>
> "Badger," he said, "my friend is trying very hard to tell his story. And I can see that you are only trying to help him, by teaching him to put the parts together in a good pattern, to speak with a pleasing rhythm, and to call on all the details of memory. But let us now see if he gets your meaning, for my friend is very smart." (44–45)

Thus Lopez manages with humor and concrete vigor to emphasize both the difficulty of effective storytelling and several of the principal techniques which emerge in his own writing: careful structure, euphony, and an abundance of particular details. When Badger asks, "Where were you when this happened?" he is not merely inquiring after a random detail, for the physical location of the storyteller during the narrated event is, for Lopez, an essential means of orienting the reader/listener. The storyteller must begin with the sense that he has a willing audience, and for this reason Badger immediately lets Weasel know of his interest in the mysterious North. But the speaker must also understand the seriousness, the underlying purpose of his narrative, or his account will be slack and incomplete.

Stephen Trimble, in describing Lopez's outdoor speech delivered near Arches National Park in May, 1989, attributes both theatrical intensity and moral seriousness to Lopez: "His college background in theater and his moral education in a Jesuit high school and at Notre Dame surely helped shape his delivery. He often sounds like an old-time preacher. He arouses and inspires and unsettles. In listening to him, I sensed a stirring in the audience" (Margolis, "Paying Attention," 50). These are precisely the traits Badger is trying to develop in Weasel, and later in Crow. Likewise, by traveling to distant places and then by reporting to us both the physical dimensions of the places and the psychological experience of coming to grips with the exotic, Lopez compels his readers either to aspire to greater awareness and concern or to face up to the irresponsibility of their disengagement from the world.

When Weasel finishes telling Badger about the north country, and Crow, with similar assistance from Badger, has told of their home in the South, Badger concludes the lesson with the following advice—advice essential to our appreciation of Lopez's own writing:

> "I would ask you to remember only this one thing," said Badger. "The stories people tell have a way of taking care of them. If stories come to you, care for them. And learn to give them away where they are needed. Sometimes a person needs a story more than food to stay alive. That is why we put these stories in each other's memory. This is how people care for themselves. One day you will be good storytellers. Never forget these obligations." (48)

In our contemporary society we have moved away from the landscape itself and certainly, until recently, from the idea of storytelling—or writing in general—as a response to moral obligation. Is it merely a quaint affectation of the traditional storyteller's sensibil-

ity that leads Lopez to write as he does and to explain his occupa-
tion in these terms? The portion of *Crow and Weasel* presented
above identifies many of the abiding issues and rationales within
Lopez's work—ones which we recognize as being so persistent and
essential that we can hardly dismiss them as affectations, despite
the initial peculiarity of a late-twentieth-century, non-Native
American invoking the aims and techniques of ancient storytelling. Lopez himself tells Kenneth Margolis that "Nonfiction writers
have taken over territory abandoned by American fiction writers.
That territory is, for example, the question of what is the relationship between the individual and God or between the individual
and the state, what is the relationship of the individual to landscape. . . . Those questions are being directly addressed by natural
history writers, or people I think of as landscape writers" (51–52).
This concern for fundamental epistemological questions is evident
in the work of all five of the writers discussed in this study, and is
something most commentators have easily recognized. However,
what is particularly significant in the approaches these writers have
taken in regard to such elemental questions is not only their
attempt to grapple with the issues themselves or with concrete
phenomena (specific landscapes or objects), but also their attempt
to understand the behavior of their own minds when confronting
such problems.

Particularizing the Exotic

I will focus my comments in this section on three specific
aspects of Lopez's particularizing of the exotic: his sense of how he
is serving "the community"; his concern for various forms of attentiveness (to place, human and animal subjects, language, and audience); and finally his interest in achieving "intimacy" with specific
landscapes, a condition strongly reminiscent of Wendell Berry's
strived-for "watchfulness."

As "a writer who travels," Lopez shoulders a special responsibility, one that goes beyond merely accounting for his private
responses to the complex landscapes he encounters. His task is to
make sense of the very process of making contact with otherness

and to describe this process in a way that will have meaning for his readers. Lopez tries to explain his fascination—and that of other natural history writers—with exotic cultures in his public dialogue with E. O. Wilson at the University of Utah:

> One of the questions that I ask myself is why so many natural history writers are so attentive to cultures other than their own, whether they are attentive to Navajo culture or to Inuit culture or to Kalahari people, or whatever. And the answer that I keep coming to is that these cultures, if you remove the tendency to make a condescending judgment, are holding on to things that, whatever the basis for them, are fundamental to the spiritual and intellectual and physical health of human beings on the planet. So it is natural that natural history writers would go back to this older form, which is to tell a story about the universe outside the human universe that helps us understand what is going on within ourselves and how we are to behave. (Lueders, 23–24)

What exactly are these things which are so fundamental to the health of human beings—these secrets of life demonstrated by other cultures? The answer seems to be that of living in daily and respectful proximity to the inhuman universe, and then recording and meditating upon and teaching this way of being by way of storytelling. (For a particularly good explanation of such storytelling, see Leslie Marmon Silko's essay "Landscape, History, and the Pueblo Imagination.") But for the writer and his readers it is simply the effort to understand wholly foreign people and places (true understanding meaning the sacrifice of preconceptions to what is actually given) that constitutes the primary challenge and the primary benefit of the journey. The process of particularizing the exotic which is so central to the goals of *Arctic Dreams*, requires that the entire landscape be regarded as "another sort of civilization we [have] to reach some agreement with" (*Arctic Dreams*, 11). Such an "agreement" means far more than a mere ceasefire or a mutually profitable contract. The "agreement" Lopez has in mind is closer to what he calls "congruence" or "coherence" or "respect" or "intimacy" on other occasions.

This task of seeing things in the exotic landscape which will "be of use to the community" (Gonzalez, "Landscapes of the

Interior," 8) is a difficult and daunting one, if taken seriously. On the occasion of his 1988 trip to China, Lopez writes:

> As a writer who travels outside his community, it is my obligation to return home now and then and say as well as I can what I have seen, to face the terror of putting this mystery into words that will serve. I am daunted by this task, as daunted as I would be in trying to describe the life of a tiger. But I know that this is what writers have been trying to do from the beginning, to make not just the familiar but the foreign comprehensible. ("Chinese Garland," 42)

It is interesting to consider the role of the individual writer who travels to exotic places – why do we, as a civilization, need such travel writers? Is it merely material constraints that keep us from journeying en masse to remote rain forests and desolate archipelagos? Aside from the disruption of remote places and cultures which would result from mass tourism, would there also be some weakening of the psychological value of making contact with otherness if we were able to do it more easily, more routinely? Is this what Edward Abbey is getting at when he writes, "We need wilderness whether or not we ever set foot in it. We need a refuge even though we may never need to go there. I may never in my life get to Alaska, for example, but I am grateful that it's there" (*Desert Solitaire*, 148–49)? Loren Eiseley once wrote that man "finds it necessary from time to time to send emissaries into the wilderness in the hope of learning of great events, or plans in store for him, that will resuscitate his waning taste for life" ("Judgment," 164). I believe we need this idea of the "emissary" and the virtually unreachable "wilderness" to convince us that there is something outside our domain, beyond our control.

Lopez is very much in the tradition of European exploration, but unlike such travelers as Alexander von Humboldt whose purpose was to illuminate distant places and accommodate them within a European worldview which had little room for the genuinely exotic, Lopez seeks to travel and write in a "tolerant" frame of mind: "I'm interested in the structure of prejudice. I am interested in tolerance. What is tolerance? What is tolerance in the biological realm? What is tolerance among human beings?" (Bonetti, 68). "Tolerance," as demonstrated in Lopez's writing, seems to be the effort to retain the exoticness of his subject matter, even in the process of making it comprehensible to his readers. By contrast, Humboldt's approach in *Ansichten der Natur* (*Views of Nature*), the famous 1808 account of his five-year journey (1799–1804) to South and Central America, is to use comparative landscape descriptions as a means of associating each American scene he encountered with scenes already imagined or witnessed by his European readers. Although Humboldt's scientific goals seem reasonable enough (he succeeded in demonstrating geographical isomorphisms and universal natural processes), the effect, in sum, was to nullify the exotic (see my 1990 article on Humboldt's comparative landscape descriptions).

The basic technique Lopez uses to maintain appreciation for the exotic is simply to "pay attention." Again and again in *Arctic Dreams* and his other writings, as well as in his many interviews, he refers to this idea of attentiveness as the essential focus of his work. This attentiveness, he tells Nicholas O'Connell, must be directed by the nonfiction writer toward both his material and his audience. "The bow of respect toward the material," he says, "means try to understand what's coming from it, not what you are trying to impose on it. Listen. Pay attention. Do your research. Don't presume." The reader, too, requires attention from the writer and, ideally, reciprocates by reading with concern and openness: "Somebody once said that what you want from a reader is someone who reads as attentively as you write. One way to get that is to cultivate a sense of respect for the reader" ("Barry Lopez," 16). Sherman Paul borrows Richard Nelson's term "gesture of reverence" to describe Lopez's habit of paying respect to the landscape itself ("Making the Turn," 377), but this gesture is directed at far more than the place. Seeking to use a language that "would leave [him], personally, on the periphery" (Bonetti, 66), Lopez carries out in his work a generalized act of respect, directed at both the subject matter and the audience, and embodying a reverence for language itself.

In his acceptance speech after receiving the 1986 American Book Award for *Arctic Dreams*, Lopez invokes the idea of "*kotodama*–that principle in Japanese [which] refers to the spiritual nature, the soul, if you will, of a word. What it means for writers is you have a responsibility that goes beyond yourself to care for the spiritual quality, the holy quality, the serious quality of language" (Keefer, "Lopez's Book on Arctic," 1B). Through his devotion to his mode of expression, Lopez contributes to the reader's inclusive sense of respect – for the text certainly, but also for the phenomena under scrutiny.

But how can the reader possibly achieve intimacy with the distant landscapes encountered only through the writer's text? The reader's contact with the landscape may be indirect, but it is still a valid encounter with the exotic and a useful exercise in Lopez's profound form of "tolerance" if the reader and the storyteller establish an intimate bond. In "Landscape and Narrative," Lopez repeats the narratives of native storytellers, but his own role is primarily that of the listener and analyst. "I listened carefully to these stories," he tells us, "taking pleasure in the sharply observed detail surrounding the dramatic thread of events" (62). This concern for detail or particularization is what Lopez generally demonstrates in his own storytelling, and what impresses and pleases us as we read. After he listened to several hunting stories, the Alaskan landscape "seemed alive" to Lopez, but he proceeds in the essay "Landscape and Narrative" to universalize this experience, to show how proper storytelling creates an intimacy between teller and listener which then extends to the landscape, too:

> This feeling, an inexplicable renewal of enthusiasm after storytelling, is familiar to many people. It does not seem to matter what the subject is, as long as the context is intimate and the story is told for its own sake, not forced to serve merely as the vehicle for an idea. The tone of the story need not be solemn. The darker aspects of life need not be ignored. But I think intimacy is indispensable – a feeling that derives from the listener's trust and a storyteller's sure knowledge of his subject and regard for his audience. (63–64)

When we, as readers, acknowledge Lopez's solicitation of trust and intimacy, we open ourselves to the possibility of making contact – but contact with what? Certainly, after reading *Arctic Dreams*, we have a deeper appreciation of the Arctic landscape, but it's hard to think of our understanding as being genuine intimacy, despite the particularity and eloquence of Lopez's account in his stories. Perhaps it is just as important – and more feasible – for us to use

Lopez's reports of the exotic to enrich our understanding of the familiar. Though many of his projects begin with excursions to remote places, Lopez says that he does most of his writing at his home on the McKenzie River in Oregon—and not only at home, but sometimes while sitting on rocks in the middle of the river. He states to Bonetti:

> In the woods, you know, you have this tremendous cerebral activity of working with these symbols on paper and your writing instrument, the pencil, actually in your hand. And then you look to the side and there will be a wolf spider making eye contact with you, and you're immediately brought into the world you inhabit as a creature, as a human being. (61)

The same goes for Lopez's readers. We use his writing as a ramp or a springboard—as a guided "preparatory meditation," to lift a term from the puritan poet Edward Taylor—toward a newly receptive state of mind. Then when we put down *Arctic Dreams*, or another such work, we are ready to see the world we inhabit, if not an Arctic tundra or a damp northwestern forest, then perhaps rolling ranchlands of fire ant mounds and subtle wildflowers, or an urban landscape with its teasing interplay of cement and vegetation.

Form and Genre: The Role of the Personal Anecdote

Without being entirely explicit about it, I have been wrestling with difficulties of genre both in this discussion of Lopez and in earlier comments on Thoreau, Dillard, Abbey, and Berry. So many different generic patterns seem at least partially descriptive of works such as *Arctic Dreams*, and yet none contains it satisfactorily. I am thinking, for instance, of George P. Landow's distinction between the "wisdom speaker" and the "sage," which describes conflicting aspects of Lopez's work, its frequent suggestion of the narrator's unity with the reader through the use of an anonymous "I" and an intimate "we" (reminiscent of the wisdom speaker's position "at a societal and cultural center") and its simultaneous eccentricity (the common perspective of the sage) in its account of an exotic landscape in which the author aspires to a nonwestern worldview (*Elegant Jeremiahs*, 23). Also there is Peter A. Fritzell's notion that "Thoreauvian nature writing" is an "attempt to meld or blend the traditions and forms of Aristotle's *Historia Animalium*, on the one hand, and Saint Augustine's *Confessions*, on the other" (*Nature Writing and America*, 3) – and indeed, *Arctic Dreams* is, in certain important respects, a convergence of natural history and spiritual autobiography. However, as speculative taxonomists such as Landow and Fritzell readily admit, the goal is not to define iron-clad categories, but to suggest generic parameters and ways of approaching types of literature – especially nonfiction – which are, by nature, eclectic. As Thomas J. Lyon puts it just before placing *Arctic Dreams* in a column labeled "Travel and Adventure": "[T]he types I have listed tend to intergrade, and with great frequency. This may be somewhat irritating to lovers of neatness who would like their categories to be immutable, but nature writing is not in truth a neat and orderly field" (3).

I am inclined to explain the intriguing form of *Arctic Dreams* not by describing its author as a hybrid of the wisdom speaker and the sage, the scientist and the autobiographer, but rather (using Lopez's own terms) as a writer who has undertaken to supplement "mathematical knowledge" with "particularized understanding" in order to achieve full appreciation – or awareness – of his subject matter. On January 27, 1852, around the time when the Journal was becoming his primary activity, Thoreau wrote:

> I do not know but thoughts written down thus in·a journal might be printed in the same form with greater advantage than if the related ones were brought together into separate essays. They are now allied to life, and are seen by the reader not to be farfetched. It is more simple, less artful. I feel that in the other case I should have no proper frame for my sketches. Mere facts and names and dates communicate more than we suspect. Whether the flower looks better in the nosegay than in the meadow where it grew and we had to wet our feet to get it! Is the scholastic air any advantage? (3:239)

It seems to me that Lopez, despite his organization of the material into "separate essays," would agree with Thoreau on an essential level that writing, particularly where nature is concerned, is best when "allied to life." The goal is not to abandon artfulness and scientific knowledge altogether – Lopez's own exhaustive use of his-

torical and scientific sources demonstrates this. But scholarship
and beguiling language alone are not enough. The nature writer
who desires a full understanding of his subject matter must experience it in person, and in order to foster this same understanding
among his readers, he must figure out a way, as Lopez writes with
regard to aboriginal storytellers in "Landscape and Narrative," to
bring "two landscapes [the internal and the external] together"
(*Crossing*, 66).

In his 1990 study of literary nonfiction, W. Ross Winterowd
applauds *Arctic Dreams*, calling it "an exceptionally interesting
book," but ultimately complains that "it lacks the intensity that the
lyric ratio, that of agent-scene, creates. It is too disunified to sustain itself" (*Rhetoric*, 133). I would agree with Winterowd that the
layers of ethos and logos, of narrative and discursive prose, never
completely melt together into an artfully homogeneous pudding in
Lopez's work. But I tend to view this as an intentional and successful effort to present two equally indispensable ways of knowing the
Arctic while keeping us aware of their distinctness. Instead of simply immersing us in the experience of the Arctic, Lopez guides us
through a learning process which alternates between immediate
sensory experience and abstract reflection, both of which contribute to achieving intimacy. The goal is not to startle and unnerve
the reader, as is frequently the case with Dillard and Abbey, but
simply to make the reader aware of the different ways in which our
minds work.

Many of the best American nature writers have long realized
that the anecdotal imagination – the affinity for the specific, the
experiential – plays an important role in our reception and expression of information about the world. It's not that nature writers
find their impersonal subject matter by itself unpiquant, unper-
suasive, but rather that writers from Thoreau to Lopez have dis-
covered how the insertion of an occasional personal narrative,
whether as a sustained structural trope or as a segue from one topic
to another, can transform a dispassionate treatise into a lush, evocative story, with the experiencing, writing self becoming an inex-
tricable part of the subject matter. Philip Rahv claimed years ago,
in his article "The Cult of Experience in American Writing," that
"experience, in the sense of 'felt life' rather than as life's total

practice, is the main . . . substance of literature. The part experience plays in the aesthetic sphere might well be compared to the part that the materialist conception of history assigns to economy," experience being "the substructure of literature above which there rises a superstructure of values, ideas, and judgments" (*Image and Idea*, 18). In nature writing the experiential element, which generally takes the form of personal anecdotes, serves various "substructural" purposes. For instance, anecdotes lend eyewitness authority to the writer's claims ("I have seen this, felt this, myself, and thus I can assure you, reader, it's true") and draw even the urban reader into proximity (if not always total sympathy) with the narrator, thus enabling vicarious experience, a surrogate for firsthand knowledge.

For numerous nature writers in the wake of Thoreau, the act of contemplating the external natural world has come to involve a simultaneous act of scrutinizing the viewing self's relationship to nature. For these writers, the personal anecdote—autobiography in miniature—becomes a powerfully appropriate tool of expression. As mentioned above, certain scholars, such as Kathleen Raine, believe that the sort of united vision of man and nature which occurs periodically in *Arctic Dreams* depends on a mystically childlike apprehension of the universe, an ability to understand that "nature is vision—epiphany—indeed theophany" ("Nature," 252). Admittedly, the raw sensitivity to nature sought by most nature writers requires an unusual stoking of awareness, but need we consider such experiences so rare and epiphanous? The point of *Arctic Dreams* seems to be that nearly everyone, from the hardy oil-pipeline worker to the visiting poet, is capable of achieving "a particularized understanding of the land itself," this being the product of imaginative scrutiny but not necessarily mystical vision. In order to perceive and respect the particular features of a given landscape, one must approach it with naivete and innocence and wonder. Lopez tells Jim Aton:

> [A]ny of us can become cynical, inarticulate with pessimism. It's important to me, though, to go into a story with a capacity for wonder, where I know I can derive something "wonder-full" and then bring this into the story so that a reader can feel it and say, "I am an adult.

I have a family, I pay bills, I live in a world of chicanery and subterfuge and atomic weaponry and inhumanity and round-heeled politicians and garrulous, insipid television personalities, but still I have wonder. I have been brought to a state of wonder by contact with something in a story." ("An Interview with Barry Lopez," 13)

This ability to accept the world with open eyes and without the burden of overpowering (and ultimately debilitating) expectations is also the subject of Peter Matthiessen's *The Snow Leopard* (1978). Matthiessen's Zen-preoccupied journey to the Crystal Monastery of remote Tibet is, like *Arctic Dreams*, "a true pilgrimage, a journey of the heart" (3), as well as a physical expedition. And though time after time Matthiessen's specific desires (a glimpse of the mysterious snow leopard, an encounter with the lama at Crystal Monastery, an answer to the koan, "All the peaks are covered with snow—why is this one bare?" (266), and a meeting with the Sherpa Tukten in Kathmandu) are left unfulfilled, he does evolve spiritually toward the condition of expectationlessness. He learns that "When one pays attention to the present [as opposed to the past or the future], there is great pleasure in awareness of small things" (96). The wonderment and pleasure—the sense of "congruence"—which result from an openness to the given world is, of course, what Lopez tries to convey in *Arctic Dreams*. Zen practitioners, native people, and children are held up as the models for this desired way of apprehending the world, and the task of the writer is to place this worldview within reach of the ordinary reader, homebound and preoccupied with mundane concerns.

The literary technique which enables the writer to re-create such experience, to make it accessible to the average reader, is the personal anecdote. By way of such anecdotes, whether presented in solid blocks or sprinkled in fragments throughout entire chapters, the reader of Lopez's book comes to see the faint stir of the Arctic willow's leaves through Lopez's own eyes. Loren Eiseley once defined his own preferred genre, the personal or "concealed" essay, as that in which "personal anecdote was allowed gently to bring under observation thoughts of a more purely scientific nature" (*Strange Hours*, 177). For Eiseley, like Lopez, it often turned out that the self was as prominent a subject for his essays as the external subject matter. Yet Eiseley's choice of the anecdotal mode seems to result more from his strategic awareness of the spark such a narrative might light in the imagination of the nonscientific reader than from any ideological design, any plan to unify the personal and the scientific in quest of deeper understanding. Lopez, on the other hand, expresses through his very use of anecdotes the need to couple our scientific knowledge with sensory and emotional experience, with the intense concern and awareness which result only from the experience of particulars.

Much like the aboriginal storyteller he describes in "Landscape and Narrative," Lopez seeks to gain the trust and sympathy of the reader, and feels an obligation "to engage the reader with a precise vocabulary [descriptive of both the external environment and his own feelings], to set forth a coherent and dramatic rendering of incidents—and to be ingenuous." Having spelled out his plan to direct the reader's attention "back to the concrete dimensions of the land" at the beginning of his book, Lopez has no hidden message in his work, no secret agenda—only the goal of depicting "various subtle and obvious relationships in the exterior landscape accurately in his story," so that "the [reader] who 'takes the story to heart' will feel a pervasive sense of congruence within himself and also with the world" ("Landscape and Narrative," 66). Congruence between the self and the world—the pinnacle of intimacy for Lopez—is what *Arctic Dreams* is working toward.

In order to promote this special understanding of the land's "concrete dimensions," Lopez makes prominent use of experiential, anecdotal passages in addition to his more scholarly or more philosophical comments about the Arctic. Many passages in *Arctic Dreams* are aloof and seemingly dispassionate—and these sections of the text would fail to show what it's like to experience the region firsthand and with intense openness. Sherman Paul argues that

> the use of personal experience to frame each chapter [in *Arctic Dreams*] is the significant literary advance on *Of Wolves and Men* [1978] and the propriety of its management a measure of his achievement. He speaks not of himself but of a narrator who is "a refinement of something that's inside of me that I found useful technically"—useful, clearly, in moderating the "enormous act of ego" always involved in writing. Yet, even though he claims that the narrator is "the num-

ber two guy . . . [and] never intrude[s] on the reader's ability to enter
the environment," Lopez himself is present and his way of entering
the environment is a notable and instructive aspect of the book. He
enacts the way to perceive about which he also writes. . . . ("Making
the Turn," 379)

Lopez's anecdotes make his discussion more human and immediate, focusing on specific encounters with Arctic phenomena, as
opposed to distilling abstract theories and supporting them with
charts and graphs, though these, too, have their place in the work.
It is important to note, though, the strangely generalized sort of
personal encounter with nature that Lopez uses in *Arctic Dreams.*
The natural particulars Lopez comes into contact with do not
function in the text as genuine particulars, but rather are immediately transformed into "symbolic particulars." The narrator, too, as
Paul suggests, is a "refinement" of the author, symbolizing the
individual's congruence with the landscape. Instead of using anecdotal narratives to dwell on minute natural specifics, Lopez makes
symbolic anecdotal gestures that advocate a respectful attitude
toward the unaltered landscape of the Arctic.

A "Proper Frame": The Primacy of the Symbolic Particular

The fourth chapter of *Arctic Dreams,* "Lancaster Sound:
Monodon monoceros"—the subtitle being Latin for narwhal—concerns the natural history and human significance of the narwhal.
The chapter is framed within the narrative of an excursion—the
traditional ploy of such nature writers as Thoreau (see "A Winter
Walk") and John Muir (see "Prayers in Higher Mountain Temples,
or A Geologist's Winter Walk" and his well-known "A Near View
of the High Sierra"). Lopez begins his chapter by emphasizing his
own presence at a precise location: "I am standing at the margin of
the sea ice called the floe edge at the mouth of Admiralty Inlet,
northern Baffin Island, three or four miles out to sea" (107). Geographical precision, together with carefully selected sensory details
and the prominent participation of the feeling self, is essential to
the anecdote's role in enabling the reader to gain a "particularized
understanding" of the narwhal and its native element, but these

aspects of the narrative also contribute to our understanding of the author himself. As Lopez tells Kay Bonetti,

> When a reader starts a story—I think a reader says, "Well, what's going on? Where are we now? What is happening?" So when you begin a story by saying where you are, offering some details of where you are, then the reader has a chance to become comfortable. I think it is imperative to be mindful of the reader's position. (62)

We become familiar with the way the writer's mind works, the way his attention drifts from external phenomena back to his own emotions, to remembered events or information and back to the primary event—the excursion to find narwhals—and we also sense his "mindfulness" of us and feel prepared to reciprocate with ingenuousness and trust. Our growing familiarity with the writer is important, because he serves as our guide, and perhaps, eventually, as an extension of ourselves. The association of the author's unique experience with feelings even the nonnaturalist might understand comes through in such generalizing assertions as "[the] attraction to borders, to the earth's twilit places, is part of the shape of human curiosity. And the edges that cause excitement are like these where I now walk . . . " (110).

The first goal of the writer is to make the scene immediate for the reader by foregrounding physical and emotional details:

> As I walk along the floe edge—the light is brilliant, the ceaseless light of July; but after so many weeks I am weary of it; I stare at the few shadows on the ice with a kind of hunger—as I walk along here I am aware of both fear and elation, a mix that comes in remote regions with the realization that you are exposed and weather can be capricious. (107)

The intensity of Lopez's perception and the powerful mixture of emotions impress us with the fact of the narrator's actual presence in the landscape (a sense of actuality augmented by the use of the present tense)—even though there is a generality to the imagery, to the sweeping references to light and shadow, which suggests a concern for the essence of the experience rather than the momentary observations. The subsequent presentation of a remembered catastrophe (men nearly stranded on drifting ice floes) and zoological information, becomes merely digression from the heart of the chapter, the personal anecdote. "I am not so much thinking of these things," Lopez writes in returning to the anecdote, "as I am feeling the exuberance of the birds around me" (108). Later, after musing for several paragraphs on the extraordinary abundance of wildlife in the region ("Three million colonial seabirds . . . nest and feed here in the summer"), Lopez snaps awake again to the primary experience. He states, "I am concerned, as I walk, however, more with what is immediate to my senses—the ternlike whiffle and spin of birds over the water, the chicken-cackling of northern fulmars, and cool air full of the breath of sea life" (109).

Strangely, though, Lopez does not show us the sight of a particular bird or even a particular group of birds, but rather uses his generalized anecdote to symbolize a "particularized understanding" of the Arctic. The scientific information, though important enough to warrant frequent and sometimes lengthy detours from the narrative (for instance, the twenty-two-page digression on biological, acoustical, mythological, and even etymological aspects of the narwhal), remains essentially digressive. The anecdote, despite its own fragmentation to allow for the informative digressions, serves as the unifying element for the chapter as a whole. With some writers—for instance, Thoreau—the relegation of science or rumination to narrative digressions would seem to imply no strict judgment about the relative importance of abstract knowledge and concrete experience. In the case of Lopez, however, the hierarchy of understanding seems clear—the experiential taking priority over the less sensory, or the "mathematical."

Again and again Lopez digresses, only to draw us back poignantly to his own walk across the ice. "I walk here intent on the birds," he writes,

> half aware of the biological mysteries in these placid, depthless waters in which I catch fleeting glimpses of cod. I feel blessed. I draw in the salt air and feel the warmth of sunlight on my face. I recall a childhood of summer days on the beaches of California. I feel the wealth to be had in an aimless walk like this, through woods or over a prairie or down a beach.
>
> It is not all benign or ethereal at the ice edge, however. You cannot—I cannot—lose completely the sense of how far from land this is. And I am wary of walrus. . . . (111)

The author's mind moves naturally from sensory impressions ("fleeting glimpses of cod") to general responses to the landscape ("I feel blessed"), and onward, by more extended association, to memories of childhood summers on distant beaches. But to dwell exclusively on the "benign or ethereal" side of the experience would be to represent it inaccurately, incompletely—hence the suggestion of lurking dread, the uneasiness of a man perched on ice above deep, cold water, far from real land, threatened vaguely by the possibility of a walrus attack. This fear, as Sherman Paul notes, "acknowledges ignorance of 'perfect harmony' and contributes to *nuannaarpog*, the 'quality . . . of taking extravagant pleasure in being alive' " (376). The full truth of the experience encompasses both bliss and fear. It also becomes increasingly apparent with each new anecdotal fragment that the experience of a narwhal hunt includes far more than the actual encounter with narwhals themselves. In fact, the particular excursion presented in the primary, intermittent anecdote of this chapter, much like the search for a similarly magical animal described in Matthiessen's *The Snow Leopard*, yields no actual narwhals. The mental state of hunting is what Lopez seeks. Just as the two types of "stalking" (active and passive) serve Annie Dillard as metaphors for elevated consciousness, hunting "becomes a metaphor that enables Lopez to speak of the requisite alertness of another kind of experience, that represented by the arduous tracking of (and in) the landscapes of this book" (Paul, "Making the Turn," 377). Thus the condition of attentiveness is both demonstrated and analyzed in *Arctic Dreams*. The unseen narwhal retains its aura of mystery—and, in fact, through its very elusiveness, teaches the narrator "a frame of mind that redefines patience, endurance, and expectation" (Lopez quoted by Paul, 376).

How is the reader supposed to respond to Lopez's first-person anecdotes? The mock self-correction in the previous quotation ("You cannot—I cannot—lose completely the sense of how far from land this is") suggests an intended identification of the reader with the author. In another passage later in the chapter, Lopez resorts to the same kind of hypothetical second-person narrative employed regularly by such Victorian word-painters as John Ruskin and John Muir:

> If you were to stand at the edge of the cliff on the north coast of Borden Peninsula, Baffin Island, you could watch narwhals migrating past more or less continuously for several weeks in the twenty-four-hour light of June. You would be struck by their agility and swiftness, by the synchronicity of their movements as they swam and dived in unison. . . . (121)

The choice of the second person is of course not accidental, nor is it made merely to achieve stylistic variety. It is Lopez's way to make his experience the reader's as well—and thus it serves implicitly as a way to transfer his wilderness ideology to the reader. Much as the regular reassertions of his own physical presence in the landscape draw the reader's attention "back [from learned abstraction] to the concrete dimensions of the land" (*Arctic Dreams*, 11), the occasional shifts into the second person serve as attempts to bridge the distance between author and reader, to make the anecdote particularly tangible for the reader.

The Mind at Work

Through the careful use of information he has gleaned from other literature, Lopez manages to avert potential tedium and numbness (the opposite of awareness) even in the more academic passages of *Arctic Dreams*. For instance, when discussing the sensitivity of the bowhead whale's skin, he writes:

> The fiery pain of the harpoon strike can hardly be imagined. (In 1856 a harpooner aboard the *Truelove* reported striking a whale that dived so furiously it took out 1200 yards of line in three and a half minutes before crashing into the ocean floor, breaking its neck and burying its head eight feet deep in blue-black mud.) (3)

The second sentence here, offered in parentheses and without emotion or additional commentary, cannot help but jar the emotions of the reader. What kind of pain could result in such a suicidal dive to the ocean floor? Such is the sensitivity of the whale's skin! The restraint Lopez exercises in presenting this kind of evocative information allows the reader's own imagination to bring the scene to life and draw conclusions.

Elsewhere, rather than merely crafting detached, reverent descriptions of exotic Arctic views, Lopez depicts himself grappling with language to get the images just right. We see him grasping for metaphors to characterize icebergs in the chapter called "Ice and Light," and this tells us not only about the physical appearance of the ice, but about the experience of viewing icebergs, the flurry of metaphor making incited by the view. He recalls, for instance:

> I wrote down the words for the tints—the grays of doves and pearls, of smoke. Isolated in my binoculars, the high rampart of a mesalike berg seemed sheared off like a wall of damp talc. Another rounded off smoothly, like a human forehead against the sky, and was pocked and lined, the pattern of a sperm whale's lacerated tun. Floating, orographic landscapes—sections broken out of a mountain range: snow-covered ridges, cirque valleys, sharp peaks. The steep walls often fell sheer to the sea, like granite pitches, their surfaces faceted like raw jade, or coarser, like abraded obsidian. (185)

Here are metaphors within metaphors, analogies between looming ice and doves, pearls, smoke, whole geologic landscapes, the "tun" of a whale, even the shape and texture of a human forehead. But this aesthetic appreciation that evolves into several additional paragraphs of measurement ("64.7 meters high by 465.4 meters long") is framed within a first-person anecdote. And the vividness of this entire discussion stems to a great extent from the image of the author himself peering through binoculars. In concluding this particular section of the chapter, while on a ship bound for the Northwest Passage, Lopez describes the rapture he felt when first encountering icebergs: "I stare for hours from the starboard window at these creatures I have never seen before. They drift past in the spanking, beautiful weather. How utterly still, unorthodox, and wondrous they seem" (186). And because we have experienced the icebergs ourselves from the author's multiple perspectives (aesthetic, scientific, and gawkingly innocent), his final emotional comments strike home with us, despite the fact that the hours of staring have been compressed into a few lines, the floating mountains of ice transformed into symbolic particulars.

Thomas J. Lyon points out, using language that echoes Annie Dillard's, that *Arctic Dreams* is not merely a study of a particular landscape, but "an investigation of the mentality of seeking itself. *Arctic Dreams*, therefore, is a highly self-conscious book." He does not mean that Lopez's work is meant to be insular, self-enclosed, egocentric. Instead, like the details of the landscape that in Lopez's work represent the very idea of particularized awareness, the author's comments about the responses of his own mind to the Arctic are intended to include the reader's possible responses as well. "Lopez's consciousness of self and nature is meant to be representative," continues Lyon, "and what develops is an exposition of two paths, two ways of seeing. We can approach the wild world (which is to say, *the* world) with designs on it, projections and preconceptions; or we can try to simply perceive it, to let it be whatever it is" ("This Incomperable Lande," 90). The ideas are reminiscent of Dillard, but when applied to Lopez, are charged with ethical implications.

Lyon's brief comment about Lopez's "two ways of seeing" is an implicit explanation of the subtitle of *Arctic Dreams—Imagination and Desire in a Northern Landscape.* The concepts of "imagination" and "desire" (encapsulated in the term "dreams") play an integral role, if not always an explicitly stated one, throughout Lopez's study of the various ways in which the human mind comes to terms with a place as exotic and overwhelming and elusive as the Arctic. But perhaps his most concentrated and effective revelation about these two mental processes appears in the chapter "The Country of the Mind." Precisely how does the mind respond to a wholly new place? How does the mind overcome "prejudice" and accept ingenuously what is there? The following quotation shows how Lopez pursues his psychological exploration:

> In the sometimes disconcerting summary which is a photograph, Pingok Island would seem bleak and forsaken. In winter it disappears beneath whiteness, a flat white plain extending seaward into the Beaufort Sea ice and landward without border into the tundra of the coastal plain. The island emerges in June, resplendent with flowers and insects and birds, only to disappear again in a few months beneath the first snowstorms. To a Western imagination that finds a stand of full-crowned trees heartening, that finds the flight and voice

of larks exhilarating, and the sight of wind rolling over fields of tall grass more agreeable, Pingok seems impoverished. When I arrived on the island, I, too, understood its bleak aspect as a category, the expression of something I had read about or been told. In the weeks during which I made some passing acquaintance with it, its bleakness was altered, however. The prejudice we exercise against such landscapes, imagining them to be primitive, stark, and pagan, became sharply apparent. It is in a place like this that we would unthinkingly store poisons or test weapons, land like the deserts to which we once banished our heretics and where we once loosed scapegoats with the burden of our transgressions. (228)

Here it is clear that Lopez uses the pronoun "I" for a variety of reasons, none of which suggests arrogance or self-absorption. Rather, the "I" represents a particular instance of a more universal psychological experience – and hardly a proud one. In this scene, the author uses the occasion of his stay on Pingok Island to confront not merely the land itself, but his own reaction to the land. He acknowledges and laments this initial reaction to Pingok as the first "way of seeing" described by Lyon above, for it results from the mind's burden of preconceptions. The ethical undercurrent of this discussion quickly becomes more than an undercurrent, as the misguidedness of approaching the world with preconceived designs is implicated with the mentality that would produce poisonous wastes and experiment with nuclear weapons.

The ethical concerns are there, and unmistakable, but they do not seem to be Lopez's primary interest. His goal, as stated in his public dialogue with E. O. Wilson and cited earlier in this book, is more epistemological than political, although the two are certainly intertwined. "[W]hat do we know? how do we know? how do we organize this knowledge?" he asks (Lueders, "Writing Natural History," 15). He responds to these questions throughout *Arctic Dreams*, but particularly in the following passage:

> The differing landscapes of the earth are hard to know individually. They are as difficult to engage in conversation as wild animals. The complex feelings of affinity and self-assurance one feels with one's native place rarely develop again in another landscape.
> It is a convention of Western thought to believe all cultures are compelled to explore, that human beings seek new land because their

economies drive them onward. Lost in this valid but nevertheless impersonal observation is the notion of a simpler longing, of a human desire for a less complicated life, for fresh intimacy and renewal. These, too, draw us into new landscapes. And desire causes imagination to misconstrue what it finds. The desire for wealth, for revivification, for triumph, as much or more than scientific measurement and description, or the imperatives of economic expansion, resolves the geography of a newfound landscape. (228–29)

The entire sequence of essays which comprises *Arctic Dreams* is, literally, an exemplary effort by an individual author to perceive, come to terms with, and eventually overcome the limitations which aggressive desire places upon the imagination. In the middle of the second paragraph just quoted, Lopez identifies three ideal objects of desire: a less complicated life, intimacy, and renewal. All three of these goals, which seem straight out of *Walden* and could fit just as well in *Pilgrim at Tinker Creek, Desert Solitaire*, and "The Long-Legged House," have less to do with affecting political change than with enhancing the life of the individual. All three goals, moreover, imply a need for freshness, openness, and innocence of sight and insight—a need for awareness.

When Lopez announces in the prologue to *Arctic Dreams* his intention to draw his reader's thoughts back to the "concrete dimensions of the land," he is referring not only to the external land, but to the human observer who participates in the land's existence through perception, imagination, and a special kind of desire for insight. In the final pages of the book, he calls this longing a "conscious desire to achieve a state, even momentarily, that like light is unbounded, nurturing, suffused with wisdom and creation . . . " (371). The landscape, though on one level respected as something distinct from the viewing self, at the same time merges with the writer who encounters it and allows the details of the place to converge with his own desire. As Sherman Paul explains it, the book shows the use of "imagination to transform desire" (377)—in other words, Lopez, imagining a condition of intimacy with the northern landscape, alters not the place, but his own expectations (presumably those of the Western mind which shudders at the bleakness of Pingok Island). This depiction of redefined expectation, of newly open awareness, is all the more powerful because it indicates the hopefulness of the narrator's ongoing conversion process, and this hopefulness envelopes the reader as well. At the conclusion of *Arctic Dreams*, Lopez, filled with intense reverence, once more emphasizes his own physical presence in the scene as he looks out over the Bering Sea from the tip of Saint Lawrence Island: "I bowed before the simple evidence of the moment in my life in a tangible place on the earth that was beautiful." But the tangible, physical reality of the earth suddenly gives way to the intangible. Or, rather, the observer's nebulous longing suddenly matches the material world: "When I stood I thought I glimpsed my own desire." The respectful observer has achieved, momentarily, an openness of mind which is in profound accordance with the unrefined, unmanipulated natural world.

"The edges of the real landscape became one with the edges of something I had dreamed," Lopez explains. "But what I had dreamed was only a pattern, some beautiful pattern of light. The continuous work of the imagination, I thought, to bring what is actual together with what is dreamed is an expression of human evolution" (371). Dreams, which are the individual's sense of how the self exists in the world, remain incomplete until one makes genuine contact with the landscape outside one's consciousness. Often landscapes are hostile and abrasive, and the typical "Western" desire is somehow to control such a landscape, to make it more comfortable or useful (even to make it a nuclear testing zone or to use it as a place for banishing heretics). What is special and exemplary—some might say epiphanous—about the experience Lopez describes at the end of *Arctic Dreams* is that the inner worldview of the dreamer is complemented, even completed, by his view of the actual world. For just one moment, "correspondence," as Emerson and Thoreau would call it, is achieved. To work toward this kind of compatibility or intimacy with the landscape is "an expression of human evolution," a continuous process. The book may conclude neatly with a moment of contact, but Lopez scarcely suggests that this is a constant condition.

"[W]hen you're working on a story," Lopez once said, "I think you're working in an ecotone, in the border country . . . , right out on the edge of yourself, at the height of your imagination . . . " (Bonetti, 76). Such an ecotone of the imagination, like the "rich biological crease" at the edge of an ice floe (*Arctic Dreams*, 111), is rich territory not only for the writer, but for his reader as well. Since (as he tells Ray Gonzalez) most members of the human community "have jobs and children [and] are unable to go to these distant places," Lopez goes himself and describes his own responses to the exotic so that "the reader can look through and under the story and feel he or she can see things as well" ("Landscapes of the Interior," 8). In this way, he achieves the final "goal of the writer," which is "to nourish the reader's awareness of the world" ("Chinese Garland," 41), helping us to "find a dignified relationship with each other and the place where we live" and giving politicians "a deep understanding of how the landscape is threatened" ("Landscapes of the Interior," 29, 9). In a *New York Times* review Michiko Kakutani claims that "It is [Lopez's] achievement in [*Arctic Dreams*] that he communicates to us a visceral sense of his own understanding and wonder, as well as his appreciation for this distant country that flickers insistently like a flashbulb afterimage in our minds long after we've finished reading." Not only does he communicate his "understanding and wonder" so powerfully, but he endeavors to explain the state of mind itself—and it is for this reason that Lopez takes his place among the other morning chanticleers in the Thoreauvian tradition.

CHAPTER 7

Coda: Excursions and Incursions

Eye-catching: Shapes in the Sky

Just making it out the front door can be the hardest part of getting outside. Shouldering my briefcase strap, my over-loaded overnight bag—Nike running shoes hanging from the handle—with the other hand I pull the front door of my house closed behind me, lock it, then fight my way around the screen door, which bangs and shudders before easing back in place.

It is the beginning of February and I am on my way to another wilderness conference in Utah. Here in San Marcos, Texas, the sun is brilliant already. Hot—or at least it seems so to someone spending his first snowless winter in six years. How can it be hotter than seventy degrees so early in the year? Can this mean "spring" already?

Leaning against the yellow brick of the house, waiting for the cab which will take me to the airport in Austin, I find my attention wandering from the still-yellow grass to the leafless trees and the seemingly uninhabited homes of my neighbors. Everyone is at work or school. "Castle Forest," as our new housing development is called, is vacant, quiet. Soon Analinda's sixth-grade science students will be on their way home, and she'll drive "Tree," a metallic gray Hyundai, to pick up our three-year-old son Jacinto at preschool. The car will whine down the block and pull into our driveway, then there will be the sounds of the emergency brake being stretched taut and the car doors opening. The neighborhood will fill up with the sounds of life as kids return from school: balls bouncing, plastic vehicles scraping the pavement, erratic chatter and complaint.

But for now the place is silent. I don't even hear any birds. Next door, the dog—large, dark, visible only in strips between the wide boards of the fence—starts to bark at me before deciding I'm not worth the effort. I put my two bags down on the driveway. An absence of bugs—sign of winter. The cab is late.

At 3:10 I notice a small plane beginning a low, nasal pass over the neighborhood. What's its business? It curves away from me and I let it go, thinking about something else – my lecture on nostalgia and defiance in wilderness literature, and then about being in the sky myself in two hours, looking down at neighborhoods with turquoise swimming pools behind each house.

Suddenly, the plane is directly above me, as if intentionally, as if aiming for me, or for something. I think – absurdly – of the plane's-eye-view footage of bombing raids against Iraq: a building, a neat square around it, and then, missile unseen, a cloud of demolition. A hard image to erase. How do I appear to the pilot above me now? Am I visible at all? If he had something for me, he could drop it now and I would receive it – or would its momentum carry it across town? If the plane suddenly lost power, would it glide to a soft landing among the cows and live oaks and cacti behind the house, or drop like a rock? I wonder this as the plane passes overhead, a few hundred feet straight up, but when I step away from the house to see it better, I notice something beyond it in the sky – also straight up – and I barely realize it when the plane is behind me. It does not return.

Eight thin shapes, dark and stiff and terribly high, circle kaleidoscopically overhead. Now nine, no fourteen. The final count is fourteen, though I feel my eyes squinting and crossing as I strain to keep the shapes distinct enough to count. A pattern of hawks, I suppose. Vultures perhaps. I cannot take my eyes away from their intricate, waltz-like circling. They seem to move in pairs, and the seven pairs cross each other's paths – their movements resembling dancers, or cars on a freeway cloverleaf, rather than the spinning of a centrifuge. I cannot fathom their motion: distant, weightless, seemingly carefree. Nor can I let go of them with my eyes, either. Vultures? Fourteen black crosses ascend to the limits of my attention, disappearing into the hazy blue Texas sky.

I am thinking of that motion, watching the shapes recede – limbs outstretched, circling in and then out, taking the updrafts and leaving the world below – when a woman's voice calls out, "Taxi?" There is a dark blue station wagon next to the curb.

Ecocriticism: The Assumed Power of Awareness

Most of us share the commonplace and frequently un-examined assumption that awareness will lead directly to corresponding action. For some people, awareness seems to imply almost automatic action. This is the assumption, of course, which underlies such nature writing as Rachel Carson's *Silent Spring* (1962). That she expects her exposé of environmental abuse to result in concrete behavioral change becomes explicit (elsewhere it is strangely unexpressed, as if her goal were necessarily obvious to her readers) when she writes:

> The fisheries of fresh and salt water are a resource of great impor-tance, involving the interests and the welfare of a very large number of people. That they are now seriously threatened by the chemicals entering our waters can no longer be doubted. If we would divert to constructive research even a small fraction of the money spent each year on the development of ever more toxic sprays, we could find ways to use less dangerous materials and to keep poisons out of our waterways. When will the public become sufficiently aware of the facts to demand such action? (152)

Carson is concerned with the particular type of awareness known as "public awareness," the collective elevation of consciousness that is considered valuable mainly because it suggests the potential for political influence. *Silent Spring*, in fact, is the classic example of literary nonfiction designed to raise public consciousness. In his 1982 *New York Times* article "20 Years After 'Silent Spring': Still a Troubled Landscape," Philip M. Boffey acknowledges that in the two decades after *Silent Spring* appeared it "has often been cited as perhaps the most influential single factor in creating public con-cern about the future of the world's ecology. It was Rachel Carson, many people agree, who initiated the modern environmental movement." So the book's influence, its raising of public aware-ness, has been tremendous, perhaps more widespread than that of any other single piece of writing about the American environ-ment, including *Walden*. Yet the punchline, as Boffey's subtitle suggests, is that "environmentalists and pesticide advocates alike

now believe that 'Silent Spring' . . . has on balance had only limited influence in the area of its chief concern – pesticides, which
include insecticides, herbicides, and other chemical pest killers"
(C1). If *Silent Spring* can achieve only "limited influence," then
what influence are such complex and obliquely ideological (or
even anti-ideological) works as *Pilgrim at Tinker Creek* and *Desert
Solitaire* likely to exert upon the general public? What are the
implications of Carson's phrase "sufficiently aware" in light of the
news that her own book, despite causing an explosion of public
awareness, has only affected the kinds of pesticides used in our
country, not the overall volume of chemicals still released into our
environment?

Despite the difficulty of creating public awareness which will
result in practical reforms of our society's environmental behavior,
writers from Ralph Nader to Annette Kolodny have worked under
the assumption that raising consciousness will do some good – perhaps that's the most that writers can hope to achieve. Roderick
Nash has written that Ralph Nader's "principal tactic in every
instance is to alert and arouse the citizenry who, through pressure
on their government, can force reforms on even the most powerful
organizations" (276–77), yet Nader's 1970 article "The Force of
Public Awareness" (in Nash's collection *The American Environment*)
seems more desirous of such "force" than convinced of its reality.
In other words, even our nation's most famous consumer advocate, who bases his work on the premise that awareness leads to
action, implies that this causal scheme is flawed because the public
has only limited access to the corridors of power and also, even
more importantly, because most people, including people of acute
consciousness, have yet to take to heart the idea that "those who
believe deeply in a humane ecology must act in accordance with
their beliefs" (283).

Other consciousness-raisers work in the humbler domain of
literary criticism, where "direct action" might mean simply thinking about literature in a new way. Cheryll Burgess, in an important 1991 paper called "Ecocriticism: The Greening of Literary
Studies" (a sequel to her 1989 talk "Toward an Ecological Literary
Criticism"), refers to Annette Kolodny's effort in *The Lay of the
Land* (1975) to detect "environmentally harmful patterns in litera-

ture [in order to] bring these patterns to public attention so that they can be rooted out and replaced with affirmative ones" (7). Here, too, there is the unexamined assumption that a problem of some kind that receives public attention is likely to be corrected. Perhaps we need this assumption because it allows us to hope that our work as teachers and writers will have a material effect in preserving the world, that we're doing more than mouthing syllables into the void. Burgess's argument, a compelling one for environmentally concerned academics, even if they are uneasy with the idea of "advocacy teaching/scholarship," begins with the idea that "Many of us [find that our] temperaments and talents have deposited us in English departments and, as environmental problems mount, we are now wondering how we can contribute to environmental health from within our capacity as professors of literature" (2). The number of "green" critics is likely to increase dramatically in the coming years in response not only to the unabating urgency of our environmental crisis, but to eloquent calls to action within the scholarly community, such as Glen A. Love's 1990 article "Revaluing Nature: Toward an Ecological Criticism," which minces no words in proclaiming, "The most important function of literature today is to redirect human consciousness to a full consideration of its place in a threatened world" (213).

Still, I have reservations—about both the enterprise of "ecocriticism" and its potential efficacy. In our role as teachers, we do have a captive audience, but even if we feel comfortable in the role of environmental indoctrinator, we'll likely find that our students are woefully inattentive. I think we would be better off—on more solid ethical ground and in richer pedagogical territory—if we took our cue from some of the writers I have considered in this book, aiming not to stimulate "the right thoughts of the righteous" (to borrow an old phrase of Cotton Mather's), but to provoke thoughts, period. Any thoughts. Perhaps the best we can hope for is, like Barry Lopez, to "create an environment in which thinking and reaction and wonder and awe and speculation can take place" (O'Connell, 16). And we can hope, with no more guarantee than the writers themselves ever get, that when our students' and readers' thoughts settle, their actions will follow suit, and the earth will be a little bit more secure.

Fences: Making Contact

Growing up in Oregon, I spent much of my youth on the run, literally. Often I ran twice, even three times a day. The hilly, winding, wooded streets of Eugene are still clear in my memory, although I haven't lived there for more than a decade. I remember the asphalt grids and the curves of terrain with pleasing detail. As I think back on my years of running there, though, I believe I was more of a passerby than an appreciative observer of the place. Running was a form of insulation, a self-imposed dreamstate, the rapid motion (usually sub-six-minute pace per mile) and hyperventilation combining to blind me to my surroundings. Caught up in internal dramas—high school projects, upcoming cross-country races—I passed through Eugene without realizing what it meant to be there. Pelting rain was merely an athletic obstacle, a way to become tougher. A hissing, menacing possum, surprised on a street during a midnight run, was a momentary horror, hardly meriting afterthought.

I remember my years as a runner in Eugene while biking to work in San Marcos. It is 1991, yet my bike still has a 1978 Eugene registration sticker. What is it, I wonder, that enables us to move beyond passivity and inattentiveness to participate deeply in the life of a place, to notice and care about what we perceive? What compels us to do so? Even now my attention is erratic. Meetings, errands, classes, grading, projects, trips, and a wearying assortment of household tasks tunnel my vision. I jump on my old bike and pedal as fast as I can, hugging the edges of the shoulderless roads to avoid pickups and hot rods, panting as I strain to climb the short but brutal hills on the way to the university. And I hardly notice what I pass, except on those rare, scheduleless days when I barely pedal, talking to myself about the distant hills, the scrubby bushes and moss-distorted trees, and the dead animals—snakes, raccoons, armadillos—on the road. But does such talking make experience real? Is this what Annie Dillard means when she says, "Seeing is of course very much a matter of verbalization"?

Much of our environmental literature is, I believe, a kind of private murmuring in pursuit of the intensification and verification of experience, an effort to sort out reality from fantasy. Jimmy

Santiago Baca demonstrates this process brilliantly in his recent *Black Mesa Poems* (1989), particularly in a piece called "What's Real and What's Not":

> . . . Following week
> Bob and I go camping.
> (Confident of his work, and proud,
> he wants to try Doris,
> as he calls his van, on steep mountain terrain.)
>
> My singleness glimmers bright,
> and my first time from home in months
> makes the land glow, the sky bluer,
> and the asphalt road
> winding to the foothills
> ignites each nerve into a sacred torch.
>
> An ex-vet Nam grunt,
> instead of going back to New York,
> Bob became a back-packing
> stick-handed hillman,
> herding goat flocks in Placitas,
> with ram-wool beard waist long,
> he roamed gopher-warted *arroyos*,
> up snake-burrowed coyote trails,
> healing himself in shady cedar groves
> and yucca patches.
>
> We snuggle in our sleeping bags,
> look up at stars,
> and want our lives to be simple
> flames of natural blue gas
> rising from ground hills,
> plentiful, innocent
> from the bowels of earth.
> From his bag, Bob stares into the dark sky,
> atop Sandia Crest, at radio transmission poles
> blink red lights of flying mortar. . . . (54–55)

Here it is not only the direct and almost-solitary contact with primitive nature that confirms the poet's sense of what's real, but also the delayed process of articulating the experience and, perhaps most importantly, the stark contrast between his own facile innocence and his companion's continued struggle to differentiate between reality and unreality, between the blinking red lights on a hillside radio tower and wartime mortar flashes. With words come clarity and firmness, a retrospective awareness. When the words are uttered at the moment of experience, the awareness is immediate. The poet's craft enables him to control and encapsulate experience, to represent what Ferdinand de Saussure calls the "vague, uncharted nebula" of thought in a few terse lines: "We enter city limits, / and the torch my body is / dims to old darkness again" (56).

But opinions about the propriety of detached, aestheticized apprehensions of the world are divided. Hildegard Binder Johnson suggested in 1979 that "Landscape per se does not exist; it is amorphous—an indeterminate area of the earth's surface and a chaos of details incomprehensible to the perceptual system. A landscape requires selective viewing and a frame" (27). Her notion is much like Saussure's theory of language—his belief that without language, thought would be structureless. It is difficult to contradict this argument, for we all realize that most human minds crave order and focus, sometimes even becoming exaggeratedly selective in pursuit of these ends. However, recent analysts of nature writing and environmental experience have tried to point out the severe limitations of rigid, inherited modes of framing and ordering perception.

Paul T. Bryant, in a 1990 lecture entitled "Nature as Picture/ Nature as Milieu," traces the historical roots of the picturesque in American literature and argues, "By rendering a scene static and stepping back from it to see it objectively, we have become separated from it" (6); however, Bryant observes that in "the most informed nature writing" the authors "put themselves into the picture and the picture becomes a scene, with action and change and interplay of humans with nature" (17). Along these same lines, John Daniel criticizes both the "cult of utility" and the "tourist seeking scenic beauty," asserting that "Neither view recognizes nature as a living system of which our human lives are part, on which our lives and all lives depend, and which places strict limits upon us even as it sustains us" ("The Impoverishment of Sight-seeing," 59). Daniel states that to achieve

> an ecological understanding of the natural world, we as people need to follow the lead of the ecological sciences and learn to live by the principles they discover. We need to heal the disruptions we have caused in the biosphere. But it is just as important, even as we scientifically study the inner workings of nature and the ways we have injured it, that we learn how to experience it again, how to apprehend it in its fullness. As Edward Abbey told us many times, you can't do that in a car, and neither can you do it with just your eyes. It can only happen by taking the time to enter the natural world, to engage it, to not only run our eyes along its surfaces but to place ourselves among its things and weathers—to let it exert, at least for intervals in our lives, the ancient influences that once surrounded and formed us. (60)

These "ancient influences" are what I often seek nowadays, even when I'm out for a morning run in San Marcos or pedaling to work. An abrasive headwind, a sudden, inescapable rainshower, or simply the tightness of muscles straining up and down hills give me a sense of contact with the world. My son Jacinto and I, after several months as tentative newcomers to Texas, have taken to stirring up fire ant nests with sticks, our shoes, even wary fingers, just trying to make contact with the ferocious, venomous ants. This is, of course, hardly an example of the benign "ecological understanding" John Daniel is calling for in "The Impoverishment of Sightseeing." But other times we're less intrusive. We crouch near bushes or holes in the ground until our legs cramp up, waiting for a movement or simply describing to each other the appearance of the place and speculating about its inhabitants. Usually we see no life, or at least nothing dramatic. Sometimes tiny black crickets will scurry away at our arrival, or a bird will burst out of the underbrush and harass us from the safety of a powerline.

I have little to offer Jacinto by way of scientific knowledge; his mother is the scientist in the family. In fact, he is the one who helps me pay attention by slowing us down, by stopping every few steps to inspect or touch something. Rachel Carson's short picture book *The Sense of Wonder* (1956) has taught me to appreciate the value of these informal nature walks with Jacinto. "A child's world is fresh and new and beautiful, full of wonder and excitement," she writes. "It is our misfortune that for most of us that clear-eyed vision, that true instinct for what is beautiful and awe-inspiring is dimmed and even lost before we reach adulthood" (42). Of course, this idealization of childhood wonder is hardly a new way of thinking, but in her brief, fragmentary narratives of excursions along the Maine coast with her four-year-old nephew Roger, Carson actually shows the give-and-take of wonder between child and adult while exploring nature. And John Daniel suggests eloquently that this feeling of wonder, this sensory attunement, can occur for adults, even without the help of a child—what's needed is time, patience, submission to the "ancient influences":

> Enough time under those influences can teach us to use our eyes actively again, as something more than receptacles. They seek a route through trees, across a creek, over a ridge, working in concert with body and mind. They follow the darts and veers of a humming-bird, a lizard skimming across stones, the quick glint of a trout. Things much smaller than El Capitan or the Tetons, things easy to miss, begin to reveal themselves—tiny white flowers of saxifrage, the quarter-sized, web-lined shaft of a tarantula's den, a six-inch screech owl flicking limb to limb in the dusk. (60)

Thus nature ceases to be mere "picture," and becomes, to use Paul Bryant's term, "milieu." This change within the individual's consciousness may at some point in the future—if enough individuals allow themselves to undergo it—have ecological ramifications, and inspire us to halt environmentally destructive practices. However, it is equally significant that such a change signals a new richness and subtlety in the mental life of an individual person, for this new attentiveness, even if achieved with the help of a child or with a group of fellow seekers, is a solitary phenomenon. Inspiration may come from the "environmental movement," and its models may be compelling narratives like Daniel's which attract imitation, but a new way of experiencing the world cannot be realized if role models and ulterior motives (however worthwhile) are too prominently in mind. New eyes need privacy and ingenuousness.

* * *

Everywhere I look in Texas I seem to confront fences. From my study window, I see a five-foot fence made of weathered red and gray boards, interlaced so tightly that it hides several houses from the rest of the neighborhood. The homes in Castle Forest have no moats, but nearly every yard on our block is protected by some kind of fence. The house we're renting seems naked by comparison, the low, chain-link fence hardly concealing the child's fort and inflatable swimming pool in the backyard. Beyond the metal fence we can look directly at the Texas Hill Country: gradual slopes, intricate live oaks, prickly pears and scrawny desert grasses, and tawny masses of grazing cows which emerge suddenly from the nearby woods, then melt back into the woods hours later, as if on cue. The images are captivating, and Jacinto and I sit for hours talking, watching the fields, daydreaming. But the fence, transparent as it is, is still there. For me it represents a psychological separation from what's on the other side, even if I can see everything. I often think about putting a chair next to the fence and jumping over, with Jacinto in my arms, to explore the vast ranchland on the other side, but something—my superego or occasional rifle blasts in the distance—keeps me from doing this. Abbey's great culprit, the entity he singled out as the arch-obstacle to perception and appreciation of the world, was the automobile. Mine is the fence. I think of cars as being fences, too—and bicycles, even rapid walking.

I wonder if books themselves are fences, or fence destroyers. I wonder what Abbey would think about my use of literature as a lens through which to view the natural world. Does the text come between me and the world, preventing a more direct and somehow *better* form of contact? If Abbey saw me at my desk with one of his books, would he rant, "[Y]ou've got to get out of the goddamned contraption and walk, better yet crawl, on hands and knees, over sandstone and through the thornbush and cactus. When traces of blood begin to mark your trail you'll see something, maybe" (*Desert Solitaire*, xii)? Or would he applaud, as he seems to in *The Journey Home* (1977)? "Stay out of there," he exhorts in "The Great American Desert." "Don't go. Stay home and read a good book, this one for example. The Great American

Desert is an awful place" (13). Is nature for one type of person, literature for another?

I find it intriguing to consider whether the direct encounter with nature—even the most glancing encounter—is aided or obstructed by the experiences that environmental literature affords. Obviously, if our eyes are glued to a page of text, we can't see the world very well. But we can, if we're sitting outside, hear it, smell it, touch it. What if we peer over the top of the page? What if we read a book, and *then* go out into the world to experience it for ourselves, to check the reality of our lives against the suppositions of the writer? It seems absurd to assume that any of our major nature writers, even those famed for exotic adventures, are wholly free of "cultural baggage," of inherited social and aesthetic "frames."

When I was in college and just beginning my plunge into literary studies, I regarded literature as an indoor phenomenon that required an indoor—that is, "closed off"—state of mind for proper consumption. I remember the pleasure of sitting in the stale vaults of the old Green Library at Stanford, conscious to the point of distraction of the feeling of enclosure and the artificiality of the book in my hands. I have trouble explaining why I used to jar open the large, semi-opaque windows near the carrels, revealing a strip of stunning green lawn and allowing eucalyptus smells and the laughter of frisbee players to mingle with the mustiness of the old library; if absolute enclosure had been my desire, I could have worked in the windowless underground catacombs. This unwillingness to abandon the vigor of the outdoors now seems a healthy anomaly in my college behavior.

During college breaks it was my impulse to take irrelevant literature with me to the mountains when I returned home to Oregon. Rather than augmenting or intensifying immediate, physical experience, these books normally served as distractions—fences. I can recall, for example, one particular morning in the Three Sisters Wilderness Area when I woke up before any of my friends. There must have been ten of us, camped near the top of a minor cliff, a hundred yards from an obscure trail. To the east we had a clear view of the solid white, almost featureless Middle Sister. It was freezing cold when I crawled out of the small tent, almost too cold for sitting still. Our campsite was still shaded from the rising sun by the mountain itself. I can remember the clarity of the blue June sky, the openness of the chasm nearby, the initial shadowy whiteness of the western flank of the Middle Sister. But the other details of the experience now escape my memory, and not only because more than a decade has passed since the trip. In fact, the sensations I've just described are probably clearer to me now than they were at the time. I actually missed – ignored – the initial phase of the sunrise, although I sat atop the cliff in full view of it as it happened. Reading. And I recall very clearly what I was reading – Proust's *Swann's Way*, a book by a man who spent much of his time in a darkened, cork-lined room! What was the point, I now wonder, of bringing a book like that to the mountains? Sitting here, starved for mountains among the arroyos and gentle mesas of Central Texas, I have difficulty believing how I took for granted and sought to escape the shimmering, wholesome, wild country of the Oregon mountains.

I would place my cliffside reading of Proust at one extreme, and Ann Ronald's rationale in designing her book *Words for the Wild: The Sierra Club Trailside Reader* (1987) at the other. Ronald explains:

> This is what nature writing, to my way of thinking, is all about. *Words for the Wild* take me places I might not otherwise visit, or they introduce me to new friends. Sometimes they join me with old ones, or they show me new perspectives of things I've seen a dozen times. On occasion, they even send me in directions I would not have dared before, challenging me to attempt the inconceivable or persuading me to try the impossible. More often, though, they just tantalize my brain. But whatever they do, they suggest new ways of thinking about and responding to the world in which I live. (xvi–xvii)

The very idea of a "trailside reader" – indeed, a backpack-sized anthology sanctioned by the Sierra Club – implies the potential compatibility of literature and primary experience in the natural world. Ronald makes it clear that the selections in her book ought to inspire responses to the world, not to the texts alone. Although my own initial literary studies occurred indoors, or in indoorlike oblivion of my wilderness surroundings, and although my own early encounters with nature writing were also physically removed from nature, I now believe that books can either separate you from the world and from your own life or deepen your engagement with reality.

At the recent North American Interdisciplinary Wilderness Conference in Utah, I commented on Abbey's statement in *Desert Solitaire* that "A man could be a lover and defender of wilderness without ever in his lifetime leaving the boundaries of asphalt, powerlines, and right-angled surfaces" (148–49). I said, "The great contribution of Abbey's work to our understanding of the wilderness is that he shows us how to enjoy the *existence* of such regions as Utah's canyon lands even in absentia – indeed, he cautions us that our own attraction to such places can result in their destruction." Could it be, I asked, that wilderness literature functions as a surrogate for actual wilderness experience? Hackles seemed to rise in the audience. I myself would not want to spend a lifetime surrounded by asphalt and powerlines, never making contact with the pre-urban world. But I believe my interpretation of Abbey's "disinvitation" is valid in two important respects. First, we must realize that our true wildernesses are becoming saturated with human use – the Three Sisters Wilderness Area, for instance, which seemed both remote and rustic when I was growing up in Eugene in the '60s and '70s, has recently suffered from overuse and the Forest Service is now restricting access during the peak season. And secondly, I believe that a lot of nature writing, with its impressive analysis and demonstration of various "awakening" strategies, helps to stoke our appreciation of daily encounters with what Don Scheese calls "humble landscapes" ("Why Nature Writing"). Of course we must do what we can to preserve and recover the world's genuine wildernesses – Prince William Sound, Lake Baikal, and even the Three Sisters. Still, it is worth remembering Eiseley's remark that "in any city there are true wildernesses where a man can be alone" ("Judgment," 165), his point being, I think, that the psychological effects of wilderness are more contingent upon point of view than geographical location. Nature writing, then, can be a fence – an obstacle, an end in itself – or it can be a pathway to more intense awareness of ourselves and our environment. Like the plane which guides my attention to the distant circling of the hawks, nature writing itself soon leaves my field of view, but its mood and perspective linger, and I see hawks, spiders, the delicate new leaves on nearby trees.

Facts and Aesthetics

In my introduction, I referred briefly to the empirical research in environmental psychology which Stephen and Rachel Kaplan, among others, have pioneered in the past few decades with the help of the time-tested theories of William James. Their work concentrates on recording and explaining, by way of "carefully designed studies," how people respond to specific environmental categories. They begin their most recent book, *The Experience of Nature: A Psychological Perspective* (1989), by defining their subject matter and their approach: "This book is about the natural environment, about people, and about the relationship between them. It is about things many have known but few have tried to study empirically. It is about things for which there is only a limited vocabulary" (2). My subject in this book is very much the same, but my methodology is wholly different. Moreover, although the "vocabularies" of my five central authors intersect in essential ways, their voices and perspectives remain strikingly individual. To believe that the study of nature and the human mind is restricted to a "limited vocabulary" would seem to cancel the possibility of rich literary treatments of the subject. And I hope I have at least managed to disprove this.

Still, much of the work empirical environmental psychologists have done and are now doing pertains to environmental literature. My own study, with its intermittent use of the Jamesian ("probable and definite") paradigm, attempts to demonstrate this application, but there are still other issues to explore. Why, for instance, do some landscapes have a wholesome or healing effect on the mind and others not? How does nature writing itself bear out or refute the psychologists' findings with regard to environmental preferences? And, perhaps most importantly, how does nature writing (and by extension the environmentally conscious teaching of literature) influence people's attitudes and behavior? Is there any discernible and empirically verifiable influence? It would also be interesting to examine cultural differences in environmental attitudes by looking at various national literatures; for instance, a friend recently recommended such Latin American novels as José Maria Arguedas's *Los Rios Profundos* (*Deep Rivers*), Miguel Asturias's *Hombres de Maiz* (*Men of Maize*), and Mario Vargas-Llosa's *El Hablador* (*The Storyteller*). These are a few topics for future study.

John Hildebidle, in his study of Thoreau as a natural historian, sums up Thoreau's approach to nature as follows:

> Thoreau, however interested he was in naturalism, was by no absolute standard a scientist, nor was he, by choice, simply a natural historian. However, the appropriate distinction between Thoreau and the tradition of amateur naturalism is not to be made on the basis of professionalism or even of accuracy. The true naturalist, to put it simply for the moment, is interested in explaining the marvelous; Thoreau's concern is to make the ordinary marvelous. (*Thoreau*, 25)

Though it may be presumptuous to associate my own approach to nature writing with Thoreau's approach to nature itself, I would say that my own hope in this study is to demonstrate what I consider to be one of the marvelous features of American nature writing, its exploration of the very topic identified in the Kaplans' more prosaic and systematic study: the point of contact between the human mind and the natural world. Yet unlike the Kaplans, who adhere—in accordance with the standards of their discipline—to the use of precise categories of both environmental stimuli and human responses, my own approach to environmental psychology, and that of the authors I have examined, has been more speculative and intuitive than scientific.

In *Encounters with the Archdruid* (1971), John McPhee notes:

> [David] Brower is a collector of rocks. Behind his desk in his office in San Francisco were rocks he had collected from all over, and notably from the canyons of the Colorado—Glen Canyon, Grand Canyon. In most cases, he did not know what these rocks were, nor did he appear to care. He had taken them for their beauty alone. (54–55)

In this study I have not "collected" such texts as Thoreau's Journal, *Pilgrim at Tinker Creek*, *The Monkey Wrench Gang*, "The Long-Legged House," and *Arctic Dreams* "for their beauty alone." But my initial attraction to all of these works was primarily aesthetic, as it has been to nature writing in general. John Tallmadge has written, "Today, with writers like Barry Lopez, Annie Dillard, and Robert Finch at work, nature writing is arguably the most exciting realm of American literature" ("Review," 64), and I heartily agree. Many other contemporary nature writers could easily fit into the patterns I have tried to illustrate in this book, but I have limited my scope to five who demonstrated with special vigor and clarity the fundamental dialectic of correspondence/otherness which found its earliest sustained consideration in Thoreau's Journal. The other four writers, to my eye, fall into rather distinct groups—Dillard and Abbey emphasizing disjunction or otherness, and Berry and Lopez emphasizing various forms of closeness or correspondence.

But as Tallmadge says, nature writing is an extraordinarily vibrant field today, and there are many important writers whose work invites a variety of critical approaches, including close readings and analyses of historical context. Scholars such as Peter A. Fritzell and W. Ross Winterowd have produced important book-length studies of nature writing and literary nonfiction lately. Other volumes, such as Chris Anderson's collection *Literary Non-fiction: Theory, Criticism, Pedagogy* (1989), offer brief studies of individual authors like Annie Dillard and Loren Eiseley. My interest in the psychological aspects of nature writing has led me lately to ponder the ideas of nostalgia, journeying, and homecoming that seem pervasive in the work of current writers, such as Peter Matthiessen, Edward Hoagland, John Nichols, and Rick Bass. In 1987, Scott Russell Sanders, in his article "Speaking a Word for Nature," deplored the lack of environmental consciousness in recent American fiction. "That a deep awareness of nature has been largely excluded from 'mainstream' fiction," he suggests, "is a measure of the narrowing and trivialization of that fashionable current. It is also, of course, and more dangerously, a measure of a shared blindness in the culture at large" (658). But perhaps, thanks to proddings like this, we're in for a surge of nature-oriented fiction, too, as in the case of the four writers I just mentioned. The audience for fiction is also changing, as I learned when I traveled to Houston in 1991 to hear Matthiessen read at the Museum of Fine Arts. Expecting the author of esoteric travel narratives and outdoor novels such as *Far Tortuga* and *Killing Mister Watson* to draw a small crowd, a friend and I lingered over dinner. When we showed up at the museum, the large auditorium was filled to capacity and dozens of latecomers were milling around outside. I didn't know whether to feel disappointed or delighted. At the time I was mostly disappointed, but now, having considered the implications of this overflowing crowd, my mood has changed.

Treetops Full of Birds

" . . . wingbeats like the breathing of an animal. A hoarse, 'chuffing' sound," I tell my class, "made by dozens of pairs of tiny wings, beating in strict, natural unison." We are discussing Imagist poetry. Normally more than a hundred students fill the lecture hall, legs lazily outstretched, heads propped up by any means available. Several speak and laugh unashamedly near the back of the room. "These people are nonmajors," I say to myself. "If only we didn't meet right after lunch." I focus on the open eyes directly in front of me—farther back in the room, I notice, another head has drooped.

"Why do we bother reading Imagist poetry?" I ask. "Does it offer a vicarious experience of the world which somehow supersedes or nullifies our own or does it serve as a model, a guide, for our process of perception and articulation?" The students can hardly bear to listen. Outside it is virtually spring. Half our class is missing, probably among the clusters of students in the Quad, visible from the windows of the classroom, gathering to laugh and wave and raise their faces to the sun. "Intensity of experience is a virtue in itself, but sometimes it can be achieved only when the mind has been prepared to pay attention. We read William Carlos Williams's lines, 'So much depends / Upon / A red wheel / Barrow / Glazed with rain / Water / Beside the white / Chickens,' and almost without knowing it our own minds become more caught up in the crisp details of our surroundings, and in the interdependence of these details, the coherence of the scene. With Ezra Pound's lines 'The apparition of these faces in the crowd; / Petals on a wet, black bough' in our heads, we view each situation with potentially figurative intensity." Faces and flower petals—the whirring of tiny wings and the breath of life itself.

* * *

We were on the "ship" when it happened. I sat leaning against a wooden post on this apparatus of logs and bars and child-sized metal passageways, with Jacinto in orbit around me, occasionally returning from a fantasy involving a combination of Batman and Ninja Turtle characters to make sure I was paying attention. But my attention is never more than intermittent. Daydreams cloud my involvement in Jacinto's games—in my head I prepare lectures, plan dinner, worry about money. When several other small children arrived and began playing separately nearby, Jacinto drifted away from me to watch.

I was staring through a group of thin, pale-barked trees when a child leaped from one of the ship's planks and landed, with an abrupt, rasping sound, in the gravel below. There was a burst of air overhead. I noticed a matrix of frantic, dark dots moving toward me from the trees I had been staring through, but in an instant they were gone. I managed to hear their wings "breathe" as they passed over me, though. And when I looked up at the treetops, they were, miraculously, full of birds again.

Identification is beyond me. I just don't care enough about names, taxonomies. This is my wife Analinda's domain as a science teacher, but she was not there to give these birds a name or category. I forced myself to see the birds' features: black wings, gray bodies, tufts of feathers atop their heads. They were bigger than sparrows and smaller than robins. When startled again by a child's shriek, they exploded into the air with fishlike togetherness, boomeranging several minutes later back to their original perches, where they sat like oversized flower buds. The trees, willows of some sort, did not yet have new leaves.

As we walked home from the Crockett School playground along streets with curbs but no sidewalks, I held Jacinto's hand and explained to him that the treetops were full of birds. Distracted by this idea which required his immediate investigation, he tripped, skinned his knee on the curb he had been walking on, and came perilously close to a fire ant mound. With a flash of parental genius, I poked the sifted lump of earth with my foot, and sure enough the tiny ants swarmed onto the surface like chocolate syrup, furious and yet almost benign when viewed from a foot away. Jacinto forgot about both his hurt knee and the marvelous birds in the trees. One awareness replaced another. As we continued our walk home, we paused to provoke more fire ants, to frighten potato bugs into balls ("I want to touch one of those caterpillars," Jacinto said, showing he'd inherited my naming accuracy), and to speculate about the aims of a large calico cat which was pawing intently at a patch of weeds. "Hey, fat cat," shouted my companion. When I started to explain about cats and mice, Jacinto looked off into the distance, beyond Castle Forest to the undeveloped Hill Country. Dark shapes, barely visible, circled miles away. "I wish we could see wolves," he said.

WORKS CITED

Abbey, Edward. *Abbey's Road.* New York: Dutton, 1979.

———. *Desert Solitaire: A Season in the Wilderness.* New York: Ballantine, 1968.

———. "On the Need for a Wilderness to Get Lost In." *New York Times.* August 28, 1972.

———. "The Great American Desert." *The Journey Home: Some Words in Defense of the American West.* New York: Dutton, 1977.

———. *The Monkey Wrench Gang.* New York: Avon, 1975.

Anderson, Chris, ed. *Literary Nonfiction: Theory, Criticism, Pedagogy.* Carbondale and Edwardsville: Southern Illinois University Press, 1989.

Anhorn, Judy Schaaf. "Thoreau in the Maine Woods: A Naturalist's Education." (Paper presented at the Society for Literature and Science Conference.) Ann Arbor, Mich: September 24, 1989.

Anscombe, G. E. M. "The First Person." In *Mind and Language.* Ed. Samuel Guttenplan, 45–65. Oxford: Clarendon, 1975.

Arguedas, José Maria. *Deep Rivers.* Trans. Frances H. Barraclough. Austin: University of Texas Press, 1978.

Asturias, Miguel. *Men of Maize.* Trans. Gerald Martin. New York: Routledge Chapman & Hall, 1988.

Aton, James Martin. "An Interview with Barry Lopez." *Western American Literature* 21 (May 1986): 3–17.

———. " 'Sons and Daughters of Thoreau': The Spiritual Quest in Three Contemporary Nature Writers." Ph.D. Diss. Athens: Ohio University, 1981.

Baca, Jimmy Santiago. *Black Mesa Poems.* New York: New Directions, 1989.

Barrio, Raymond. *The Plum Plum Pickers.* (1969) Binghamton, N.Y.: Bilingual Press, 1984.

Berry, Wendell. "A Country of Edges" and "The Making of a Marginal Farm." *Recollected Essays 1965–1980.* San Francisco: North Point Press, 1981.

———. "A Few Words in Favor of Edward Abbey." (1985) *What Are People For?* San Francisco: North Point Press, 1990.

———. "Getting Along with Nature." *Home Economics.* San Francisco: North Point Press, 1987.

———. "The Long-Legged House." *The Long-Legged House.* New York: Audubon/Ballantine, 1969.

———. *The Memory of Old Jack.* New York: Harcourt Brace Jovanovich, 1974.

_____. "Notes from an Absence and a Return." *A Continuous Harmony: Essays Cultural and Agricultural*. New York: Harcourt Brace Jovanovich, 1972.

_____. *The Unsettling of America: Culture & Agriculture*. New York: Avon, 1977.

Bloom, Harold. "Emerson: The Glory and Sorrows of American Romanticism." In *Romanticism: Vistas, Instances, Continuities*. Ed. David Thorburn and Geoffrey Hartman, 155–73. Ithaca and London: Cornell University Press, 1973.

Boffey, Philip M. "20 Years After 'Silent Spring': Still a Troubled Landscape." *New York Times*. 25 May 1982.

Bonetti, Kay. "An Interview with Barry Lopez." *The Missouri Review* 11 No. 3 (1988): 57–77.

Bryant, Paul T. "Echoes, Allusions, and 'Reality' in *Hayduke Lives!*." *Western American Literature* 25 (February 1991): 311–21.

_____. "Nature as Picture/Nature as Milieu." (Paper presented at the annual meeting of the College English Association.) Buffalo, N.Y.: April 1990.

Buell, Lawrence. *Literary Transcendentalism*. Ithaca: Cornell University Press, 1973.

Burgess, Cheryll. "Ecocriticism: The Greening of Literary Studies." (Paper presented at the Third North American Interdisciplinary Wilderness Conference.) Ogden, Utah. February 7–9, 1991.

_____. "Toward an Ecological Literary Criticism." (Paper presented at the annual meeting of the Western American Literature Association.) Coeur d'Alene, Idaho. October 11–14, 1989.

Caldwell, Patricia. "Why Our First Poet Was a Woman: Bradstreet and the Birth of an American Poetic Voice." In *Prospects: An Annual of American Cultural Studies*. Ed. Jack Salzman. 13 (1988): 1–35.

Cameron, Sharon. *Writing Nature: Henry Thoreau's Journal*. Oxford and New York: Oxford University Press, 1985.

Carruth, Hayden. "Attractions and Dangers of Nostalgia." *The Virginia Quarterly Review* 50 (Autumn 1974): 637–40.

Carson, Rachel. *Silent Spring*. (1962) Boston: Houghton Mifflin, 1987.

_____. *The Sense of Wonder*. New York: Harper & Row, 1956.

Catton, William R. "The Quest for Uncertainty." *Humanscape: Environments for People*. (1978) Ed. Stephen Kaplan and Rachel Kaplan, 112–15. Ann Arbor, Mich.: Ulrich's, 1982.

Channing, William Ellery. *Thoreau, the Poet-Naturalist*. Ed. F. B. Sanborn. Boston: Charles E. Goodspeed, 1902.

Clark, Suzanne. "Annie Dillard: The Woman in Nature and the Subject of Nonfiction." In *Literary Nonfiction: Theory, Criticism, Pedagogy.* Ed. Chris Anderson. Carbondale and Edwardsville: Southern Illinois University Press, 1989.

Coleridge, Samuel Taylor. *The Friend.* Ed. Barbara E. Rooke. Princeton, New Jersey: Princeton University Press, 1969. (Quoted in Rossi, William John [see below].)

Daniel, John. "The Impoverishment of Sightseeing." *Wilderness* 54 (Fall 1990): 56–60.

Deemer, Charles. "Up the Creek." *The New Leader,* 18–20. 24 June 1974.

Dillard, Annie. *An American Childhood.* New York: Harper & Row, 1987.

———. *Holy the Firm.* New York: Harper & Row, 1977.

———. *Living by Fiction.* New York: Harper & Row, 1982.

———. "Living Like Weasels" and "Total Eclipse." *Teaching a Stone to Talk.* New York: Harper & Row,1982.

———. "Notebook," *Antaeus* 61 (Autumn 1988): 84–87.

———. *Pilgrim at Tinker Creek.* (1974) New York: Harper & Row, 1988.

———. "To Fashion a Text." In *Inventing the Truth: The Art and Craft of Memoir.* Ed. William Zinsser, 53–76. Boston: Houghton Mifflin, 1987.

———. "Why I Live Where I Live." *Esquire,* March 1984, 90–92.

———. *The Writing Life.* New York: Harper & Row, 1989.

Dunn, Robert Paul. "The Artist as Nun: Theme, Tone and Vision in the Writings of Annie Dillard." *Studia Mystica* 1 (1978): 17–31.

Eiseley, Loren. *All the Strange Hours: The Excavation of a Life.* New York: Scribner's, 1975.

———. "The Enchanted Glass." *The American Scholar* 26 (Autumn 1957): 478–92.

———. "The Judgment of the Birds." *The Immense Journey.* New York: Random House, 1957.

———. "Walden: Thoreau's Unfinished Business." *The Star Thrower.* New York: Harcourt Brace Jovanovich, 1978.

Elder, John. *Imagining the Earth: Poetry and the Vision of Nature.* Urbana and Chicago: University of Illinois Press, 1985.

———. "John Muir and the Literature of Wilderness." *The Massachusetts Review* 22 (Summer 1981): 375–86.

Emerson, Ralph Waldo. "Biographical Sketch." In Thoreau, Henry D. *Excursions,* 7–33. Boston: Ticknor and Fields, 1863.

———. *Journals.* Quoted in Hotson, Clarence Paul. "Emerson and the Doctrine of Correspondence." *The New-Church Review* (January 1929): 47–59.

_____. *Nature.* In *The Writings of Ralph Waldo Emerson.* Ed. Brooks Atkinson. (1836) New York: Random House, 1940.

Finch, Robert. "North Beach Journal." *Outlands: Journeys to the Outer Edges of Cape Cod.* Boston: Godine, 1986.

Franklin, Phyllis, ed. *MLA Newsletter.* Winter 1990.

Fritzell, Peter A. *Nature Writing and America: Essays upon a Cultural Type.* Ames: Iowa State University Press, 1990.

Freud, Sigmund. "The Uncanny." *Studies in Parapsychology.* (1919) New York: Macmillan, 1963.

Gonzalez, Ray. "Landscapes of the Interior: The Literature of Hope. An Interview with Barry Lopez." *The Bloomsbury Review* (January/February 1990), 8ff.

Gunn, Giles. *The Interpretation of Otherness: Literature, Religion, and the American Imagination.* New York: Oxford University Press, 1979.

Harrison, Jim. Review of *The Monkey Wrench Gang. New York Times Book Review.* 14 November 1976.

Hartman, Geoffrey H. "The Romance of Nature and the Negative Way." In *Romanticism and Consciousness: Essays in Criticism.* Ed. Harold Bloom. New York: Norton, 1970.

Hawkes, John. Remarks during " 'Nothing but Darkness and Talk?': Writers' Symposium on Traditional Values and Iconoclastic Fiction" at Unspeakable Practices: A Three-day Celebration of Iconoclastic American Fiction. Brown University: Providence, Rhode Island. 4–6 April 1988.

Hepworth, James. "The Poetry Center Interview." In *Resist Much, Obey Little: Some Notes on Edward Abbey.* Ed. James Hepworth and Gregory McNamee, 33–42. Salt Lake City: Dream Garden Press, 1985.

Hildebidle, John. *Thoreau: A Naturalist's Liberty.* Cambridge: Harvard University Press, 1983.

Hoagland, Edward. "From the Land Where Polar Bears Fly." *New York Times Book Review.* 16 February 1986.

Hotson, Clarence Paul. "Emerson and the Doctrine of Correspondence." *The New-Church Review* (January 1929): 47–59.

Howarth, William. *The Book of Concord: Thoreau's Life as a Writer.* New York: Viking, 1982.

Humboldt, Alexander von. *Ansichten der Natur.* (1808, 1826, 1849) Nördlingen: Greno, 1986.

James, William. *Psychology: Briefer Course.* (1892) Cambridge and London: Harvard University Press, 1984.

_____. *Varieties of Religious Experience.* (1902) New York: Macmillan, 1961.

Johnson, Hildegard Binder. "The Framed Landscape." *Landscape* 23, No. 2 (1979): 26–32.

Kakutani, Michiko. Review of *Arctic Dreams*. *New York Times Book Review*. 12 February 1986.

Kaplan, Rachel, and Stephen Kaplan. *The Experience of Nature: A Psychological Perspective*. New York: Cambridge University Press, 1989.

Kaplan, Stephen. "Perception of an Uncertain Environment." In *Humanscape: Environments for People*. (1978) Ed. Stephen Kaplan and Rachel Kaplan. Ann Arbor, Mich.: Ulrich's, 1982.

Keefer, Bob. "Lopez's Book on Arctic is Best in America." *The Eugene Register-Guard*. 19 November 1986.

Keller, Joseph. "The Function of Paradox in Mystical Discourse." *Studia Mystica* 6 (Fall 1983): 3–19.

Landow, George P. *Elegant Jeremiahs: The Sage from Carlyle to Mailer*. Ithaca: Cornell University Press, 1986.

Lavery, David L. "Noticer: The Visionary Art of Annie Dillard." *The Massachusetts Review* 21 (Summer 1980): 255–70.

Lichtenstein, Grace. "Edward Abbey: Voice of Southwest Wilds." *New York Times*. January 20, 1976.

Lopez, Barry. *Arctic Dreams: Imagination and Desire in a Northern Landscape*. New York: Bantam, 1986.

———. *Crow and Weasel*. San Francisco: North Point Press, 1990.

———. "A Faint Light on the Northern Edge." *The North American Review* (March 1982): 12–21.

———. "Landscape and Narrative." *Crossing Open Ground*. 1984. New York: Scribner's, 1988.

Lopez, Barry, with Charles Wright and Maxine Hong Kingston. "A Chinese Garland." *The North American Review* 273 (September 1988): 38–42.

Love, Glen A. "Revaluing Nature: Toward an Ecological Criticism." *Western American Literature* 25 (November 1990): 201–15.

Lueders, Edward. *Writing Natural History: Dialogues with Authors*. Salt Lake City: University of Utah Press, 1989.

Lyon, Thomas J. *This Incomperable Lande: A Book of American Nature Writing*. Boston: Houghton Mifflin, 1989.

McConahay, Mary Davidson. " 'Into the Bladelike Arms of God:' The Quest for Meaning in Thoreau and Annie Dillard." *Denver Quarterly* 20 (Fall 1985): 103–16.

McFadden-Gerber, Margaret. "The I in Nature." *American Notes & Queries* 16 (September 1977): 13–15.

McPhee, John. *Encounters with the Archdruid*. New York: Farrar, Straus and Giroux, 1971.

Maitland, Sara. " 'Spend It All, Shoot It, Play It, Lose It.' " *New York Times Book Review*. 17 September 1989.

Major, Mike. "Annie Dillard: Pilgrim of the Absolute." *America*. 6 May 1978: 363–64.

Margolis, Kenneth. "Paying Attention: An Interview with Barry Lopez." *Orion Nature Quarterly* 9 (Summer 1990): 50–53.

Marsh, George Perkins. *Man and Nature; Or, Physical Geography as Modified by Human Action*. (1864) Cambridge: Harvard University Press, 1965.

Matthiessen, Peter. *The Snow Leopard*. New York: Bantam, 1978.

Miller, James E., Jr. *Word, Self, Reality: The Rhetoric of Imagination*. New York and Toronto: Dodd, Mead, 1973.

Miller, Perry. *Consciousness in Concord: The Text of Thoreau's Hitherto "Lost Journal" (1840-1841) Together with Notes and a Commentary*. Boston: Houghton Mifflin, 1958.

_____. "Thoreau in the Context of International Romanticism." *The New England Quarterly* 34 (June 1961): 147–59.

Mitchell, Don. "Dancing with Nature." *The Bread Loaf Anthology of Contemporary American Essays*. Ed. Robert Pack and Jay Parini, 188–97. Hanover, New Hampshire and London: University Press of New England, 1989.

Muir, John. "A Near View of the High Sierra" (1894) and "Prayers in Higher Mountain Temples, or A Geologist's Winter Walk" (1918). Reprinted in *Mountaineering Essays*. Ed. Richard F. Fleck, 23–64. Salt Lake City: Gibbs M. Smith, 1984.

_____. *The Yosemite*. (1912) Garden City, NY: Doubleday, 1962.

Nabokov, Vladimir. *Lolita*. (1955) New York: Berkley, 1977.

Nader, Ralph. "The Force of Public Awareness." (1970) In *The American Environment: Readings in the History of Conservation*. Ed. Roderick Nash, 276–83. Reading, Mass.: Addison-Wesley, 1976.

Nash, Roderick, ed. *The American Environment: Readings in the History of Conservation*. Reading, Mass: Addison-Wesley, 1976.

Nelson, Richard K. "The Gifts." *Antaeus* 57 (Autumn 1986): 117–31.

Niebuhr, Reinhold. Introduction. *The Varieties of Religious Experience*. By William James. (1902) New York: Macmillan, 1961.

O'Connell, Nicholas. "Barry Lopez." *At the Field's End: Interviews with 20 Pacific Northwest Writers*. Seattle: Madrona, 1987.

Olney, James. *Metaphors of Self: The Meaning of Autobiography*. Princeton, New Jersey: Princeton University Press, 1972.

Paul, Sherman. "Making the Turn: Rereading Barry Lopez." *Hewing to Experience: Essays and Reviews on Recent American Poetry and Poetics, Nature and Culture.* Iowa City: University of Iowa Press, 1989.

———. *The Shores of America: Thoreau's Inward Exploration.* Urbana: University of Illinois Press, 1958.

Peck, H. Daniel. *Thoreau's Morning Work: Memory and Perception in A Week on the Concord and Merrimack Rivers, the Journal, and Walden.* New Haven, Conn.: Yale University Press, 1990.

Polanyi, Michael. "The Structure of Consciousness." In *Knowing and Being.* Ed. Marjorie Grene. Chicago: University of Chicago Press, 1969.

Polanyi, Michael, and Harry Prosch. *Meaning.* Chicago: University of Chicago Press, 1975.

Powers, Ron. " 'Don't Think of It as Art': Nonfiction and the Inflected Voice." *The Kenyon Review* 11 (Summer 1989): 139–52.

Rahv, Philip. "The Cult of Experience in American Writing." *Image and Idea: Fourteen Essays on Literary Themes.* New York: New Directions, 1949.

Raine, Kathleen. "Nature: The House of the Soul." *Temenos* 9 (1988): 251–68.

Robbe-Grillet, Alain. "Nature, Humanism, Tragedy." *For a New Novel: Essays on Fiction.* Trans. Richard Howard. Evanston: Northwestern University Press, 1965.

Ronald, Ann. *The New West of Edward Abbey.* Reno and Las Vegas: University of Nevada Press, 1982.

———, ed. *Words for the Wild: The Sierra Club Trailside Reader.* San Francisco: Sierra Club, 1987.

Rosenwald, Lawrence. *Emerson and the Art of the Diary.* New York and Oxford: Oxford University Press, 1988.

Rossi, William John. "Laboratory of the Artist: Henry Thoreau's Literary and Scientific Use of the Journal, 1848-1854." Ph.D. Diss. Minneapolis: University of Minnesota, 1986.

St. Armand, Barton L. "Topics for Discussion." Unpublished "Preliminary Examination for the Ph.D., Part II – Writtens" for Scott Slovic. Providence, Rhode Island: Brown University, 1988.

Sanders, Scott Russell. "Speaking a Word for Nature." *Michigan Quarterly Review* 26 (Fall 1987): 648–62.

———. "The Singular First Person." *The Sewanee Review* 96 (Fall 1988): 658–72.

Saussure, Ferdinand de. *Course in General Linguistics.* Ed. Charles Bally and Albert Sechehaye. Trans. Wade Baskin. New York: Philosophical Library, 1959.

Scheese, Don. "Nature Writing: A Wilderness of Books." *Forest and Conservation History* (October 1990): 204–8.

_____. "Why Nature Writing." (Paper presented at the Third North American Interdisciplinary Wilderness Conference.) Ogden, Utah. February 7–9, 1991.

Silko, Leslie Marmon. "Landscape, History, and the Pueblo Imagination." In *On Nature: Nature, Landscape, and Natural History*. Ed. Daniel Halpern. San Francisco: North Point Press, 1987.

Slovic, Scott. "Nostalgia, Defiance, and the Southwestern Wilderness: Graves, Abbey, Nichols." (Paper presented at the Third North American Interdisciplinary Wilderness Conference.) Ogden, Utah. February 7–9, 1991.

_____. " 'The eye commanded a vast space of country': Alexander von Humboldt's Comparative Method of Landscape Description." *Publication of the Society for Literature and Science* (May 1990): 4–10.

Smith, John. *Captain John Smith's History of Virginia*. (1624) Indianapolis: Bobbs-Merrill, 1970.

Solheim, Dave and Rob Levin. "*The Bloomsbury Review* Interview." In *Resist Much, Obey Little: Some Notes on Edward Abbey*. Ed. James Hepworth and Gregory McNamee, 79–91. Salt Lake City: Dream Garden Press, 1985.

Tallmadge, John. Review of *The Norton Book of Nature Writing* and *This Incomperable Lande: A Book of American Nature Writing*. *Orion Nature Quarterly* 9 (Summer 1990): 63–64.

Teale, Edwin Way. "Making the Wild Scene." *New York Times Book Review*. 28 January 1968.

Thoreau, Henry David. *The Journal of Henry D. Thoreau*. Ed. Bradford Torrey and Francis H. Allen. Volumes 1–14. Boston: Houghton Mifflin, 1906.

_____. *Walden*. (1854) Princeton: Princeton University Press, 1971.

_____. "Walking." In *The Natural History Essays*. Ed. Robert Sattelmeyer. Salt Lake City: Peregrine Smith, 1980.

Trimble, Stephen. *Words from the Land: Encounters with Natural History Writing*. Salt Lake City: Gibbs M. Smith, 1988.

Vargas-Llosa, Mario. *The Storyteller*. Trans. Helen Lane. New York: Farrar, Straus and Giroux, 1989.

Wakoski, Diane. "Edward Abbey: Joining the Visionary 'Inhumanists.' " In *Resist Much, Obey Little: Some Notes on Edward Abbey*. Ed. James Hepworth and Gregory McNamee, 102–7. Salt Lake City: Dream Garden Press, 1985.

Ward, Patricia. "Annie Dillard's Way of Seeing." *Christianity Today*. 5 May 1978: 30–31.

Welty, Eudora. "Meditation on Seeing." *New York Times Book Review*. 24 March 1974: 4–5.

Winterowd, W. Ross. *The Rhetoric of the "Other" Literature*. Carbondale and Edwardsville: Southern Illinois University Press, 1990.

Wolfe, Linnie Marsh, ed. *John of the Mountains: The Unpublished Journals of John Muir*. Madison: University of Wisconsin Press, 1979.

Wymard, Eleanor B. "A New Existential Voice." *Commonweal* (24 October 1975): 495–96.

Index

Abbey, Edward, 3, 150; aesthetics and morality in works of, 11, 18, 101; as anti-ideological, 138, 140; and the automobile, 177; correspondence, disjunction, and unpredictability in works of, 5, 8, 11–12, 39, 84, 96, 116–17, 118, 124, 125, 130, 135, 152, 183; death of, 93; as environmental advocate, 107, 113, 138; goal of, 101, 113, 152; journal of, 18; humor of, 11, 103; language of, 10–11, 18, 116, 118–19; metaphors of, 116; and separation of man and nature, 84, 177–78; and Thoreau, 6, 12, 97; on wilderness, 113–14, 147, 180. See also similar subheadings under Desert Solitaire; The Monkey Wrench Gang

Abbey's Road (Abbey), 106–7

Abbzug, Bonnie (The Monkey Wrench Gang), 102, 108, 109–10, 111

Agee, James, 117

Alcott, Bronson, 22

Allen, Francis H., 53

American Childhood, An (Dillard), 67; awareness in, 9–10, 61–62, 65, 92; awareness as process in, 89–91

Anderson, Chris, 183

Anhorn, Judy Schaaf, 25

"Annie Dillard: The Woman in Nature and the Subject of Nonfiction" (Clark), 65–66

"Annie Dillard's Way of Seeing" (Ward), 77

Anscombe, G. E. M., 69

Ansichten der Natur (Humbolt), 148

Antaeus, 86

Arctic Dreams (Lopez), 18, 37, 148, 182; anecdote in, 16, 156–58, 159, 161; attentiveness in, 141–42, 148, 159, 164; compared to

Matthiessen's Snow Leopard, 154, 159; compared to works of other nature writers, 156, 164; and genre, 150, 151; geographical precision in, 156, 157; goals of, 137, 140, 146, 152, 155, 163–64; imagination and desire in, 88, 162–63, 164–65; and intimacy with the landscape, 15, 17, 88, 152, 155, 164, 165; language of, 15, 139–40, 161; and man's estrangement from nature, 16, 137, 138–39; metaphors in, 17, 159, 161; participation of feeling self in, 156, 159; particularized understanding in, 15, 141–42, 149, 151, 153, 156, 158, 162; and the reader, 139–40, 157, 159, 162; scientific information in, 15, 16, 158, 160; sensory detail in, 152, 156, 158, 159; subtitle of, 162. See also similar subheadings under Lopez, Barry

Arguedas, José Maria, 182

Aristotle, 151

"Artist as Nun: Theme, Tone and Vision in the Writings of Annie Dillard" (Dunn), 63

Asturias, Miguel, 182

Aton, James, 84, 94, 153

Augustine, Saint, 151

Baca, Jimmy Santiago, 172–73

Bacon, Francis, 34, 141

Barrio, Raymond, 104

Bass, Rick, 183

Berry, Wendell, 3, 150; on Abbey, 100; awareness gradually deepening in works of, 11–12; belonging/understanding in works of, 99, 121, 128, 183; compared to other nature writers, 9, 11–12, 121, 130,

to author in, 111; tension between aesthetics and morality in, 11, 103, 112. *See also* similar subheadings under Abbey, Edward

Muir, John, 120, 156, 159

Nabokov, Vladimir, 11, 106
Nader, Ralph, 170
Nash, Roderick, 170
Nature (Emerson), 21, 24, 29
"Nature as Picture/Nature as Milieu" (Bryant), 174
Nature writing: and appreciation for "humble landscapes," 180; and awareness, 3, 4, 7, 172–74; effects on readers of, 14–15, 139, 169, 181; encounters with nature aided or obstructed by, 178–79; and environmental awareness of public, 15, 170–71; and environmental psychology, 181, 182; in a journal, 6–7; as obstacle or pathway, 180; and personal anecdotes, 152–53, 154; and picturesque, 174–75; as prescriptive, 137–38; and relationship of self to nature in, 153, 182; as surrogate for nature experience, 180; Thoreau's Journal as prototype of, 5
Nature Writing and America: Essays upon a Cultural Type (Fritzell), 112
Nelson, Richard, 148
New West of Edward Abbey, The (Ronald), 11, 102–3
New York Times, 113, 169; *Arctic Dreams* reviewed in, 140, 166; *Monkey Wrench Gang* reviewed in, 102, 103
Nichols, John, 183
Niebuhr, Reinhold, 76
"Notebook" (Dillard), 87
"Notes from an Absence and a Return" (Berry), 13, 122, 124–27
"Noticer: The Visionary Art of Annie Dillard" (Lavery), 62

O'Connell, Nicholas, 140, 148
Olney, James, 75

"On the Need for a Wilderness to Get Lost In" (Abbey), 113
Origin of Species (Darwin), 33

Paul, Sherman, 34, 148, 155–56, 159, 164
Peck, H. Daniel, 38, 44
Pilgrim at Tinker Creek (Dillard), 63, 131, 164, 182; anthropocentrism in, 66; attunement to nature in, 64–65, 80, 85; critics of, 8–9, 62, 66–67; awareness provoked by unexpected in, 9–10, 72, 85–86; and environmental awareness of public, 170; and James, 76–77, 80; language in, 78–79, 81, 91, 117; mysticism in, 61–62, 66, 76, 77, 78, 81, 82, 83, 84, 85–86, 91; "seeing" in, 78, 79–80, 82, 91; self-consciousness in, 61–62, 66–67, 77–78, 81, 82, 83, 90; study of visionary process in, 80–82, 85
Plum Plum Pickers, The (Barrio), 104
Polanyi, Michael, 56, 112–13
Pohrt, Tom, 142
Pound, Ezra, 184
Powers, Ron, 117, 119
Prelude, The (Wordsworth), 57
Proust, Marcel, 179
Psychology: Briefer Course (James), 80

Rahv, Philip, 152–53
Rahm, Dave, 70–76, 88
Raine, Kathleen, 64, 88, 153
"Revaluing Nature: Toward an Ecological Criticism (Love), 170
Rexroth, Kenneth, 134
Robbe-Grillet, Alain, 4–5
Ronald, Ann, 11, 102–3, 107, 179
Rosenwald, Lawrence, 50–51
Rossi, William, 25, 39, 43–44, 56
Rousseau, Jean Jacques, 106
Ruskin, John, 159

St. Armand, Barton, 34
Sanders, Scott Russell, 119, 183
Sarvis, A. K. *(The Monkey Wrench Gang)*, 102, 108, 109, 110
Saussure, Ferdinand de, 174